A History of Religion in 5½ Objects

A HISTORY OF
RELIGION IN
5½ OBJECTS

Bringing the Spiritual to Its Senses

S. BRENT PLATE

BEACON PRESS
Boston

Beacon Press
Boston, Massachusetts
www.beacon.org

Beacon Press books
are published under the auspices of
the Unitarian Universalist Association of Congregations.

17 16 15 14   8 7 6 5 4 3 2 1

This book is printed on acid-free paper that meets the uncoated
paper ANSI/NISO specifications for permanence as revised in 1992.

Text design by Wilsted & Taylor Publishing Services

Library of Congress Cataloging-in-Publication Data

Plate, S. Brent.
 A history of religion in 5½ objects : bringing the spiritual to its
senses / S. Brent Plate.
   pages cm
 ISBN 978-0-8070-3311-1 (hardback)
  1. Religion and culture. 2. Senses and sensation—Religious aspects.
3. Religion—History. I. Title. II. Title: History of religion in five and
a half objects.
 BL65.C8P52 2014
 203'.7–dc23   2013039786

This is what life is all about:
salamanders, fiddle tunes,
you and me and things,
the split and burr of it all,
the fizz into particulars.

—Annie Dillard,
  Teaching a Stone to Talk

Contents

½

half. 1. Being one of the two equal parts
into which a thing is or may be divided.
—*Oxford English Dictionary*

*Less solace in these songs half-ourselves
& half-not.*
—Colin Cheney,
"Half-Ourselves & Half-Not"[1]

After making eight mostly successful movies, Federico Fellini
set to work on *8½*. Since its release a half century ago, the surre-
alistic, self-reflexive motion picture has hit the tops of "all-time
best" lists the world over. Fellini's film within a film portrays
a middle-aged filmmaker, Guido Anselmi, played by Marcello
Mastroianni. Between love and lust, desire and creativity, Guido
quests for something, but seems unsure exactly what that might
be. His life is incomplete and he knows it. He gestures toward
love, often lasciviously, but as the beautiful Claudia suggests,
he doesn't know how to love. Guido rhetorically queries her:
"Could you choose one single thing, and be faithful to it? Could
you make it the one thing that gives your life meaning . . . just
because you believe in it? Could you do that?"[2] The apparent

answer is no, at least in his case. But the quest remains, and Guido's limited life persists.

Two and a half decades later, Julian Barnes inserted what he called a "Parenthesis" between chapters 8 and 9 of his novel *A History of the World in 10½ Chapters*. Equally as eccentric as Fellini's film, Barnes's fictional writings speculate on love, history, and artistic creation, meanwhile self-referentially questioning the author's role in it all. The parenthetical half chapter asks what it means for two people to love each other and the effects that may or may not have on a "history of the world." Among other felicitous phrasings, Barnes likens love to a "windscreen wiper across the eyeball." Even so, he wonders whether love is a "useful mutation that helps the race survive." Or maybe it is a luxury, some value-added option to our lives: unnecessary but persistent. Regardless, "we must believe in it, or we're lost."[3]

Two different works of art that examine love, desire, creativity, and the meaning of life, and both use "1/2" in their titles. What can this possibly mean? Is the half some extra value, like a baker's dozen? Or does it reflect something taken away, as if it was supposed to be the ninth but part of it was lost, or never finished? The beginnings of an answer were laid out a long time ago.

Almost two and a half millennia before Fellini and Barnes, the philosopher Plato wrote a work known as the *Symposium*, another meditation on the nature of love. In the midst of the convivial conversations of the story, Aristophanes stands up and presents what is perhaps the first artistic, amorous exploration of the half. The ancient playwright waxes mythological as he tells a comic tale of human origins: The first creatures were different from us, doubled in form from our present appearances; they had spherical bodies, with four hands, four feet, one head with two faces, and two sets of genitals. Because of their multiple hands and feet, they could move quite fast, and as such made a cartwheeled attack on the gods, which sent shock waves through the heavenly realms. Instead of killing the human creatures in retribution, the great Zeus decided to split them all in half so that they would be "diminished in strength and increased in numbers."[4] The result is the human body we each have today, living our lives as incomplete creatures, always looking for our other half. Love, the story suggests, completes us by coupling us, making us whole again with the perfect fit of another creature.

Aristophanes's halving is, I suspect, what Fellini and Barnes were after in their approaches to the topic of love. The "1/2" in their titles, and mine, stands as a symbol of our incomplete natures, the need for a human body to be made whole through relations with something outside itself. "No man is an island, entire of itself," as John Donne's seventeenth-century text declares. "Every man is a piece of the continent, a part of the main." Except that we get disconnected from our surroundings, from each other, from our gods, from the natural world, becoming floating islands. Our lives are half-lives, and we desire fulfillment, completion, wholeness. Aristophanes's mythologizing intimates that a perfect fit exists, somewhere out there, for our half bodies.

But this is not a book about finding a soul mate, one other human body that completes us. Many such books are readily available. This is about another kind of fullness, another kind of bonding for our coupling bodies, another kind of love. This is about a religious love, though not necessarily the love of a god.

This book tells the story of the human half body, such as we are, and some of the objects we connect with in our quest for religiously meaningful, fulfilling lives. Because, let's face it, Aristophanes tells a nice tale, but another body *doesn't* actually complete us. We humans may experience a few, fleeting moments of all-consuming, all-connecting ecstasy that grow rarer as life goes on, but we don't, can't, live in that state. We still need to eat and explore, to touch and talk, to breathe plant-produced oxygen and drink from one stage of nature's water cycle. Moreover, our ability to love can be amazingly vast, well beyond directing our affections toward one other single creature. We love (and *love* is indeed the word) a very good meal, our children and their imaginary plays, the color orange just so at sunset, the feel of our cat's fur as we pet it, a film that makes us laugh, a book that makes us cry. All these things too we love. They link us with a world beyond our own skin. Taken collectively, these experiences make us feel as if we are not one-half but one.

Beginning with our incomplete half body, the following chapters discuss five types of objects that humans have engaged and put to use in highly symbolic, sacred ways: stones, incense, drums, crosses, bread. These objects are ordinarily common, basic, profane. *Profane* stems from the Latin roots *pro* and *fanus*, meaning "outside the temple"; in other words, the deep meaning of the profane is not inherently negative, just everyday life: houses, trinkets, bakers, and post offices are all outside the temple. Such is the paradox of religious experience: the most ordinary things can become extraordinary. We often forget this, overlooking the commonplace because we're trained to respond to mass media spectacles, expecting an overwhelming lightning-bolt transmission from on high. Or we do the opposite and believe that spiritual truths are to be found in some remote setting, far from the quotidian, in a pretense of utter silence and absence, usually a mountaintop, desert, or other spectacular natural setting. Situated in between these two extremes, the spiritual objects discussed here are things that many readers will come across in the course of the next twenty-four hours. Chances are, you will find them where you didn't expect to find them, right under your noses, at your fingertips, on the tips of your tongues.

Connectors: USB ports, HDMI cables, DVI outlets, VGA adapters, 110-volt three-prong plugs, 220-volt two-prong plugs. If you don't have the right connectors, you can't watch your high-definition television, project your PowerPoint presentation, or

use your hair dryer when traveling abroad. In the world of electronics much is incompatible, which makes it so nice when the
right fit is found, when that crystal-clear connection is established and the show can go on.

We humans also *plug in*. Our bodies are a matrix of connecting points that, when used appropriately, allow us to relate to
and draw breath, meaning, and inspiration from the environment around. James Cameron's blockbuster film *Avatar* portrayed something like this, as the blue-being Na'vi had neural
ponytails that directly jacked into the flora and fauna of their
world, linking nervous systems across species. And we watched
this bright new time-space in 3-D, thinking: "How cool is that?"
Meanwhile, we forgot that we already have such connectors
inherent in this very mortal coil.

The primary contact points between the self and the world
are the sense organs: the mouth, nose, eyes, ears, and skin.*
So vital are these to our being in the world that the ancient
Greek philosopher Protagoras once claimed, "Man is nothing but a bundle of sensations." These sense connectors are
the meeting places for us to experience the world, the comings
and goings that flow through the organs and open our bodies to life itself. We plug in with them. The human body feels
the world, engages the sights and sounds, tastes and smells of
one's setting, incorporating (literally, "bringing into the body")
the environment around. As the painter Paul Cézanne once
claimed of his process, "The landscape thinks itself in me, and I
am its consciousness."[5] Similarly, Diane Ackerman's wonderful

---

* There are other ways of numbering the senses—there may be only one sense or
as many as hundreds, depending on the perspective—but we will begin with the
contemporary, commonplace conception that there are *five* senses. The five senses
noted here are technically called the *exteroceptive* senses, relating the internal and
external worlds, while there are also *interoceptive* senses that tell us about our
internal state of being, such as our sense of pain, thirst, and hunger. There is also a
sense of balance, a sense of decorum, a sense of humor, and that critical kinesthetic
sense that lets us know where we are in relation to the rest of the world.

work *A Natural History of the Senses* explores many of these connections:

> There is no way in which to understand the world without first detecting it through the radar-net of our senses. . . . Our senses define the edge of consciousness, and because we are born explorers and questors after the unknown, we spend a lot of our lives pacing that windswept perimeter: We take drugs; we go to circuses; we tramp through jungles; we listen to loud music; we purchase exotic fragrances; we pay hugely for culinary novelties, and are even willing to risk our lives to sample a new taste.[6]

To become more than a half being, more than a drifting island, we use our senses, the primary place of communion with the physical world, including the communion with other human bodies. And each of the senses has their appropriate objects of connection. Apart from some striking synesthetic experiences, basil's fragrance is not heard, a computer keyboard is not tasted, words on a page are not smelled. Proper connectors matter so that we can make sense of the objects in the world.

Because human experience and understanding is primarily a sensual bodily exercise, making a whole out of a half through the sense organs, religion itself is also deeply sensual. Ackerman doesn't name it as such here, but the explorations and questings she describes are the stuff from which religion is made. Religion is more about such quests and questions than any answers and arrivals. Too often religion is explained as a "set of beliefs," which primarily exist in the thought processes of the brain. The answers, having been found, are guarded behind the fortress of the forehead. The quest is over, we're all cleaned up, and life goes on. Religion, on this popular but ultimately misguided account, is about intellectual decisions regarding theism or atheism or polytheism, about correct thinking—orthodoxy (*ortho*, meaning "right" and *dox*, meaning "thinking") with regard to prophets and scriptures, about theological treatises and the content of preachers' sermons. Symbols, rituals, and bodies are believed to be merely secondary expressions of some primary intellectual order. But this is to put the proverbial cart before the horse.

There is no thinking without first sensing, no minds without their entanglement in bodies, no intellectual religion without felt religion as it is lived in streets and homes, temples and theaters. Long before intellectual, systematic thoughts arise in the cognitive workings of humans, long before abstract ideas emerge about deities who create and destroy, the senses actively receive and process information about the world and make meaning of it. Religion, being a prime human activity throughout history, is rooted in the body and in its sensual relations with the world. It always has been and always will be. We make sense out of the senses. This is the first true thing we can say about religion, because it is also the first true thing we can say about being human. We are sentient beings, and religion is sensuous.

The prolific Romanian-born historian of religions Mircea Eliade thought long and hard about what makes certain activities, gatherings, objects, people, and beliefs "religious" and not just some other part of mundane existence. Reading across multiple languages, modern and ancient, Eliade articulated some of the most important ideas for the scholarly study of religion, and his influence still continues to be felt a quarter century after his death. While many aspects of religious experience (myths, rituals, and symbols most prominently) are found in most cultures and times, Eliade is also clear about the role of the senses in making and shaping religion: "Broadly speaking, there can be no religious experience without the intervention of the senses. . . . Throughout religious history, sensory activity has been used as a means of participating in the sacred and attaining to the divine."[7] Eliade goes on to examine anthropological and mythological accounts of shamans, magicians, and healers and how they undergo a profound reshaping of their sense perceptions in order to achieve their appointed vocation. The shaman does not see, smell, or hear like ordinary people but "through the strangely sharpened sense of the shaman, the sacred manifests itself."[8] Which is not unlike the role often ascribed to the artist and poet in secular societies, who offer new ways of seeing, new ways of being. The parallels between artists and shamans, poets and priests will be one of the underlying aspects of the following chapters.

While shamans are his prime examples, Eliade notes that *all* religious people experience the sacred primarily in and through the senses. This should be obvious to anyone who reflects for long on religion and how it happens: incense fills the nostrils of a Krishna devotee in a temple in Vrindavan, India, letting him know he is in a sacred place; Muslim worshipers heed the muezzin's amplified call to prayer from the minaret of a Moroccan mosque; a girl tastes bitter herbs at a Passover Seder in Brooklyn, reminding her of the harshness of her ancestors' slavery in Egypt; a Greek Orthodox woman gazes reverently upon an icon of Jesus Christ and sees the gaze returned, knowing she is blessed; a Zen Buddhist acolyte strolls meditatively through gardens in Kyoto, experiencing form and emptiness. These sensual experiences are part and parcel of the *stuff* of religion. Myths, rituals, symbols, acts of devotion, prayer, and faith itself do not occur without sensual encounters.

To learn about religion we have to come to our senses. Literally. We have to begin to discover, as the anthropologist Paul Stoller did some years ago, that we cannot know the worlds of any other culture, let alone our own, unless we get inside the sensational operations of human bodies. Stoller began doing anthropological fieldwork with the Songhay people in Niger in the 1970s, initially returning from his visits troubled by the fact that the world he experienced there could not be communicated to his professional circles back home. Most important, the sense experiences he encountered operated in ways distinct from those he learned in the United States. After continued visits, he eventually realized that for the Songhay, thought, feeling, and action are inextricably linked, and that these bonds are made in and through the senses. His revelation finally led to a new way of understanding: "Now I let the sights, sounds, smells, and tastes of Niger flow into me. This fundamental rule in epistemological humility taught me that taste, smell, and hearing are often more important for the Songhay than sight, the privileged sense of the West. In Songhay one can taste kinship, smell witches, and hear the ancestors."[9]

Stoller's interest in the sensuality of social life led him to reflect on his own process of conducting scholarly research, and especially the linguistic and cognitive biases on which our idea of "knowledge" relies. In short, knowledge is believed to be about rational thoughts, communicated in verbal language, at the expense of the body and its perceptions. Even so, the body makes itself known:

> Stiffened from long sleep in the background of scholarly life, the scholar's body yearns to exercise its muscles. Sleepy from long inactivity, it aches to restore sensibilities. Adrift in a sea of half-lives, it wants to breathe in the pungent odors of social life, to run its palms over the jagged surface of social reality, to hear the wondrous symphonies of social experience, to see the sensuous shapes and colors that fill windows of consciousness.[10]

The bodily senses—of the scholar, shaman, and layperson alike—awaken, begin to desire, to seek out the missing half.

My daughter once had an African dwarf frog, all of a full-grown inch. It's a perfect pet for a five-year-old since it doesn't require much cleanup. But she still wanted a dog, because, as she emphatically told me, dogs can be petted. When she first got the frog, she wanted to take a bath with it. That was her way of making an amphibious connection, and since she can't really get into its little cube of a home, she thought they could meet in a mutually agreeable aquatic atmosphere. There is at least one reason elephants and kangaroos are not pets, just as there is a reason dwarf frogs are not hugely popular; they can't be petted. Petting a dwarf frog would nearly kill it; elephants are relatively immune to the smallness of the human hand. My daughter inadvertently taught me that what is meant by a *pet* is directly tied to *petting*, which has to do with having a meaning-ful encounter with a creature beyond our body. We feel the need to touch, and we need the feel of touch. And while the pet who is petted benefits—the dog pumps his leg rhythmically, the cat purrs—the petter also gains. We crave interaction: sensing half bodies need objects to sense.

When I set out to write this book, I thought I was writing a book about the role of the senses in religious experiences. In a sense, that's what this is. But more honestly, the objects took over. My daughter and her frog showed me that while touch is important, the thing touched is equally so. Things got turned inside out. And that's because it's impossible to talk about the senses in abstraction, to smell without an odor, to hear without a sound, to touch without some thing to bump up against. The half body meets its missing parts. Experience is a two-way pro-cess, a mutual give and take.

The strangest part of all this is the assertion that, for example, a rock can have character, agency, power, and not just when it trips us on the sidewalk. Walt Whitman's poem "There Was a Child Went Forth" tells of the child who engages objects and these become a part of him as he grows: "And the first object he look'd upon, that object he became." Whitman tells of the objects we engage with in life, of lilacs and morning glories, "the noisy brood of the barn-yard" and "His own parents." For our interests in this book, drums and bread and incense have the ability to *correspond*, becoming correspondents, and we take them with us, as Whitman declared, "for the day, or a certain part of the day, or for many years, or stretching cycles of years." It takes two to tango, and meanings are created from the dance—the interactions, relationships, and exchanging of information. Which means that while it may seem I am doing the sensing and meaning making, the objects themselves are giving me input, speaking to me. Purring, perhaps.

Many people in many times and places have believed in the power of fetish objects, material things endowed with magical powers that must be treated with proper respect. The Songhay people Stoller lived with for many years, for instance, often use carved wood fetishes in their rituals because they hold power. The sculptures help in fertility, in connection to the ancestors, and with other life necessities. These objects are thought to cure and bless and kill; they have agency, the ability to act upon the world and change it in some significant way. Such things, and the people who hold them dear, will be discussed in these pages. But modern, secular people also have their own meaningful objects, and they are affected by their power, even if they don't *believe* in the fetishistic nature of the object. I give two examples here that have resonated in my own deeply felt senses about the power of objects and the effect they have on our lives, ancient and contemporary.

Thirty years ago MIT physicist and philosopher of science Evelyn Fox Keller wrote a biography of the geneticist Barbara McClintock. McClintock was a modern scientist who devoted her life, almost monastically so, to the understanding of genetics by engaging with generation after generation of corn crops. Her unorthodox methodologies brought insights and sometimes scorn from fellow biologists. As Keller begins to conclude McClintock's life story, she asks, "What enabled McClintock to see further and deeper into the mysteries of genetics than her colleagues?" Keller tells us that McClintock's "answer is simple.

Over and over again, she tells us one must have the time to look, the patience to 'hear what the material has to say to you,' the openness to 'let it come to you.' Above all one must have 'a feeling for the organism.'"[11] This last phrase became the title of Keller's book. McClintock was accused of being too mystical when she talked like this, but she knew this was the path to good science, and she did not think being a mystic was an altogether bad thing. Good science takes time. It takes receptivity. It takes insight. We must have open eyes and ears. Listen to the corn and it will tell many things.

Another example comes from the work of Sherry Turkle, the Abby Rockefeller Mauzé Professor of the Social Studies of Science and Technology at the Massachusetts Institute of Technology. For a long time now, Turkle's research has responded to questions about how new technologies are changing human identity, how we continue to evolve sometimes in contrast to and sometimes coextensive with the machines we make. She has edited a collection of autobiographical essays written by scientists, artists, designers, and scholars, each musing upon one object that has been significant to them in some way or another in their life: a suitcase, a camera, a car, a cello, a train. (Evelyn Fox Keller considers slime mold.) The result is a delightful insight into the material realities that lie beneath even the most abstract thinking. "For every object they have spun a world," says Turkle.[12]

Turkle introduces the book, entitled *Evocative Objects: Things We Think With,* by reflecting on her childhood memories, and in particular a certain closet in her grandparents' house. Inside the closet were keepsakes, photographs, notes, address books, and other things that allowed her a deeper insight into the lives of her ancestors. This is where, in retrospect, she began to feel her calling:

If being attentive to the details of people's lives might be considered a vocation, mine was born in the smell and feel of the memory closet and its objects. That is where I found the musty books, photographs, corsages, and gloves that made me feel connected. That is where I determined that I would solve mysteries and that I would use objects as my clues.[13]

Turkle's memory, and thus identity, and ultimately vocation are shaped by the closet stuff she sensually engaged decades ago. Such objects are *evocative*: they call us, shape us, and identify us.

It is really just a coincidence that both examples here come from scholars currently working at MIT, but the fact that they are at one of the world's elite institutions of scientific learning shows us how narrow can be the gaps between premodern and postmodern worldviews, between the fetishists and the scientists. In human settings across time and space, objects have power. They remind, shape, overtake, startle, stir, and speak. Turkle suggests, "We think with the objects we love; we love the objects we think with," just as McClintock thought *with* corn, not simply *about* it. This is part of what it means to love things, and for objects to help complete us.

Objects, things, stuff, belongings, mementos, goods, and artifacts all have the ability to speak, to call out, to meet the human body in particular times and places and alter the course of our lives. One person's trash may be another's treasure; meanwhile, there are many instances in which objects have helped steer entire cultures and civilizations and, if you believe the subtitles of recent books, "changed the world." Philosophers and historians have begun to recast their eyes on overlooked objects, writing stories of such mundane things as salt, maps, cod, mathematical equations, tea, sugar, the Fender bass guitar, shoes, coal, potatoes, tulips, guns, germs, and steel and how these have altered the history of civilization.

In 2010 the British Broadcasting Corporation and the British

Museum joined forces to produce a marvelous series of broadcasts entitled *A History of the World in 100 Objects*. Written and narrated by Neil MacGregor, director of the British Museum, each of the programs focuses on one object from the museum's collection. Rather than being a staid overview and description of these artifacts, MacGregor does something grander and tells of the ways these objects are imbedded within historical processes and came to actually set the stage for major world events to emerge and cultures to evolve. A two-million-year-old piece of stone found in Tanzania marks the emergence of modern, tool-using humans. A three-millennia-old Egyptian papyrus demonstrates the use of mathematics in ancient societies. A pair of five-hundred-year-old Japanese porcelain elephant sculptures is entangled with the emergence of our contemporary global economy. Human history is not just a story of big ideas and bloody battles that erupted across the earth for eons. It is also a history of the objects that humans have forged out of natural materials, how we have used them and how they have simultaneously used us.

The BBC programs, like this book, use the modest indefinite article *a*. Not *the* history of the world or *the* history of religion but *a* history. As if to say, "Here's a way to look at it. Not the only way, but one we've found to be of interest, and we hope you will too." A century ago, a perusal of a local library would reveal multiple titles beginning with "The History of . . . ," though not many books make such an assertion anymore. We've grown skeptical of such approaches, and rightly so, since they claim something that is not possible: a single, conclusive, all-encompassing history. This book is decidedly not that.

At the same time there is an argument going on here about how to examine *any* history of religious traditions and practices. This is to say that religious history is incomplete if it ignores the sensing body and the seemingly trivial things it confronts. Years ago I attended a Protestant seminary and took courses in church history, which meant we read the writings of intellectual theologians who wrote about abstract ideas that a tiny minority of literate people have understood. Nowhere did we learn about how the masses of people ("the church") actually experienced life, practiced rituals, or sensed the world. Which is to miss much. My research since that time has convinced me that religion must be understood as deriving from rudimentary human experiences, from lived, embodied practices. This is not to disregard the intellectual writings—far from it—but to resituate them in actual space and time and to write many histories beginning with the indefinite article.

One rainy day a few years ago, I stood at the confluence of the Kamo and Takano Rivers in Kyoto, Japan, with a group of researchers who had come to learn about the history of Japanese gardens. Our guide was about to show us the nearby ancient Shinto shrine called Shimogamo, but felt it important for us to begin a bit farther downstream, at the meeting of the rivers, in order to understand the power of place that the shrine held. The rivers, flowing in from the mountains north of the city, have brought life to the urban valley of Kyoto for well over a thousand years, and the shrine's location between the two water sources draws a kind of sacred hydroelectric energy from them.

I stood on the riverbanks in a rain jacket long past its utility, and some lines from T. S. Eliot's *Four Quartets* came to mind: "I do not know much about gods; but I think that the river is a strong brown god." Eliot—who grew up in the Mississippi River city of St. Louis—goes on to tell of how the river is at first seen as a frontier to those who confront it and need to get to the other side. Then, once bridges and barges are built, the river is forgotten by city dwellers, those "worshippers of the machine," who go about their business crossing from one side to the next or pushing commerce upstream.[14]

As the rain came down that day and the water rose on both

sides of us, it slowly struck me that these rivers had surely also brought death and destruction on more than one occasion. The unpropitiated river "keeps his seasons and rages," as Eliot put it, offering a reminder "of what men choose to forget."[15] This was without a doubt also part of the power tapped into by the ancient diviners who saw the site as a point of contact for the *kami*, the nature-dwelling spirits of the Shinto tradition. Sacred sites hold energy in reserve, forces that can rise up and kill. Meanwhile, humans wage technological war against the raging gods of nature, making tools such as flood containment devices that aim to tame the threats of the wild. The need to control the natural world, to make order out of chaos, produces great inventions and proves the ingenuity of human survival mechanisms. At the same time, technological taming facilitates forgetting. When we forget how our existence depends on our technologies—whether a bridge over a river, a stone arrowhead for hunting, or an Internet connection over continents—we begin to lose connection, remaining in our half-lives.

This is also to say that religion, at a certain base level, operates in accord with basic, natural experiences of eating and breathing, seeing and speaking. The natural world—from flora and fauna to the sun, moon, and stars—has its cycles, its seasons, and its smells and colors. Religious life grew up in correspondence with these cycles, keeping humans in tune with nature's rage and blessings. To make sense of it all, we humans began to tell and listen to stories about the rivers and crops, night skies and blue seas; we acted out audiovisual performances to ensure fertility of family and fields; we burned substances and breathed their scented smoke; we cooked foods and savored their flavors; and we began to become more extravagant with the twists and turns of abstract meaning we assigned to the sensually evocative objects we encountered. Religious life, like other aspects of culture and society, engages basic, cosmic forces, producing sense-laden myths, rituals, and symbols that allow us to embrace the rhythms of the natural world, share with other humans, and commune with God. Culture is at heart the cultivation of nature, and religion has been a key human force of cultivation. Cults, culture, and cultivation are not merely etymological relations, as each of the following chapters will illustrate.

We modern people, so the story of history goes, don't need the cycles of the moon to tell us when to start fasting for Ramadan, since we have calendars; we don't need to know when sunset begins and the candles are to be lit for the Sabbath meal, because we have clocks; we don't even need buildings for Sunday morning church services, because we have live streaming on the Internet. We have thus lost touch with cosmic cycles, and in so doing have lost touch with the basic ebbs and flows of religion. But let's be clear here too: religious institutions are as much to blame for any of this.

The objects explored in these pages each navigate the distinctions between nature and culture and their impact on religious histories. Each object is initially embedded in the natural world, but becomes part of culture through a series of ritualistic, mythic, and symbolic interactions with human bodies. Rock exists throughout the earth's crust and mantle, but when pieces of it crumble, tumble, or erupt, they become human sized and we interact with them as *stones*. Fire burns matter with or without human involvement, yet when some burning smoke is produced and used for particular rituals, the scented substance is called *incense*. Animal skin, stretched taut across wood supports from felled trees, are the foundational material for *drums*. One of the primary marks scribbled by toddlers is that of two crossed lines, and the near-universal primacy of this figure makes the symbol of the *cross* appear natural, emerging across continents and cultures. Naturally occurring materials like wheat, water, eggs, and yeast are harvested, processed, and baked into *bread*. Cultivating nature is what makes nature meaningful, useful to us as humans, just as we humans evolve in relation with these objects—they act on us as much as we act on them. In and through these varied objects, we are able to explore the religious cultivation of nature, thus telling particular histories of religion.

The nature-culture nexus is also the birthplace of art. So, by simultaneously placing religion at this connecting point, I also aim to give a privileged place for the arts, as religion comes to its senses. This is then an aesthetic religion as much as a religious aesthetics. Poets like T. S. Eliot, Gary Snyder, and Walt Whitman and visual artists like Paul Cézanne, Agnes Martin, and Andy Goldsworthy have as much to teach us about a history of religion as the philosophers and theologians. Actually, more so.

One of the odd and ironic things about this book is that it takes words to point toward sensual objects and bodies. Just as physical bridges are built over rivers, verbal viaducts span the physical experiences of our lives. When we do so we invoke another vital connection: that between words and things, the key connection of *metaphorical* language. The term *metaphor* stems from Greek linguistic roots that have do with "carrying across." À la Eliot, we might say metaphors carry us across a godly, raging river.

The contemporary philosopher Mark Johnson argues that metaphors are most often manifestations of basic bodily, sensual encounters with the physical world. He has discussed the idea of "primary metaphors" that grow from our bodily perceptions and interaction with our environment as we grow up and try to make sense of things. Our bodily experience and engagement with physical reality is so permanent, so all-pervasive that our language can only come back to these most elemental interactions. Thus, ideas are *grasped* or they go right *over our heads*; good friends are *close*, but sometimes even our partner feels *far away* and we *drift apart*; some days we wake up feeling *up* and other days we are *down*, even though our height hasn't changed. The physical basis of our existence aids communication, letting others know how we feel through the use of metaphor. This allows connection between people and collectively enables us to reach for *higher*, more abstract ways of thinking.[16] To come back to the aquatic metaphor: the river is made up of the primary physical experiences of our sensual body, and the bridge is the language we use to build upon these experiences and make them intelligible to others and to ourselves. Without the bridge, we are just swimming in the current. With only the bridge, we are forgetful, disconnected creatures.

Metaphors are not just flowery words or decorative flourishes for our speech and writing. Instead, James Geary's 2011 book on metaphor suggests that "metaphorical thinking—our instinct not just for describing but for comprehending one thing in terms of another—shapes our view of the world, and is essential to how we communicate, learn, discover and invent."[17] Metaphor is our bridge of understanding, carrying our communications to a farther shore we could not otherwise reach. Metaphor is imaginative, allowing us to travel, feel, and comprehend the places, experiences, and knowledge to which we do not have immediate access. This is true not only technologically and theologically but also ethically. Novelist Cynthia Ozick explains how metaphors are "one of the chief agents of our moral nature, and that the more serious we are in life, the less we can do without it. . . . Those who have no pain can imagine those who suffer. The strong can imagine the weak. . . . We strangers can imagine the familiar hearts of strangers."[18] We rely on the known to understand what is unknown. One thing suggests another: the familiar, already experienced, carries us to the strange, as yet unexperienced other shore.

To think up and put up bridges across rivers, to engineer our protection from nature's rages and diseases, abstract thinking is necessary. Our most lofty, abstract language about angels and afterlives, gods and demons, heavens and hells uses metaphorical crossings to carry us to the unknown. It is, for example, humanly impossible to comprehend a Creator God who can establish the entire universe; so devout monotheists have referred to this god metaphorically, calling him Father, King, Judge, Protector, Provider. The gendered *him* is also a metaphor. But even the down-to-earth dimensions of religious discourse are based on our physical-sensual environment: Evangelical Christians gather to discuss their "walk with God"; the most basic prayer in Judaism begins with the sensual injunction, "Hear, O Israel . . ."; Quakers seek an "inner light"; the name Qur'an means "recitation" and invokes the first words the angel Jibrail spoke to Muhammad on Mount Hira: "*Iqra!*" meaning, "Recite!"; and Buddhist sutras and sayings constantly evoke the imagery of the mind as a clear mirror.

To experience metaphor in its full sense is to bask in the comfort of walking dryly across the bridge, while simultaneously appreciating the potentially hazardous crossing that is taking place. Part of the purpose of this book, therefore, is to remind us of these two aspects, to bring the spiritual to its senses. Too often we forget the forging it once took to make that crossing. Scholarly histories of religion, as well as many self-help spirituality books, are filled with such forgetful language, turning the realities of religious life into disembodied, detached verbal constructions. Meanwhile, the best of poetry and prose can simultaneously bring us to the dizzying heights of metaphor, just as they remind us of the engineered scaffolding that has brought us there. Without the comprehension of why the bridge is there in the first place, the power of it is lost. Thus also, to understand religions from places around the world and times through history, we have to approach them metaphorically, which is to say sensually *and* verbally.

Bringing the river and the bridge together, bringing the spiritual to its senses, means thinking about religion itself in a new light. We have to divest ourselves of the idea that we can get to know something about a tradition by reading their sacred texts or by following the decrees of religious leaders. Instead, I suggest we imagine religious histories as histories of *technology*. The term derives from the ancient Greek root *techne*, which refers to an "art, skill, or craft." Technology deals with human connections to and uses of natural and human-made materials, as well as the artistic, religious, social, and pragmatic means of repurposing these materials for human use. Turning geological rocks into sacred stones for a temple, wheat berries into bread for Christian Communion, and smoldering cinders into incense for protection from malicious spirits are all technological activities. Here, the artist is just as crucial as the engineer, and a history of religion relies on know-how as much as knowledge. Libraries and the Internet may store information and records of previous knowledge, but the human body stores know-how. People who practice religion do not necessarily *know* about the history or doctrinal elements of that religion, but they *know how* to do that religion. Religious people are not *believers* so much as *technologists*.*

Ultimately, it is physical objects like stones, incense, drums, crosses, and bread, and our technological encounters with them, that give rise to our religious language and make sacred utterances meaningful. We see, hear, smell, taste, and touch well before we speak. Sensual experiences with these objects constitute the rushing river; language about them creates the bridge over which we cross. If these chapters do nothing more than make you put the book down and pick up that stone or feather or drawing or knickknack on your desk or by your bed or in your purse and think about the sensed significance of that object, then they will have achieved one part of their aim.

---

* And thus many polls that seek to chart religious demographics are doomed to inadequacy since they merely ask about what people believe. What people *say* and what they *do* are often two different things.

In the concluding chapter I will return to some of these broad takes on religion and technology and suggest that the sensually religious activities described herein are bound up with *soul*. Soul, I will suggest, is a technology. But before we get to that, we have to wind through the histories of the objects themselves, to metaphorically imagine them as they are sensually approached and apprehended within specific times and places. Interactions with objects as well as words are and always will be sensual engagements, whether that technology is the burning sap of a myrrh tree or a computer network, whether we are face to face or interfaced. Religion in a high-tech, media-saturated, global-economic age is as reliant on objects as it is in smaller scale societies. Humans are fetishists through and through.

STONES

*I had to forget my idea of nature and learn again
that stone is hard and in so doing found that it is also
soft. . . . I am no longer content to simply make objects;
instead of placing works upon a stone, I am drawn to
the stone itself. I want to explore the space within and
around the stone through a touch that is a brief moment
in its life. A long resting stone is not an object in the
landscape but a deeply ingrained witness to time and
a focus of energy for its surroundings.*

—Andy Goldsworthy, *Stone*[1]

Stones are set, cut, clutched, chiseled, and hurled. They ride in
our pockets for luck on journeys or climb into our boots, turning
travels into travails. Five small ones and a sling can take down
a giant, while one alone might kill two birds. They are fingered
for protection, worn as rings and necklaces, studied for scientific
discovery, used as a tool in capital punishment, and seen as sites
of supernatural power. If all that sounds too grand, we might
just put them in a box, call them our pet and sell them by the
millions.*

---

* Originally sold in 1975, "Pet Rocks" made their creator, Gary Dahl, a million-
aire within a few months. A new release hit the market as I was writing this book.

Stones solicit attention, usually subtly, almost inaudibly. Among the vast number of stones, rocks, pebbles, and gravel on the planet earth and beyond, a handful are occasionally selected, unearthed, transported, and repurposed for sacred means, becoming talismans, amulets, altars, or memorials. Stones can be manifestations of a divine force, provoking people to pilgrimage over hundreds, even thousands, of miles to bask in their presence. Others are ritual objects, helping to keep ceremonies centered and flowing smoothly. Some offer curative powers when touched, healing various maladies. Still others survive as markers of special events from ages past, inviting people to engage memories in a present, physical form. They can mark space in the form of boundary markers, delineating mundane distances as well as precincts of sacred sites, while specially set stones symbolize microcosmic events like fertility and macrocosmic occurrences like the rhythm of the stars and planets in the sky. Reaching back through time, they are mediums for ancestors long gone. In each case, stones are objects sensed, felt with fingertips, seen with the eyes, and felt deeply within. Stones show us the way.

This chapter tells the story of stones large and small, ancient and recent, white and black, striated and marbled, smooth and rough that have found their way into personal and communal sacred settings, engaging the sensual human body. Somehow, in spite of their assumed nature as hard, cold, heavy, deaf, dumb, blind, and unmoving, humans have taken a shine to stones. Stones confront us with object lessons in permanence and change, protection and vulnerability, the stability of home and the instability of the journey, and ultimately, the transitions between life and death. Such ambiguities allow insights into the power of religious traditions, institutions, beliefs, and practices.

Three stones. Three faiths. Situated at the zero point of the Abrahamic, monotheistic religions known as Judaism, Christianity, and Islam are stones. Making up more than one-half of the world's population today, and stretching back for millennia, these three religious traditions have spread around the world through missionaries, militaries, and media. The Peoples of the Book have collectively produced libraries upon libraries of learned writings, given birth to modern science, waged wars, mourned and praised their long-gone mythological heroes, and performed simple and elaborate rituals filled with songs and objects, and they continue to challenge the sociopolitical structures of the modern and postmodern world. If we head to the heart of their globally sprawling bodies, to the nave of their sacred spaces, we find stones. A wise man builds his house upon rock, while a foolish man builds it on sand. After the storms come and go, the house on the rock stands firm.[2]

These three Western traditions clearly built their houses on rock, and that metaphor can be taken literally. Singular stones help orient the global spaces of the religious traditions, serving mythic and ritual functions as they mark the *axis mundi*, the "cosmic axis," the absolute center of the world around which all else revolves. In turn, stones have become central as pilgrimage sites of the faiths, standing patiently as throngs of people come to gaze, touch, and be in the presence of this hard substance's witness, there at the nexus of existence.

At the geographical center of Judaism is the city of Jerusalem. Within that holy city today are the remains of the temple, first built by King Solomon about three thousand years ago, destroyed by King Nebuchadnezzar of Babylon around 586 BCE, later rebuilt, and destroyed again by the Roman Empire in 70 CE. The stone bricks of its western wall (the Wailing Wall) still remain, as does the foundation stone, thought by many to be the location for the ancient Holy of Holies, the most sacred space for Judaism and the site where people believe Abraham came close to sacrificing his son Isaac. Jutting up from the earth, the outcropping is nothing spectacular, but it stands its ground.

Through a series of concentric circles of increasing sacredness—Israel, Jerusalem, Temple, Holy of Holies—the foundation stone holds forth as the central spot on all the earth for sacred stability, the navel of the world. Synagogues the world over orient themselves toward Jerusalem, and ultimately to this stone site; and observant Jews come to make their requests, pleas, and petitions. The mystical Kabbalistic writings found in the Zohar, as well as other Talmudic literature, consider this stone to be the same one through which God created the world by throwing a great stone down to earth. Over the years, the stone has been chiseled, wept upon, hammered, grazed and gazed upon, lasting through crusades and constant political shifts. None of this has stopped the devout from making treacherous journeys to connect with the potency of the stone's presence.

The foundation stone became crucial to Islam as well, and today the Muslim-made Dome of the Rock sits atop the ancient outcropping. The Dome was erected as a shrine (not a mosque) around 691 CE and marks the legendary place where Muhammad the prophet underwent his mystical Night Journey seventy years earlier. Muhammad began the journey while in Mecca, when the angel Jibrail brought him the horse-like steed Buraq, who took him to Jerusalem. Moving farther into sacred space, Muhammad is brought to the site of the ruinous Jewish temple, and the furthest mosque of the time, al-Aqsa, on Temple Mount. From that pivotal location, Muhammad ascended into the seven heavens (a journey known as the *mi'raj*), spoke with past prophets, and received instruction about ritual observances for those who would submit to Allah, those who would later be called Muslims.[3] Over the centuries, devout Muslims have made pilgrimages to the shrine, somewhat replicating Muhammad's journey and showing their own piety. The Islamic tradition's reuse of the older Jewish tradition, at the stable site of a standing stone, shows how the newer revelation to Muhammad did not simply cancel the older Jewish one. According to traditional Islam, it actually continued and updated the previous traditions.

The seventh-century emergence of Islam as a dominant world power resulted in the replacing of that most sacred location. While evidence suggests that early Muslims prayed facing toward the stone at the center of Jerusalem, it wasn't long until Islam's cosmic center shifted to Mecca, and today it is the Ka'ba (literally "cube") that serves as the *axis mundi*. Islam has its own concentric circles of increasing sacredness, paralleling Judaism's: Mecca, Grand Mosque, Ka'ba, and ultimately within the Ka'ba lies a particular stone known as the Black Stone, now set at the shrine's southeast corner. There are historical indications that the Black Stone was originally a meteorite, and ancient, pre-Islamic people saw its arrival on earth as a sign from the heavens, and thus to be exalted. Such meteorite worship is well documented in ancient Greece, as black stones called *baitulia* stood at the center of cultic rituals. Islamic traditions and archaeological findings also hint at the Black Stone's origins in Abu Qubays, a mountain near Mecca. Whatever the case of its geological and devotional origins, the reality is that a relatively small stone stands at a central site for the global practice of one of the most influential religions in the history of the world. Within the massive pilgrimages to Mecca, during the hajj and other smaller pilgrimages, the Black Stone has been greeted through touching and kissing. Today it exists smoothed and broken into pieces from years of devotional caresses. The power of the stone to draw people to it is so strong that a series of silver frames have been placed over it for protection. Over time these frames themselves are dented, scratched, and buffed from millions of fingers touching them. Once the frames fall into disuse they end up in various cultural collections and serve as sacred objects in their own right. (I saw one of these in Istanbul's Topkapi Palace a few years ago and watched people stand reverentially in front of it, though now, because of museum regulations, the devout are not allowed to touch it.)

Not far from the Western Wall and the Dome of the Rock stands the Stone of Anointing within the Christian Church of the Holy Sepulchre in Jerusalem. In the fourth century the emperor Constantine had the church built on the site held to be the place of Jesus's death and burial, though the building of today dates from the twelfth century. Observant Christians believe the Stone of Anointing to be the site where Jesus's body was prepared for burial. Since at least the fourth century Christian pilgrims have made their way there to be absolved of sins, but also to be able to say, "I was there," as might be witnessed by the proliferation of images of the stone found across the Internet today. Entering the church, one will often catch sight of someone kneeling over the stone, perhaps stretching their arms across it, touching and kissing it, and thus understand blessings to flow as the once rough surface is smoothed away. Like rivers over rocks, lips and fingertips smooth the stone. In the process, one's soul is smoothed. Fires, earthquakes, and invasions have come and gone over the centuries at this site, but the stone remains. Or at least it is believed to remain, to be the one and same as that from long ago.

There are many other centers of the world, and across Christendom the pious and curious flock to sacred stones. Like Islam, Christianity's center shifted away from Jerusalem to farther and farther places on earth, most prominently Rome and Constantinople, but myriad local spots have emerged, grounding religious rituals and mythologies. Every mid-August, for example, hundreds of thousands of people descend on Quillacollo, Bolivia, for the festival surrounding the Virgin of Urkupiña, whose mythology is based on the Marian visions of a shepherd girl a few hundred years ago. At one point during the festivities, people venture several kilometers away, to Calvary Hill and chisel a stone out of the ground, carrying it home with them in expectation of good fortune, returning the stone the following year "with interest." The ritual is based on the activities of the original shepherdess whose vision of the Virgin Mary told her to take a stone home with her. When she did, it turned to silver, thus providing sustenance for her poor family. Meanwhile in Ireland, from the time of the Protestant Reformation until today, "Mass rocks" have indicated hidden, outdoor spaces in which it was relatively safe to meet for Catholic Mass in a Protestant-infused society. These stones serve as ports of call and altars on which priests can conduct Mass. These stones now, well after direct threat, continue to summon people to them, and thousands of Christians every year make pilgrimage to the sites.

Stones help hold certain spaces as sacred, literally and figuratively weighing them down. Stones are significant in part because of their relatively stable positions within space. Solomon's, Jesus's, and Muhammad's physical bodies have left the earth, but millennia later we can feel the same stones they felt. Like religion itself, the stone's lessons are situated between quests and aims, questions and answers. The pilgrim goes to the stones in hopes of healing or a new chance in life or to set distance from past events. Stones help show the way, imperceptibly urging us onward, even as they become resolutely situated at the end of the way: they are there waiting at the journey's terminus.

Perhaps it is the ubiquity of stones in human life—their pure pragmatic nature, their durability and simultaneous malleability—that has prompted us to bestow certain stones with spiritual power, beyond their use as a weapon or roadside marker. As with bread, incense, crosses, and drums, the sometimes-sacred status of stones begins with the substance's simplicity and pervasiveness across cultures. This is a curious thing about sacred objects: the type of object is common—pieces of bread, sticks that burn, a rock—while some specimens of the type are taken to be holy. Or, more specifically, the common objects become holy when placed within a unique time and place, and humans find power within them.

In the early twentieth century, French sociologist Emile Durkheim categorized religious life and thought as involving a series of distinctions between the sacred and the profane. While "anything can be sacred," Durkheim suggests, "the sanctity of a thing is due to the collective sentiment of which it is the object."⁴ This is not to say all things are sacred, but that anything *can be*. As with real estate, it's all location, location, location. The philosopher Nelson Goodman says something similar: "Stones are normally no work of art while in the driveway, but may be so when on display in an art museum."⁵ What matters is the location of an object within a particular social setting, the ways it is meaningful to groups of people for specific purposes. In many times and places around the world, groups of humans have come to collectively believe that this stone, this one right here in front of us, is given by the gods, is provided as a token, and should be set up as a centerpiece in a garden, an altar, or a device for the keeping of collective memories. While I tend to agree with the social dimensions of Durkheim's analysis, objects can also gain a kind of sacred power within more individualized settings and encounters.

The top of my seven-year-old daughter's dresser contains one plastic watch given to her by a favorite aunt, one Captain Jack Sparrow Lego figure, one wooden die from a board game, and a baseball-sized stone. Like any good altar, it's a hodgepodge of ingredients that heeds nothing to consistency in style, material, or form. Instead, it's a collection of materials brought together in a single location and unified through the intentions (however unconscious) of a collector, such as my daughter. The objects are set there, and not down in her toy box or left under the bed, because they stand out from her other toys and games. The stone in the collection was found on the beach in San Diego on the last day we vacationed there a few years ago. My daughter had been having a good time that day, splashing through the shallows, chasing seagulls, digging tunnels in the sand, and searching for shells and stones. At the end of the day she didn't want to leave, and it being our last day of holiday, she somehow, almost instinctively, had this notion that she needed to bring something with her. If she couldn't stay, then part of that environment could—must—come along. My reasoned pleas about it being too big, too heavy, too something to fit into baggage on the airplane back to New York amounted to little; its current situation in her room evidences its bicoastal journey.

Individuals as well as communities gather objects, place them in one location, and allow those objects to hold a significant, sacred place in their lives. Makes no difference whether these objects belong together in accord with some ancient manual of myths and rituals or aesthetic school of thought, nor has it ever mattered much. An online search for contemporary "images of personal altars" reveals an arresting array of the ways people continue to bring objects, human-made as well as naturally found, into a new space, repurposing the profane for sacred ends. Altars reflect personal tastes, even as the social mores and cultural products of the individual's environment are profoundly influential. While altars can include ephemeral objects, they continually, the world over, incorporate solid substances, things that will last and remind the devotee of places and times and people long gone. And, I suspect, many who are reading this have at one time pocketed a stone and carried it from its original setting to a special shelf, desk, or table, often across great distances.

The taking of stones from certain locations may seem to be a benign activity, but it is not always. Sometimes it is theft, as a controversy in Central Australia shows. Again, location matters. The iconic natural landmark called Uluru (Ayers Rock) is a UNESCO World Heritage Site and part of the Uluru-Kata Tjuta National Park, which sees a half-million tourists each year. The rock formation itself is considered sacred by the Anangu people, who esteem it in their mythologies, and the monolith has long been a place for ritual performance. Because it is understood as a sacred site, full of power, tourists have made a habit of taking sand or stones from the park, illegally bringing them back home with them, hoping to garner some blessing from the place. In 1998 a German-based company even sold Uluru stones for hundreds of dollars, calling the stones "children of Uluru," until a group of Anangu stated their objections and the company ceased the selling. Another report indicates that "a genuine piece of Ayer's Rock" was advertised on eBay in 2005, with a bid starting at fifty US dollars. In the midst of these stone thefts, curious reports have emerged, as many who have taken them have complained about bad luck and misfortune after returning home: marriage troubles, family illnesses, even deaths. So now over the past two decades, the stones have been consistently returned by post to the Australian National Park from all over the world. Some people write accompanying letters, apologizing for taking the sacred objects. Others seem to believe that returning the rocks will reverse their bad fortune. The returned objects have become known in the park as "sorry rocks."[6]

Contrary to the sorry rocks of Uluru, the stone on display in my daughter's room is just a chunk off some bulkhead. It is not beautiful, nor is it sacred by any traditional definition. But it has a heft to it; it is solid, like it can carry the weight of memories of a place and time across a continent. I should perhaps be forgiven in extending the definition of stone to include a hunk of rough, graveled concrete found on a beach and winding up on my daughter's stack of drawers. Yet if gravel-concrete is made by human means, compressing various types of mined and milled rock together, rock itself is nature's equivalent. All rock, whether sedimentary, igneous, or metamorphic, is formed from other types of rock, forced together by means volcanic, geologic, and catastrophic. As solid and unchanging as natural rock seems, it is itself in a constant state of flux.

The point is to suggest that stones are themselves on a journey, even when they seem stable. They are formed, reformed, and transformed over long periods. They are washed smooth by a river through the years, while our fingertips feel erosion's polished results. We might even be provoked from time to time to stop and contemplate the paradoxical effects of as supple a substance as water on the solid stuff of stone. Or we might gaze at a banded stone, the beauty of a rainbow of colors striped together, and be astonished by the tremendous geological forces necessary to press various minerals together in so permanent a way.

The stones of Jerusalem and Mecca, Uluru and my daughter's dresser, each demonstrate one key aspect of the appeal of stones: the stone's voyage is felt and seen by our sensual bodies. The stone's journey meets the human journey, provoking memories, contemplation, a respect for the immense energies at work in the universe, all contained in a small object that can be tossed aside, skipped across the surface of still water with an ever so supple wrist, set up along the trail, used as a tool, or placed in an altar setting. As poet William Blake once famously suggested, "To see a world in a grain of sand / And a heaven in a wild flower / Hold infinity in the palm of your hand / And eternity in an hour." In such sensual experiences with objects the macrocosmic wonders of the world connect to the microcosmos that is our sensing body. The journey of one body is mirrored in the body of the other.

The Italian poet Petrarch once said, "I do not know whence its origin, but I do know that innate desire to see new places and to change one's home. There is something truly pleasant, though demanding, about this curiosity for wandering through different regions."[7] Petrarch's intuition about travel seems to have been proven correct through history, leading contemporary biologist John Janovy to suggest, "Pilgrimages seem to be almost instinctive, or at least derived from behaviors now so ingrained in our species that it's difficult to distinguish between genetic and social origins."[8] Religious traditions have worked with this restless facet of human life and developed simple and extensive pilgrimage rituals. In the midst of these we find stones aiding travelers in the midst of encounters in and with the unknown. They are protective devices to ward off evil spirits and unwanted strangers, markers to describe distance to and from a sacred site, or piles that testify to those who have gone before.

In the Detroit Metro Airport stands a beautiful black granite water fountain created by WET Design, the same group who created the Bellagio Fountains in Las Vegas and remade the Lincoln Center fountains in New York City. The fountain is a wonderful spectacle and watching it helps pass the time, yet on a recent layover my attention was drawn elsewhere. Near the fountain are several trees in large containers. In these containers are smooth stones covering the potted dirt. It's not clear who started the process, but people have begun to write on the stones, offering their names and the places they are traveling to or from, in multiple languages, and often including visual symbols like hearts and peace signs. There are no instructions nearby telling people to leave their contribution; rather, it seems to have started on an impulse that was then followed somewhat instinctively by others. I spoke with the airport's media relations office, and they told me that Northwest Airlines initially felt this was "like graffiti" and worked hard to eliminate the marked-up stones. Over time the stone writings returned and the airlines gave up trying to get rid of them. This improvised ritual is remarkable for what it tells us about the nature of stones and how they connect to humans, and something about the nature of humans, particularly in the midst of a journey.

I suspect most of the people who have made their contributions to the stone collection in the Detroit airport do not know much about the ancient Greek myth of Hermes, the messenger for the Greek gods and protector of travelers (like a proto–Saint Christopher). Scholars have suggested that Hermes took his name from the root term *herm*, which in ancient times signi-fied a stone heap, and was later used as the name for a sacred boundary marker or roadside altar, often a sculpted bust upon a pillar. The ancient Greeks often interacted with stones, carving into them or leaving them in a seminatural state as protective de-vices, but also as pragmatic markers of distance along roads and borders. Magic and math have not always been so far apart.[9]

A herm was also a talisman, placed at borders and sacred spots to protect a local group from any strangers they might encounter there. The heaps offered protection as people trav-eled, something perhaps intuited by modern airline travelers. And not dissimilar to the Hindu use of images of Ganesha (stone or other) or the Jewish use of a mezuzah, herms were also set outside one's house to offer luck and blessings to guests who entered.

While the Detroit airport stones are a recent phenomenon, they unwittingly continue ancient traditions and practices, such as the global phenomenon of creating cairns. From the Gaelic, a cairn is simply a pile of rocks. Sometimes they have religious connotations, sometimes not. Crucial here is the fact that a cairn is made up of more than one stone, and they indicate some sort of human expression, somewhere between nature and culture, usually situated in the realm of ritual. Like the airport stones, cairns connect the traveler to those who have gone before and will come after. And like the airport stones, cairns become re-positories for stories. Cairns are civilized markers within the wild, among the chaos of unknown, threatening lands, whether airport terminal or mountain pass. They become especially critical in more desolate climates, when snow has covered trails or where pathways are at risk of being covered or washed away. The significance of the pile of stones depends on its placement and on who is looking and listening. Cairns, and other collections of stones, have much to tell us. But we have to know how to listen.

In Mongolia, atop mountain passes and hills stand large cairns called *ovoo* (literally, a "heap") made up of stones, wood, bones, and other materials. The Mongols are traditionally nomadic and shamanistic, and the worship of certain mountains is not uncommon; Genghis Khan himself was a worshiper of Burkhan Mountain. The shape of an *ovoo* mimics a mountain and can be found in high elevations, becoming a key site for rituals. Some ceremonies take place near the heaps, and others at the base of the mountain on which they stand. In older times, *ovoo* were typically shrines dedicated to the local Mongol deities Nibdah, Shibdagh, or Luus, the "dragon king." In the shamanistic religious environment, it is also believed that certain shamans can control nature, causing rain, wind, and so forth, through engagement with a sacred stone called a *jada*.

Tibetan Buddhism eventually came to dramatically influence Mongol culture, triggering a number of changes in traditional rituals and myths. Yet, as with most new religious movements, the old is adapted and reincorporated into the new. In the older traditions, animal sacrifices were often made, and the *ovoo* were, in part, composed of animal bones. In the newer renditions, Buddhist prayer flags began to be placed within the *ovoo*, while Tibetan prayers and scriptures were written directly on the stones. And instead of the shamanistic deities being worshiped at the *ovoo* sites, devotion shifted to various Buddhist lamas.[10]

From one religion to the next, over centuries of rituals and rain, piles of stones remain. Living now in an age of technological, planned obsolescence, Detroit airline passengers evidence a desire for that which lasts, something that makes a mark on the future, communicates not in the ephemerality of texts and tweets and talks but in the hard, lasting language of stone. They mark our presence in a physical place for people and ages to come. Facebook and Twitter accounts are filled with updates on people in transition. And yet, in a real sense, humans have been checking in and sending status updates for millennia. Stones never become obsolete as social media.

Two sculptors offer further meditative forays into the human relationship with stone, and their works allow us to examine the distinction between nature and culture. The artists are not creating art for religious purposes—an object set in a place of worship within a specific religious tradition for a specific ritual outcome—but their work allows us to think about how art functions religiously. Their art is analogous to religious objects, borrowing similar principles, symbols, and compositions, and allows some insights into how and why religious traditions have used stone in the ways they have for so many eons.

Isamu Noguchi grew up between Japan and the United States, trained as a modern artist in the Euro-American mode, but later undertook a study of Japanese gardens, particularly their Zen Buddhist aesthetic styles. He saw a parallel aim in emerging modern artistic sensibilities and the ancient tradition of garden making in Japan: both seek a heightened awareness of one's environment, a distillation of the cosmos, and a conscious disturbance of the natural realm. Through these two contrasting influences, Noguchi eventually settled on stone as his primary medium: various types of granite, basalt, and marble quarried around the world. In his unique hybrid way, Noguchi took the Japanese garden art of stone setting and modified it by etching and cutting and smoothing parts of stone.

His 1971 piece *To Intrude on Nature's Way* condenses many of Noguchi's artistic tendencies. Here the basalt monolith is left natural in places, cleaned of clinging dirt but otherwise unaltered from its found state. But Noguchi chisels into it at other points, intruding on nature's own artistic processes. The work remains in limbo, somewhere between the natural and the artistic, allowing viewers to think about what art does that is different from, but also similar to, nature. Natural rock becomes sculptural artifact, made meaningful within an artistic location. The human hand, using tools, transforms the object into something other than it was in nature. Nature is brought into culture. In so doing, the artist works in a way parallel to the cultivating, artistic work of religious traditions.[11]

Similarly, the contemporary British artist Andy Goldsworthy works with all manner of matter, exploring relations between stone and time, nature and culture. His almost-animistic sculptures are typically temporary as he uses ephemeral substances like twigs, leaves, snow, and mud. Or he uses stone but without the setting of mortar, so even these structures eventually fall apart. Many of his works are set far from any urban museum environment and the only lasting artwork is simply a photograph taken before his sculptures return to their natural setting. A pile of rocks is left on a beach. The coming high tide submerges and disassembles the heap, tossing the stones through ebbs and flows.

Goldsworthy gets a feel for a place and proceeds with an intervention that both alters nature and respects it. He speaks of particular stones that "proffer some radiating anime, some soul and intention, witnessing to the past in this time and in this place." And, he claims, "a rock is not independent of its surroundings. The way it sits tells how it came to be there. The energy and space around a rock are as important as the energy and space within. . . . When I touch a rock, I am touching and working the space around it."[12] Goldsworthy's work is striking, often leaving viewers mesmerized by the simplicity that good art can take. Leaves, stones, sticks, water, mud, snow: all fleeting, yet powerful while they exist. Reflecting on such work, we might scratch our heads and realize: this stuff, this matter, these sticks and stones, might be alive. There is anime, soul, and intention in these objects.

Taking Noguchi's and Goldsworthy's cues, it is possible to

productively rethink a difference between *stone* and *rock*. While the terms are often used interchangeably in everyday English, I tend toward the geological understanding that rock is a natural material. In fact, little else on earth is so thoroughly natural. Rocks *become* stones when humans interact with them and use them in cultural settings, often after smaller chips have fallen off the old block. Under the artistic caress of Noguchi and Goldsworthy, stones become symbolic of human engagement with nature. Unlike rock, a stone stands between nature and culture, at once harkening back to whence it came and forward to where it may become further entrenched in human affairs. Thus, to give a working definition: stones are humanly used pieces of rock. Just as the stones use us.

As such, the Stone Age was given its name because humans used stones as tools. It wasn't the "Rock Age," even though, scientifically speaking, the substance used was indeed rock. A pivotal era in history, the Stone Age lasted more than three million years and spanned the difference between *Homo erectus* and *Homo sapiens*. During this time, modern humans emerged out of the Rift Valley of East Africa as rocks were fashioned into stone axes, blades, chisels, knives, awls, and scrapers used to hone, dig, pierce, chop, cut, crack, and kill. Along with the use of handheld, shaped stones, this era gives the earliest evidence we have today of the beginnings of art, social organization into settled communities, the cultivation of plants, and, ultimately, religion.

The discovery in the 1960s of the great stone rings of Gobekli Tepe in southeastern Turkey evidence ritual gatherings, aesthetic creations, and the use of stone more than eleven thousand years ago. Dating six thousand years before Stonehenge, and seven thousand before the stone structure known as the Great Pyramid of Giza, this is the place of the oldest known temple on earth. While we are still years and perhaps decades from firm conclusions about this archaeological find, one current theory suggests that Gobekli Tepe supports the presence of an organized religious site in the midst of foragers. In other words, as Klaus Schmidt, the lead archaeologist at the site speculates, religious ritual, sacred space, and even the practice of pilgrimage preceded the rise of agriculture and civilization as we tend to define it. This places organized religion at an earlier point in evolutionary history than previously believed. Modern humans do not exist apart from stone, and religion itself is built upon such rock.

The difference between rock and stone is the difference between nature and culture, which is also to say stones speak to the differences and connections between nature and religion. The difference lies in *technology*, as noted in this book's introductory chapter. A stone axe and a stone monolith standing in an art museum or archaeological dig are products of technology, as are drums and bread. They may not take batteries to operate, but they are technological just the same. The stone does not even need to be physically altered but simply put to use in some humanly meaningful, creative way.

Sen no Rikyu was the greatest designer of Japanese tea gardens and ceremonies in the sixteenth century, and his creative impact is still felt today. He received Zen training at the Daitoku Temple in Kyoto, and his lasting influence on the architecture of the teahouse and gardens is due to the aesthetics produced from a Zen sensibility. The graceful yet rigid actions of the traditional tea ceremony find roots in the Buddhist practice of mindfulness, one step of the eightfold path that Siddhartha Gautama, the Buddha, taught millennia ago. Legend has it that drinking tea, usually green and thus caffeinated, developed as monks spent long periods of time in meditation and needed something to keep them awake, though it also had medicinal uses, as contemporary dieticians are now realizing. With deliberate and careful attention to every minor activity in the preparing of tea for guests, Rikyu suggested the ritual provides for harmony, respect, purity, and tranquility.

Drinking tea is not so much the goal of the ceremony as it is one step along the way. The term used is *cha-do*, literally the "way of tea." Rikyu was influential, in part, because he redefined the implements used. Cups, pots, and whisks were selected for their *wabi* (rustic) quality, giving the assurance and appearance of being well used even if recently made, and of being accessible to people of various means and not simply the fancy gold-plated utensils of the upper classes. He also designed the architecture and landscape of the *teahouse*, a term that includes not merely the building but also the surrounding gardens and, crucially, the *roji* (path) leading up to it. The short walk from street to teahouse, through use of winding walkways, carefully selected and pruned foliage, becomes a compressed pilgrimage, a sacred journey. Entering the tea garden is a journey into a sacred space.

Among other innovations attributed to Rikyu is the use of a *sekimori ishi* ("barrier stone"), a small stone typically placed on top of larger stepping stones. The stone directs foot traffic and even can indicate that the teahouse is closed. If the *roji* forks and the visitor is unsure which way to go, a *sekimori ishi* will direct the way by barring one path. No fortified gate or imposing No Trespassing signs are needed, just a small stone tied up with a length of rope, looking like a geological birthday present.

One key difficulty in setting this up, for those taking the aesthetic implications of the teahouse and ceremony seriously, is finding just the right stone. Not any one will do. Preference is for a flat-bottomed stone with a nice rounded top, large enough to be noticed but small enough to be carried around. Anyone could easily step over or around a *sekimori ishi*, but for those who understand the symbol, the message is clear. It is one of those light, whimsical touches that made Rikyu so famous.[13]

Other stones that serve as barriers in Japanese culture carry more gravity. After being ignored and often hidden for centuries, several hundred tsunami stones became apparent after the devastating earthquake and tsunami hit northern Japan in April 2011. Placed on slopes, safely above rising ocean waters, the stones were carved with warnings not to build below this level, or they would provide lists of previous death tolls, or serve as markers for mass graves. Itoko Kitahara, a specialist in the history of natural disasters at Ritsumeikan University in Kyoto, is quoted in the *New York Times*: "The tsunami stones are warnings across generations, telling descendants to avoid the same suffering of their ancestors."[14] These are messages from those who have gone before, offering protective warnings and telling stories through the medium of stone.

The Pulitzer Prize–winning author Annie Dillard tells a quirky story about a reclusive neighbor named Larry who keeps a stone on his shelf ("a palm-sized oval beach cobble whose dark gray is cut by a band of white which runs around and, presumably, through it"). The neighbor is ritualistically teaching the stone to talk. No one is sure how he is going about it, but Dillard speculates that this strange activity is really about the need to listen, to hear silence. It takes practice. "The silence is all there is," Dillard writes. "It is God's brooding over the face of the waters."[15] Yet, the reverse activity can also be true. Stones teach *us* to talk.

Stones are metaphorically meaningful in human life since almost everyone, at some point, has encountered pebbles, stones, rocks, cliffs, or rocky mountains. More to the religious point, the metaphorical weight of rock and stone finds its way throughout sacred scriptures. To give one initial, solid example, the primal naturalness of rock and stone is so insistent that it becomes one key way to speak about God and God's nature in the Hebrew Bible. God is the "rock of Israel," "my rock and my fortress," "the rock of your refuge," "an everlasting rock." Or as God queries: "Is there a God besides me? There is no Rock; I know not any."[16] This sense of solidity and permanence, this connection with the raw materials of the God-made earth, makes rock a key part of divine language. In fact, the Hebrew Bible makes dozens of references to God as a rock and no more than a handful to God as Father. How much different would the Christian creed be if it reflected the biblical usage: "I believe in God, the Rock Almighty . . ."

Language is deeply material, and the rhetorical usage of rock and stone stems from their real physical nature. They are, to give the three simplest descriptions, solid, hard, and heavy. These attributes give way to others such as permanent, unchanging, and foundational. Expressions like "free as a rock," "the stone-like softness," or "light as a stone" simply don't make sense.

But, metaphors aside, surely stones are inert, aren't they? They lack animation, a soul that gives them life. After all, they just lie there until someone picks them up. Or they roll, "with no direction home," as Bob Dylan had it. We use them metaphorically to indicate inactivity and disability: stone-blind, stone-deaf, still as a stone. Or as the heavy metal band Metallica grinds out an answer to the question of what has happened to one's wasted life: "Stone dead forever, that's right."

Building on their physical existence as objects sensed primarily through touch and vision, myths and rituals from around the world have continued to speak of stones and their life and death functions within human cultures. In Greek mythology, Niobe turned to stone after the loss of her children, crying rivers of tears. In the Lakota traditions the story is told of a woman who turned to stone after her husband and village abandoned her; the remaining woman-stone was in turn considered sacred and was carried with the repentant community as they traveled. Conversely, in Maori traditions the deity Rakahore is a personified form of stone who reproduces various stones and rocks across land and sea. And Hawaiian cultures tell stories of stones having sex (solid rocks are male, porous rocks are female), producing smaller pebbles. Stones, like so many religious symbols, can mean one thing and also the opposite: they stand at the point of death, but also produce life.

The Christian New Testament at first might seem to follow the soulless, directionless stone metaphor. Jesus's sermons are littered with references to them as inert objects acted upon by the will of God. The itinerant preacher of the Gospels speaks of God's power as "able from these stones to raise up children." He queries what kind of person would give their son a stone rather than bread, or he notes that if his own disciples did not praise God, "the very stones would cry out." Even the devil knows the power of God to turn stones into bread, and so tempts the proclaimed Son of God to do likewise. In each instance, stones are lifeless nature standing in contrast to some animating life force. To prove the potency of God, the stone must be impotent.[17]

Such lifeless language dovetails with the many biblical accounts of capital punishment: death by stoning, a brutal form of execution by torture as stones break bones and pelted bodies collapse after repeated blows. Death comes slowly. Throughout Jewish, Christian, and Islamic scriptures are accounts of stonings and warnings not to behave in particular ways because the penalty is death. (To be clear, the Qur'an does not mention stoning, though several hadith do.) One man is found gathering sticks on the Sabbath day, "and all the congregation brought him outside the camp, and stoned him to death with stones, as the Lord commanded Moses."[18] The Bible is full of many such accounts that associate stones not just with lifeless matter but also with the taking of life. Many of the early Christian martyrs, including Saints Stephen and Timothy, were killed by stoning. Stoned to death. Stone dead.

One more famous case involving laws of stoning is found in the Gospel of John while Jesus is teaching at the temple in Jerusalem. Interrupted by a group of people who bring in a woman accused of adultery, the Pharisees recite the law to Jesus: Moses commanded that punishment for such actions is stoning. They ask Jesus's opinion on the matter. Jesus, who was often called rabbi and knew the law well, did something unexpected: he turned the tables and indicted everyone by claiming, "He who is without sin among you be the first to throw a stone at her."[19]

Through such descriptive retellings, stones are connected with judgments, taking on connotations of guilt and innocence, functioning within the sacred stories as symbols, and even agents, regarding matters of life and death. All this aids in the lead-up to the Passion story, the narrative of the death and resurrection of Jesus. After some close calls with groups of upset people ready to kill him, sometimes with stones in hand, Jesus is eventually executed on a cross, in the Roman manner of capital punishment. After his death and deposition from the cross, he is taken to a tomb and embalmed on the Stone of Anointing. The Gospels then tell of a "great stone" rolled across the entrance to the tomb and a seal set on the tomb with a guard standing by. In each of the four Gospel accounts, the stone is miraculously moved away from the tomb entrance sometime during the night. When the women come to visit on Sunday morning, they are startled by the empty tomb, with the stone rolled away. The rolled stone becomes the first symbol of the resurrected Jesus, the triumph over death that stands at the heart of Christianity. A fragment of this is called the Angel's Stone and stands within the Church of the Holy Sepulchre in Jerusalem, not far from the Anointing Stone.

If the Christian scriptures tell of Jesus being tempted by the devil to turn stones into bread, the Islamic tradition also connects devilish temptation and stonings, with a nice twist. One key rite enacted as part of the hajj, the great pilgrimage to Mecca, is the stoning of the devil. Three stone pillars (*jamarat*) stand in the city of Mina, a few kilometers east of the Masjid al-Haram, the grand mosque of Mecca. In the midst of multiple rituals, including the wearing of special white garments (*ihram*), praying on Mount Arafat, running between two hills, drinking water from the Well of Zam Zam, sacrificing an animal, and circumambulating the Kaba, pilgrims throw stones at the *jamarat*. As numbers of pilgrims have increased (several million have performed the hajj in recent years), the pillars have also grown, due to the fact that stray pebbles thrown by other pilgrims were accidentally hitting people across the way. Old images of the *jamarat* show them to be small pillars, about two meters high. In 2006, the pillars were rebuilt into great walls with bridges towering around them, enabling millions of pilgrims to pass by and throw stones from upper or lower levels.[20]

Each of the smaller rituals that comprise the hajj stem from ancient stories, connecting contemporaries to the original hajj made by Abraham (Ibrahim) and also to the critical figures of Hagar, Ishmael, and Muhammad. The relevant story about stoning the devil for the hajjis, as those who complete the hajj are called, goes back to Abraham, the great patriarch of the Israelites and Arabs and ancestor of Muhammad. The Qur'an tells us how Abraham was commanded by Allah to sacrifice his son Ishmael in a way parallel to the Hebrew scripture account of Abraham's sacrifice of Isaac.[21] Later traditions tell us a fuller account and state that along the way, Abraham was tempted three times by the devil not to sacrifice his son, and thus to disobey Allah's commands. Ever available in times of need, the angel Jibrail fortifies Abraham's commitment and tells him to take stones and "Pelt him!" Contemporary hajjis mimic the ancient story by pelting the symbolic pillars with stones. In so doing, they are repelling the devil and his temptations, and showing their own resolve and faithfulness.

The mythical-metaphorical use of stones, whether in words or in the hand, is complex. On one hand, they are inert objects, a mere conduit to prove power. On the other hand, they begin to speak as they are bound up with activities of temptation and judgment, guarding and killing, death and resurrection.

Taking another look at the New Testament conversation about stones, we find their active role as a prime building material. In the midst of telling parables, Jesus quotes from the Psalms, "The very stone which the builders rejected has become the head of the corner."[22] Jesus mentions the cornerstone, at once rejected but then used, as himself. And later writings in the New Testament make this claim more boldly, as Christ Jesus is the cornerstone of the temple of God for the people of God.

When constructing a new church, post office, synagogue, bank, temple, house, or mosque, the cornerstone is the first material set in the foundation, and all other materials are based on this primary stone.* Its placement becomes crucial to the orientation, height, and balance of the rest of the building; if the cornerstone is off kilter, the whole building will be. But to be on kilter in a religious building also entails a spiritual sense of balance, some perfectly perpendicular metaphysics. Because cornerstones are so fundamental to a building, rituals often accompany their setting. Animals are sacrificed, dignitaries (secular and religious) perform gestures, prayers are spoken, and music is played. Meanwhile crowds of people take part in these foundational moments, directing their sacred energies toward raising the building. Varieties of similar rituals are evidenced across the world at many times and places and across religious traditions.

The Roman Catholic Church has a rite dating back at least a half millennium and probably earlier titled, "Of the Blessing and Laying of the Foundation Stone for the Building of a Church." In the rite a bishop sprinkles holy water on the foundation stone, engraves crosses on each side of the stone, and recites prayers and Bible verses in the presence of a group of congregants. In

---

* Many modern buildings pour concrete as a foundation, and so the cornerstone becomes metaphorical, though the concrete must still be well squared.

some accounts, money is also thrown into the foundations or laid on the cornerstone, though that is not part of the official liturgies.

The Catholic rituals, like many in the Christian church, have ancient pagan roots. The Christian rite takes after a pagan ceremony dedicating the Roman temple of Jupiter, just after the time of Jesus. Accounts of this ceremony tell how the "great stone" (at the foundation of the temple) was washed with lustral water and dragged into place by a collective.[23] Meanwhile, the oldest known cornerstone ceremonies go back thousands of years before Jesus, to the times of the ancient kingdoms of Akkad and Egypt. For almost as long as structures have been built, people have ritualistically participated in placing the first stone, the cornerstone.

In extreme cases, humans have been sacrificed at the foundations of a building. The nineteenth-century German poet and satirist Heinrich Heine tells of how "in the Middle Ages the opinion prevailed that when any building was to be erected something living must be killed, in the blood of which the foundation had to be laid, by which process the building would be secured from falling." And Jacob Grimm's *Germanic Mythology* relates how "It was often thought necessary to build living animals, even men, into the foundations on which an edifice was raised, to induce the earth to bear the burden laid on it."[24]

In the New Testament, Jesus proves himself the punster, playing on words and perhaps a sense of cornerstone history, as he gives a nod to one of his followers, Simon. Jesus renames him Peter, saying, "And I tell you, you are Peter, and on this rock I will build my church."[25] In Greek, Peter is *Petros*, while the term for *rock* used here is *petra*: "I tell you, you are *Petros*, and on this *petra* I will build my church." Rhetorically following Jesus's earlier parable of the wise man who builds his house upon a rock—as opposed to the foolish man who built his house on sand and winds and rains knock it down—Peter is the solid rock that supplies the foundation for the house-cum-church. In Roman Catholic tradition, Peter is seen as the first pope, who helps to establish the Christian church, the rock that is firm, solid, able to hold up large structures over the centuries.*

Scholars debate whether this same Peter, the disciple of Jesus, actually wrote the biblical books that bear his name, but this much is true: the author of 1 Peter picks up right away on the stone and rock metaphors that Jesus provides in the Gospels. Chapter 2 of that book strings together a series of scripture verses pointing to Jesus as a "living stone" and how each follower might themselves too become such a stone, being built into a "spiritual house." Peter's language reembodies Jesus's earlier language. Stones are living, and the house built from them is spiritual. The church has its foundation on rock. So does religious discourse. Upon this rock, sacred language will be built.

As I write this, it is summertime here in Central New York, an all-too-short period when we rush outside to soak up as much sun and green as we can before winter sets in again. This also entails a scramble to get things planted, hoping for a bounty of homegrown tomatoes, beans, corn, and other tasty veggies. During the season the local libraries appeal to our literary green thumbs, prominently displaying their collections on gardening. The garden manuals, as one would expect, describe the growing rate and height, hardiness, uses, and arrangements of plant material: trees, perennials, annuals, grass, vegetables, and herbs. Maybe some vines. Every once in a while the books might explain how to make a trellis or pathway.

Yet, one of the oldest surviving garden manuals in the history of the world begins by telling us that gardening is "the art of setting stones." This is the first line of the eleventh-century

---

* See Matthew 7:24; Luke 6:48. Peter's primacy continues in Roman Catholic theology, while the Protestant argument against it is still very evident today.

treatise *Sakuteiki* (Records of garden making) attributed to a minor court official during Japan's Heian period (794–1185). During the Muromachi era three hundred years later, another manual, *Senzui narabi ni yagyo no zu* (Illustrations for designing mountain, water, and hillside field landscapes), appeared. As with any good garden manual, the two records provide instruction on arrangement and design, how to work with particular materials, and the development of a humanly cultivated space in conjunction with natural surroundings.

What is striking to modern Western sensibilities is the importance placed on stones in the midst of it all. From the first line of the *Sakuteiki* through the end of the *Senzui*, the manuals offer training in stone use and arrangement, instruction on how to complement certain stones with other materials and elements of the natural world, as well as strategies for connecting stones to the humans who participate in the garden. The *Sakuteiki* explains the cornerstone-like importance of beginning with a "particularly splendid stone and set it as the Main Stone. Then, following the request of the first stone, sets others accordingly." Note how the first stone "requests" other stones. The *Senzui* even sets out a vocabulary of names for the shapes of the garden stones, for example, the *furoseki* ("never-aging rock"), *mizuuchi-ishi* ("water striking rock"), *mangoseki* ("rock of ten thousand eons"), *kamoi-ishi* ("ducks' abode rock"), or the *shuseki* ("rock of perfect beauty"). Records show that from the Heian period, and especially into the Kamakura period (1185–1333) when Zen Buddhism was widespread through the islands, the work of priest and gardener was often inseparable. The name for this occupation was *ishi-tate-so,* or "stone-setting priests," a term that continued on in the Zen tradition far into the Muromachi period. Stones have qualities, personas, and characteristics, and if the human gardener is attentive enough, he might be able to decipher these and set them properly.[26]

Very few places in the world (save China) cherish, use, and, in many cases, deify stones as in Japan. Japanese gardens are rife with indications of the potency, vitality, and cosmic significance of stones as they merge ancient Shinto practices and beliefs with Buddhism. Buddhism itself came from India, filtered through Chinese religious, aesthetic, and philosophical attitudes, including Taoism and Confucianism, before arriving in Japan in the sixth century. Japanese religious traditions today continue to mix and merge each of these in unique ways, and the gardens provide a palimpsest, an archaeological layering, of religious and cultural histories.

Within the indigenous traditions of Shinto, otherwise known as the "way of the *kami*," are many gods and goddesses. Similar to other polytheistic and animistic traditions, these include spirits of the ancestors who have died and passed on; deities of storms, fire, the sun, and the sea; gods of longevity and of foods like rice; and patrons of vocations such as sword smiths, musicians, and peddlers. The classic eighth-century text *Kojiki* states that there are eight million *kami*, which is another way to say the number is infinite. And the other eighth-century classic chronicle *Nihongi* chronicles the ancient "age of the kami," a time when "trees and grasses had the power of speech."

The *kami* also inhabit rocks and stones. Not unrelated to the Hawaiian and Maori stories noted above, accounts of Shinto mythologies involve beliefs and narratives about stones that produce offspring, grow, and move on their own accord. Particular rock outcroppings are seen as residences for the deities and are known as *iwakura*. Some accounts suggest that people saw something in a particular natural arrangement and realized the spirits were there, while other accounts describe an unusual setting and use it as a place to set up rituals to invoke the *kami*. As a result, various Shinto shrines exist across Japan, built upon more ancient geologically natural manifestations of the *kami*, like trees and hills and rock. Very often too, a local shrine will recreate the sacred presence of nature on a smaller, more human scale. The natural setting might be a mountain (e.g., Mount Fuji) standing tall and ever present over the valleys and plains below. The mountain, in turn, could be suggested by an *iwasaka* ("god boundary") made of upright stones or a circle of horizontal stones around a central stone, which thereby demarcates a sacred boundary.

The oldest existing Shinto shrine in Kyoto is the Kamigamo Shrine, and is now a UNESCO World Heritage site. Its origins derive from the worship of the deity *Kamo-wake-ikazuchi-no-kami* atop the sacred mountain of Koyama, two kilometers from the present shrine. Originally, people journeyed up to the mountain, but the devout were eventually able to experience down in Kyoto the sacred presence of the *kami*, now enshrined in the Kamigamo grounds near town. The sacred power was transported down to the valley and, standing at Kamigamo's entrance, twin cone-shaped *tatesuna* symbolize Mount Koyama. The one-and-a-half-meter-high mounds are formed from loose gravel. Because there are two, the mounds are also meant to invoke the binary forces of yin and yang, and thus create a harmonious experience through the shrine. And because a single sprig of pine branch is usually stuck at the pinnacle, they also can represent the trees that were used as part of sacrifices in the ceremonies. As with many dimensions of Japanese gardens and shrines, there is no single symbolic meaning. Within Kamigamo's *torii* gates stands the *Gan-jo*, the sacred rock highlighted during the annual *Aoi* ("Hollyhock") festival. During this time the chief priest kneels before the stone to receive a blessing, since the chief *kami* resides in that very stone during the festival period.

Shinto traditions continued to place importance on the *kami* that reside in natural objects like stones, eventually influencing the later Buddhist gardens. As Buddhist practices and ideas began to grow across Japan, a repurposing of the old symbols took place. The stones and shrines to the deities in nature did not disappear but changed forms to meet new ways of seeing and being. One of the more remarkable developments in gardening involved the creation of dry stone gardens. In the earlier gardens, water was the dominant element in the form of ponds, streams, and waterfalls. These gardens are called *sansui*, literally, "mountain-water," and derive much of their compositional form from Chinese landscape painting. Under the aesthetic austerity of Zen, stone and rock replaced water elements, generating an *impression* of ponds, streams, and waterfalls in the perception of viewers. These are known as *kare-sansui* ("dry mountain-water") gardens, and are thought to have originated with the work of the fourteenth-century Rinzai Zen monk and designer Muso Soseki. Both garden varieties, dry and wet, and other genres such as the tea garden, stroll garden, and imperial garden continue to be created now.

A diversity of garden forms can be seen within the Zen Buddhist temple complex in Kyoto called Daitoku-ji. Set up in the early fourteenth century by Shuho Myocho (or Daito Kokushi), this center for the Rinzai school of Zen comprises twenty-three subtemples operating today, even though Japanese people demonstrate less and less interest and involvement in Buddhist monastic rituals, save funeral rites. Significant among the spaces within the temple complex are tea gardens, graveyards, moss gardens, and pathways. Daitoku-ji is also home to some of the most intriguing *kare-sansui* gardens in the world, from the centuries-old gardens found in Daitoku-ji's subtemples of Daisen-in and Ryogen-in to the modern abstract spaces created by Mirei Shigemori—one-time collaborator with Isamu Noguchi—in the mid-twentieth century.

In Ryogen-in lies the so-called smallest rock garden in Japan, a *tsubo-niwa* ("small enclosed garden"), created by Gakusho Nabeshima in the 1950s. Named Totekiko, this garden—like its older and better-known *kare-sansui* ancestor in nearby Ryoan-ji—can be seen as containing the entire cosmos in its small site. All the tensions, all the forces, all the important objects are reduced to the tight space of this enclosure.* Many summaries of the garden claim that Totekiko represents a Zen adage about how "the harder a stone is thrown in, the bigger the ripples." In this way, the carefully raked gravel represents a body of water while the larger stones are the stone thrown into the gravel-water.

Observers also see the five large stones as islands in the sea, with waves lapping against them. Three stones are on one end and two on the other, which also harkens back to the Chinese mythology of the five Isles of the Immortals. And then again, perhaps these are mountains, another vital component in Japanese mythology, emerging from a surrounding foggy landscape. More down to earth, as with the famous mother tiger and cubs interpretation of the stone garden at Ryoan-ji, the stones might be animals or humans crossing a stream, caught in the currents of life. Or it may just be an abstract but captivating arrangement of varieties of rock, between white and black, vertical and horizontal, one end and another, carrying out multiple yin and yang contrasts. Some scholars have even looked at *kare-sansui* gardens like the famous Ryoan-ji through visual Gestalt theories, suggesting that it is the empty spaces between the larger stones that become harmonizing and contain a subliminal meaning.[27] As usual within religious symbolic structures, simple one-to-one correspondences give way to deeper realities: the ambiguous mysteries of myth, ritual, and symbol sensually absorbed.

A stone's throw from my office deep in Oneida County, New York, stands the Hamilton College Cemetery. Its current residents go back two centuries and include the founder of the college, a Presbyterian minister and missionary to the Oneida Indians named Samuel Kirkland, and the eighteenth-century Oneida Indian chief who became Kirkland's friend and a

---

* It is approximately 1.5 × 5 meters.

Christian convert, Skenandoa. The stone monument at Ske-
nadoa's gravesite reads: "You have laid a permanent foundation for a great school, and you propose our children shall be
benefited by it. . . . Possibly you may find that the difference
between us consists only in the color of skin." Their graves are
side by side, which by no means indicates that the relations
between European whites and the native Oneida have always
been cozy.[28]

Oneida is the anglicized name of Onyota'a:ka (pronounced
O-ni-yo-da-ah-ga), which translates into English as "People of
the Standing Stone." Before Kirkland, French Jesuit missionaries were in contact with the Oneida, and a 1700 treaty with
the French displays a signature of the Oneida nation simply as
a drawing of a stone. In fact, a standing stone has continued
to be at the physical and ceremonial heart of Oneida identity
for hundreds of years. It is an oblong gray syenite boulder that
has been an object of special veneration for as long as written
history allows. According to several older sources, the stone
was at the center of harvest and new-year festivals, dances, and
general worship of the Great Spirit. The old stories told of how,
whenever the Oneida people moved, the stone followed them.

The Oneida Stone caught the attention of the nineteenth-
century American geographer and ethnologist Henry Schoolcraft, who recorded a good deal of Native American mythology,
and whose work would inspire Henry Wadsworth Longfellow
to write his famed *Hiawatha* in 1855. Schoolcraft tells of the
relations between the stone and the Oneida people as being "in-
dissolubly" linked. "The stone is spoken of, in their traditions,
as if it were the Palladium of their liberties, and the symboli-
cal record of their very nationality."[29] But as the Oneida were
largely driven out of central New York, the stone was taken
and moved in 1849 to the emerging urban center of Utica and
placed at Forest Hill, a cemetery on the edge of the city. As the
Erie Canal remade prosperity for European immigrants across

the Northeastern United States, so rose the need to conquer land and bury people.

In a curious account, somewhere between eulogy and triumph, is the Reverend George Hardy's report of the Oneida Stone as it stood on a hill above Stockbridge, New York, just before it was taken to the cemetery: "This was the resting place of the stone when the white man appeared in the land, and the red skinned children of the Great Spirit began to give way before him. . . . It saw its people themselves waste away at the stranger's presence, their council fires extinguished, their festal days unobserved, their sacrifices unoffered."[30] As the stone was then moved to its cemetery site, Rev. Hardy's implication is that what is being buried is a whole people. The stone stood as a memorial, witnessing to their lives.

Today, after decades of change, the Oneida Stone has been returned to the Oneida Nation and now stands at the entrance to the Shako:wi Cultural Center in Oneida, New York. The Oneida have rallied to preserve their land, their culture, and, most important, an economic base that can retain their sense of power into the twenty-first century, and to repurchase land on which their ancestors lived. Among other works, the Oneida have set up a casino-resort, which now brings in millions of dollars in revenue. With this they are working to preserve their heritage, history, and language, in part by making generous donations to the National Museum of the American Indian in Washington, DC. (Forty large, uncarved stones called Grandfather Rocks, surround the NMAI itself; they were blessed in an inaugural ceremony and now serve to ensure a safe journey and carry messages to future generations.) The name the Oneida have taken for the casino metaphorically reflects both their past and their future: Turning Stone.

When I was a child, my mother created a scrapbook of our family, years before the multibillion-dollar scrapbooking industry took hold. The book contained images, some hand drawn and some photographic, and narrative bits and pieces of the stories of our family's life. As I remember it, the bound book with its needlework cover displaying the title "Plate's Pile of Stones" lay prominently on the coffee table of our living room. The book was a pile. The stories within were the stones.

My ancestors drew much of their lived mythology from the Christian scriptures, and our family scrapbook's title was taken from an Old Testament passage. At the beginning of the story told in the book of Joshua, we learn that Moses has just died, having been denied entrance into the Promised Land because of his disobedient indiscretion when the people he was leading were thirsty. He had angrily struck a rock with his staff, which caused water to pour out. With the death of Moses, Joshua becomes the leader and takes the Israelites across the Jordan River into the land of milk and honey. As they finish fording the boundary waters, marking the end of a long journey from slavery in Egypt and the beginning of a promised good life to come, God gives Joshua a few instructions: "Take twelve stones from here out of the middle of the Jordan, from the very place where the priests' feet stood, and carry them over with you, and lay them down in the place where you lodge tonight." God understands the permanence of a stone monument, its connection to a place, lasting through time, and so God concludes the directives: "When your children ask in time to come, 'What do those stones mean to you?' then you shall tell them that the waters of the Jordan were cut off in front of the ark of the covenant of the Lord; when it passed over the Jordan, the waters of the Jordan were cut off. So these stones shall be to the Israelites a memorial forever."[31] An ancient pile of stones marks time and triggers stories, which is just what my family intended with their modern version. (Something along these lines is enacted when stones are placed on grave markers in Jewish cemeteries.)

Decades later, when I visit my mother's house and read our

family's "Pile of Stones," I encounter a memorial, and I remember the times of loss, whether lost lives or lost youth, and the times of gathering, whether weddings or reunions. In so doing, I learn again where I come from, and ultimately the construction of who I am. One primary metaphor for my life has become this object, this pile of stones. Throughout history and across the world, stones and the stories they are witnesses to, let us know where we have been, where we are, where we are going, and at last, who we are.

Stones stand. And they can stand in the same place for a long time. Wind and rain, sleet and snow cause erosion, and human hands wear them down even farther, changing the color and texture of the durable matter. Yet, on a human time scale, stones seem virtually impermeable, imperceptibly changing in a lifetime. This fact makes them the ideal material to mark special, sacred spaces, memorials for generations to come. We find this in the gravestones of the Old Burying Grounds in a New England village, as well as in a crowded Tokyo cemetery; in the Washington Monument and the Vietnam Veterans' Memorial in Washington, DC; in the Holocaust Memorial in Berlin and the pyramids of Egypt; in the Taj Mahal in Agra, India, as well as the Pyramid of the Sun in Teotihuacán outside Mexico City. Stone is globally pervasive as a medium for remembering what has come before, for reencountering what no longer is. People feel connections with stones; they fondle them, touch them, kiss them, and tell stories by them.

In a 1928 work, the poet Francis Ponge pondered "The Pebble." Ponge sees a long geological process evolving over time, as each and every pebble emerged from a "single enormous ancestor," a "cadaver" that has now crumbled into pieces. We are left with smaller rocky chunks from that initial unity, the greatest of which are "sown about under woods by Time." There they crack, smile, and eventually become silent. Along the way, disintegration continues and the rock fragments grow smaller and smaller: a boulder, stone, pebble, sand, "smaller from day to day but always sure of its form." While a great wind can uproot a tree but not move a pebble, the pebble itself eventually turns into sand, and dust. Human time, distinct from the extensive unfolding of geological time, allows rocks, stones, pebbles, and sand to appear immutable. Sometimes—as Ponge and William Blake and so many others have demonstrated—we get a glimpse inside the process, the eternity in a grain of sand, arrested in development and devolution. Through this glimpse we encounter the mortal-bound nature of all life. Ponge suggests, "The great wheel of stone seems to us practically immobile and, even theoretically, we can only understand a part of the phase of its very slow disintegration."[32] When the stone speaks, and we hear, we realize the inevitability of its and our turn toward dust. Though life spans differ, the stone and the human share this humble trait. Whatever other effects they produce—protection in travel, cosmic wonderings, links to the natural world, marking sacred space, grounding speech—sensual encounters with stones ultimately trigger the human encounter with mortality.

Along the way, as we have seen in the preceding, stones just might be teaching us to speak a word or two. At least—if we are listening—they are telling us something about life itself: performing for us, whispering, standing up and down, killing, drawing us near or pushing us away, pointing here and there, reviving, ticking down the moments of eternity, allowing us to stand in awe and contemplation. And in so doing, they are acting religiously. Religions may tell us to take up stones and throw them at each other, but religious traditions also encourage us to stop, look, and listen, to be aware of the nature of everyday existence, of our physical lives and dependence on earthly matter.

INCENSE

Oil and incense gladden the heart,
And the sweetness of a friend is better
than one's own counsel.

—Proverbs 27:9

There is a familiar story in the Christian tradition about a few wise men, magicians of a sort, who discerned star signs and similar celestial occurrences. One night they are led by an exceptionally bright star to pay a visit to a special child born in the Roman-occupied town of Bethlehem. Like the much earlier visitation of seers to the infant Siddhartha Gautama (who became the Buddha), these wise men also saw it written across the sky that this child was going to be a world changer, a king. And so they brought the now well-known gifts: gold, frankincense, and myrrh. Two thousand years later, only one of these might be found on Santa's wish list.

Gold has been a relatively stable commodity over the millennia and across the world, valued by kings who kill for it, worn by women willing to pay good money for it, sought by athletes who train for years to have it hang around their necks, and seen as a sign of sacred status as it embellishes texts, ritual implements, and holy sites. Gold sets a standard, and global economies are linked to its value. In contrast, frankincense and myrrh come from harsh desert climes where the oozing wounds of scrubby trees are processed and ultimately burned to offer an aroma in a variety of social settings. Burning tree embers seems a bit dim in light of the gleam of gold, yet so strong was the ancient desire for specific scents—and so far from our contemporary sensual interests—that incense was offered as a gift fit for a king.

Incense is often called "food of the gods," reflecting the belief that it emerges from the realms of the gods, and thus we are to make offerings of sweet smells back to them. In Mesoamerica, copal is the name of incense burned at various rituals, and the story is told about how at one point the gods gathered and cast themselves into a pit of live coals. From this was produced the sun and moon, bringing light to the world; the gods became incense, and thus was light created. In the Iroquois and other Native American traditions, the Creator gave four gifts to the people: sweetgrass, sage, cedar, and tobacco. The four gifts correspond to the four directions. They are made into braids, and then burned to accompany prayers and smudging ceremonies. On the other side of the world, as we will see later in this chapter, Agni, the Vedic god of fire, has incense burned for him in order to reconstitute his body, which had been mythically dismembered. And the deities of Babylon, Egypt, Israel, Japan, and elsewhere all have longstanding relations to burning substances, as smoke and smell are offerings that connect the here below to that up above.

Yet, over the past few centuries, incense has become more accessible to more people, becoming widespread outside temples, and the smells linger in homes and streets from Mumbai to Miami, Singapore to Senegal. It is used not only in worship settings but also for purification, protection, healing, memory, marking time, and creating space, as we will see through this chapter. Sacred and profane objects are not always easily separable, and questions emerge about how set apart a thing should be to be considered holy.

The smell of certain substances can change our life in minor ways, like feeling relaxed in the presence of lavender, or in more drastic ways, as in the story of Marcel Proust's whiff of a madeleine, setting him on a writing journey that uncovered elements of his past life long forgotten. When I was writing my PhD dissertation in Atlanta, I walked to and from the university's library through a park. The foliage was lush, and in the summertime the honeysuckle vines that climbed over fences and choked out small shrubs—beaten only by the kudzu—would produce small yellow-orange flowers. I could smell the flowers long before I saw them. The aroma was sweet and intense, and mixed with the sultry Georgia air, permeated my nostrils and seemingly my whole body. It was like taking a bath in sugar. On the way home from a long day, feeling tired and a little sweaty, the smell halted me in my tracks. This was no passive rose saying, "Stop and smell me," this was a flower that *made* me stop. I was helpless against it. I breathed deep, letting go of the receding day. The tension in my shoulders subsided, my chest expanded. It wasn't necessarily a light feeling that I had, but the fragrance changed me.

Neuroscientists and psychologists tell us that the olfactory system is made up of some of the most ancient machinery in the sensing body. Unlike the other senses, olfactory nerves head straight for the limbic system and directly trigger the amygdala, a small region of the medial temporal lobes in the brains of higher vertebrates like primates. Here, memories are processed and emotions are born. Smell touches our species' deep desires and fears.* Among others, Rachel Herz at Brown University has shown how smell triggers a greater emotional response than other sense perceptions, and, like Proust, our autobiographical

---

* One brief indication of this is that people with anosmia ("smell blindness") are more prone to depression.

knowledge is shaped by scent.[1] We know ourselves by our
smells, as they transport us to the past through a present experience. The blind and deaf Helen Keller once stated, "Smell is a
potent wizard that transports us across thousands of miles and
all the years we have lived."[2] And the French philosopher Jean-
Jacques Rousseau related smell to memory and desire, claiming,
"Smell is the sense of the imagination; as it gives tone to the
nerves it must have a great effect on the brain."[3]

Walking into sacred spaces like temples, mosques, and
churches, several sensual actions are often undertaken that
mark the passage from profane space to sacred space. (Recall
that *profane* is not a negative term but synonymous with the everyday, the quotidian; it comes from the Latin *profanus*, meaning literally that which "outside the temple.") Muslims and
Shinto practitioners, for instance, will use water to wash hands,
face, and mouth,* while Roman Catholics perform the more
symbolic action of dipping fingers into holy water and touching the forehead. Other spaces are noted by taking off one's
shoes, bowing or genuflecting, or ringing a bell. These motions
are performed so that our bodies can tell our minds that it is
time to focus. We are trained through our senses. Objects and
spaces educate us.

When we walk into a space for a religious ceremony, a key
trigger is the smell of incense. It changes our attitudes; it changes
our actions. Incense is used in a striking number of places across
the world, in a variety of religious traditions. As we purify ourselves and get ready to leave the dust of the profane world behind, we also begin to smell the burning of various materials.
While incense is the main subject here, we might also remember
that perfume too has its roots in a similar activity: *per-fume*
literally means "through burning" (from the Latin *fumar*).

Scents change our moods, or put us in the mood, affecting

---

* The Islamic *wudu* also includes washing of the feet.

our appetites and libidos, our mindful and prayerful interests, our ways of thinking, acting, and feeling, our engagement with the past and prospects of the future, just as they place us in a time and space that is deeply *present*. Along with food and sex, not in contrast to them, smells also get us in the mood for worship.[4]

Does holiness have a scent? And if so, does it smell like flowers? Fresh cut grass? Cooking food? Rain in the desert? The top of a newborn baby's head? History gives us one clear answer, and that is the wide-ranging use of frankincense for sacred means.

Frankincense is also known as olibanum, and dhoop in India. From the Old French, *frank* means "pure" or "of high quality," while the name olibanum stems from the Arabic roots *luban*, indicating "whiteness," thus implying purity. Frankincense, then, is the "true" incense. Records indicate that the ancient Babylonian temple of Baal burned two and a half tons of frankincense every year. Egyptian mythologies say that it came to Egypt via the phoenix, and pellets of it were found in King Tutankhamen's tomb. The Roman historian Pliny reports the Roman emperor Nero to have burned one entire year's crop of it at his wife's funeral. At athletic events hosted by King Antiochus Epiphanes in ancient Syria, almost two centuries before the birth of Christ, spectators were given gifts of frankincense and myrrh at the conclusion of the games in a gesture of hospitality. If our contemporary associations with incense reach no further than hippies and some smelly stuff at churches, we might begin to realize how much our sensual worlds have changed since the birth of Jesus.[5]

Frankincense is derived from trees of the genus *Boswellia*,* native to the southern Arabian Peninsula and the Horn of Africa, in landscapes notoriously rife with venomous snakes.

---

* *Boswellia sacra* and *carteri* are the most commonly harvested, though the *papyrifera* and *serrata* species are also used.

Harvesting entails etching the outer bark of the tree so that a milky-white resin drips out, dries, and crystallizes. The crystals are collected, cured in caves, and sold. Because of the material's sacred nature, the ancient gathering of it was performed within a ritualistic framework. It is a labor-intensive process that has continued relatively the same way for thousands of years. The harvesting and selling of the material has long been part of the economic framework of the Arabian Peninsula, paving the way for the "Incense Trail" and the financial infrastructure that made the prophet Muhammad's hometown, Mecca, a bustling intersection of cultures, languages, goods, and religious traditions. Frankincense has played a key role economically, architecturally, spiritually, and sensually in Western religions, particularly in the history of Judaism.

Along with the rest of the biblical book, Exodus 30 was probably written and compiled around twenty-five hundred years ago, telling of an age another thousand years previous. Several centuries before the temple and the establishment of life in the Promised Land, we find, as part of the covenant that God enacted with Moses at Mount Sinai, the establishment of the ancient Israelites' central worship space, the tabernacle. This "meeting tent" was portable, and transported across the Sinai desert as the people wandered in the wilderness. As the home for the Holy of Holies, in which sat the Ark of the Covenant, strict details were given for architectural structure and interior design. Next to a table for showbread, the importance of incense is made clear, establishing it as a central aspect to worship of the one true God:

> The LORD said to Moses, "Take sweet spices, stacte, and onycha, and galbanum, sweet spices with pure frankincense (of each shall there be an equal part), and make an incense blended as by the perfumer, seasoned with salt, pure and holy; and you shall beat some of it very small, and put part

of it before the testimony in the tent of meeting where I shall meet with you; it shall be for you most holy. And the incense which you shall make according to its composition, you shall not make for yourselves; it shall be for you holy to the LORD. Whoever makes any like it to use as perfume shall be cut off from his people."[6]

God provides a secret recipe to be used only in this one setting for this one purpose. This mixture is holy, sacred, *kadosh*. Regulations regarding the practice of burning incense offerings were strict, as the Israelites would one day witness. On this occasion, Moses's brother Aaron had been consecrated as High Priest and his priestly sons, Nadab and Abihu, offered a "strange fire" before the Lord, "and fire came forth from the presence of the LORD and devoured them, and they died before the LORD."[7] A harsh justice for a seemingly slight slip in ritual etiquette, creating a textual passage on which many a scholar, rabbi, and theologian has also stumbled. Whatever else it suggests, we find the often dangerous power of the sacred and the constraints through which ritual and space are established.

If we moderns imagine a ritual sacrifice, we tend to think of meat, the offering of animals. But ancient texts and rituals continually place the burning of incense and the burning of meat side by side, meaning that incense itself is a sacrifice and thus also highly valued. Just as a lamb for slaughter had to be pure, so too was the incense to be pure. And sometimes the flesh and the incense were offered up together. Leviticus 2 instructs the priests to put oil and frankincense on the meat offering and burn it all together. Herodotus tells of a more involved mix of meat and scent in the Egyptian mode of sacrifice in which the young ox is prepared with a stuffing made from consecrated bread, honey, raisins, figs, frankincense, and myrrh. And when archaeologists uncovered the temple at Tenochtitlán in present-day Mexico, they found sacrificial stone knives that had a special copal ball on the hilt, very directly mixing the fleshy sacrifice and incense.

Discussing the offerings proscribed in the Torah, the great philosopher, physician, and rabbi Maimonides suggested a practical reason for the burning of incense: the aroma counteracted the smell of animals slaughtered for sacrifice with their entrails cut open, making the place stink like an abattoir. "If there had not been a good smell," he says in the *Guide for the Perplexed*, "let alone if there had been a stench, it would have produced in the minds of the people the reverse of respect; for our heart generally feels elevated in the presence of good odor, and is attracted by it, but it abhors and avoids bad smell."[8] Here and throughout the *Guide*, the medieval sage gives practical interpretations of the seemingly obscure requirements of Levitical law, offering a pragmatic apology. The severe codes for worship are there to enhance basic, sensual dimensions of religious practices. When one sees and sniffs within the great temple, he says, "certain emotions are produced in him."

The special recipe remained with the Israelites after they settled into the land on the east shore of the Mediterranean, established a monarchy, and began work on the great Temple of Solomon in Jerusalem. As in the tabernacle, incense is given a prime place, and two main altars were established: the Altar of Burnt Offering and the Altar of Incense. Offerings, made according to the recipe given earlier, were burned twice a day as the priest lit candles, and on Yom Kippur the high priest was required to burn incense in the censer within the Holy of Holies, not just on the altar outside. The tremendous nature of the temple was such that the Queen of Sheba traveled to visit. She was overwhelmed, presenting King Solomon with gifts of gold, precious stones, and spices.

According to various passages in the ancient oral tradition collected and codified as the Mishnah, the Abtinas family oversaw the secret incense recipe to be used in rituals during the time of the Second Temple. One of their claims to fame was that they could mix up a recipe to produce a stream of smoke that shot straight up like a pole, hit the ceiling, spread, and descend around the room, creating a vaporized version of a palm tree. Their family secret was kept intact, and many tried but failed to imitate this bit of pyrotechnics. Partly because of the secrecy of the recipe, today we have no clear idea what is meant by two of the four main ingredients: onycha (Hebrew, *shekheleth*) or stacte (Hebrew, *nataf*). Arguments have ranged from onycha being part of a mollusk or part of a rock rose, or possibly even amber, while the eleventh-century Talmudic sage Rashi argued that it was a benzoin, taken from a root in the ground. Stacte seems to have been a plant resin, but of which plant is unclear.

Secret knowledge often gives way to mystical dimensions. The economy of mysticism runs on the currency of secrecy. As esoteric elements within Judaism developed and Kabbalistic literatures spread, the presence of incense and smoke was seen to contain forces for mystical unification, syntheses of contrasting energies. The Zohar, the collected literature in the mystical tradition of Kabbalah, indicates how the smoke of offerings conjoins the up above with the down below, meanwhile uniting male and female principles, as well as purifying. Incense smoke precedes, and thus underlies, everything. Indeed, we read Rabbi Yosi's comments that "incense does more than prayer by creating unity and bringing light and removing filth from the world." According to the Zohar, not only does the actual offering of the incense work its wonders but also the words surrounding incense have power. Simply reciting the incense recipe from Exodus is powerful enough to help fight off death, including that brought by the plague. The literature even indicates how the ancient priests saw the letters of the Holy Name emerging in the rising smoke of the offering.

Holy incense can destroy evil influences: "Nothing is as effective as incense for doing away with death in the world, for incense is the connecting of Judgment with Mercy with the sweet savor in the nostrils," says the Zohar. Not only that, but within Kabbalistic traditions, reading and studying about the ingredients and preparing incense will protect one from illness. Similarly, in the Egyptian Book of the Dead, incense burning is prescribed for the safety of the souls of the departed as they move toward heaven, while the earliest Japanese accounts of incense use place it at sites of funerals. Pragmatic logic mixes with sacred sentiment.

Beyond the olfactory sensation, the burning of incense in sacred sites has a visual logic: smoke rises. And since the gods and goddesses reside in the heavens above, the incense ascends to meet them. King David makes the vertical analogy of worship and smoke: "Let my prayer be counted as incense before thee, and the lifting up of my hands as an evening sacrifice!"[9] Smoke from incense and burnt offerings become lines of communication with the deities.

Precisely because incense is so holy, contains so much power, it is not generally burned today in Jewish holy places for ritual purposes. As the First and Second Temples were the central sacred sites for ancient Judaism, the space of synagogues have typically been seen as distinct places of gathering, learning, and prayer. Offerings, including the incense offering, are not made here. The destruction of the Second Temple by the Romans in 70 CE also entailed, in essence, the end of the incense offering. Some Orthodox Jewish communities continue to claim that they kept the secret recipe safe and will make it again if the temple is ever rebuilt.

Try to grab smoke and it vanishes. Take a sniff and it lodges in the nostrils, shooting signals up through olfactory nerves and into the limbic region of the brain. But eventually the smells dissipate, exiting the nose and the conscious mind alike. Smoke, like light, paradoxically can be seen but not possessed. It can pass in and out of our sensing bodies, but it cannot be held. Smoke is physically sensed and spiritually suggestive—there is a reason ghosts and spirits are often portrayed looking like wisps of smoke. Theologically, light and smoke are not possessable objects, and therefore sidestep prohibitions on representing divinity, even as they remain within reach. Yet smoke possesses us, affecting our sense of space, memory, and feelings of pleasure and pain.

Not all people through history have delighted in smoke and scents the way the God of the Torah did. The concern in many cases, particularly in later monotheistic traditions, has to do with the tangible, object-centered aspects of worship. This smacks of idolatry, since the God of Christianity, Islam, and post-exilic Judaism has tended to be utterly transcendent and immaterial. To offer material goods to an immaterial God is problematic, not because people are worshiping the smoke, as might be the concern with images, but burning offerings indicates an external form of worship, when what God seemingly wants is an interior, contrite heart. Religious reformers' arguments against material rituals assert that external expressions move in the wrong directions: we should be cultivating an interior spiritual life instead of an exterior one.

A few centuries after the Incense Altar and the Golden Age of Israel, the prophet Isaiah bespeaks a God in which "incense is an abomination,"[10] and Jeremiah worries over and over about the people burning incense to other gods, particularly Baal. King Solomon himself made such concerns legitimate. According to the book of 1 Kings, Solomon "loved the Lord," built the great temple in Jerusalem, and burned incense to God, yet he also built incense altars to the gods of some of his seven hundred wives who came from other lands and were devotees of Moloch, Chemosh, and other deities. Later, Pliny, born within Jesus's lifetime, expressed his own concerns: he was disturbed to see the wastefulness of all these burnt offerings within Roman pagan rituals—remember Nero's burning an entire year's crop at his wife's funeral.

As Christianity emerged out of its pagan and Jewish roots, its leaders renounced the use of incense. If burning sacrifices offer a "pleasing odor to the Lord" of Genesis, Exodus, and Leviticus, a millennium and a half later Saint John Chrysostom would reverse such anthropomorphic tendencies and declare, "God has no nostrils."[11] The highly influential Christian theologian Origen, writing in the third century CE, suggested that one clear way to distinguish Christians from pagans was by the burning of incense. Jesus Christ, Origen claimed, will "defend us from the earth-spirits intent on lust, and blood, and sacrificial odors, and strange sounds, and other sensual things."[12] Origen interpreted many of the physical activities outlined in the early Jewish scriptures and turned them into metaphors, so that "burning" became an interior condition and not entirely to do with actual fire. Another great theologian of the time, Tertullian, scolded that burning odors are idolatrous. Writing to his wife, he laid out an ethical and behavioral guideline for her, indicating that the "handmaid of God" will be "agitated by the odor of incense."[13] The new tradition called Christianity began to coalesce and create its own unique identity, and so certain symbolic objects and actions needed to be left behind. New religious movements and reformations often bring with them a purging of sensual-ritual activities, claiming to aspire to something higher, by which is meant something more interior, and the emerging church was no exception.

Roman emperors similarly saw the use of incense as a method of marking identity, though from the other perspective. Christians refused to make offerings to Roman gods, as was the custom for citizens of the age. One better-known story recounts Habib, a deacon in a local church in the early fourth century who refused to make offerings, including the burning of frankincense, for Zeus. For his act of civil disobedience Habib was executed, becoming one of many early martyrs for the still-persecuted religion. In a curious poetic homily exalting the martyrdom, a sixth-century bishop in Syria named Mar Jacob sings the praises of Habib, reworking the death so that Habib becomes a burnt sacrifice, and the smell of his burned flesh becomes incense to God, "and there rose up the sweet perfume of the martyr."[14]

John of Ephesus gives another odiously odored sixth-century account. Best known today for his works *Ecclesiastical History* and *Lives of Eastern Saints*, John recounts some controversies surrounding the emerging doctrine of the Trinity. Mainly it hinged—as does so much in Christianity—on the dual nature of Jesus Christ, his full divinity and full humanity. Some claimed that if Jesus were actually two parts, then there were not three but four parts of the godhead Those who detracted from the dual-nature Christology carried this out to its logical extreme, calling those who saw two natures in Christ believers in a quaternity, not a trinity. Because of the seeming absurdity of this, many simply said Jesus was just one in nature, and they came to be called the Monophysites, ultimately coming out on the bottom of the theological tussle. In spite of their logic about not having another part of the Trinity, they were persecuted by the emerging Orthodox consensus confirmed by councils in the fourth century and later. In *Lives of Eastern Saints*, John discusses the heretics, those who opposed the dual-nature creed and who were thus thrown into fire, noting that the smoke wafted to heaven and seemed to please God. The God of the early Christians did not want incense sacrificed, but martyrs and heretics seemed to be an acceptable sacrifice at times. Human bodies became smoldering censers.

With such early resolve against offerings, it would seem that incense would have been swept away forever and not have become part of the Christian tradition. But walk into churches around the world today and that pungent air tells a different story. In spite of notions that God wants an interior, contrite heart, we are externally, sensually motivated beings. The very fact that early church leaders had to continually speak out against the use of incense surely implies that the practice continued among many people who called themselves Christian. After all, there is no need to denounce something that doesn't exist.

Around the same time as Habib's incensed martyrdom, Constantine rose to power, famously converted to Christianity, and issued the Edict of Milan, offering tolerance of all religions across his empire. Many of Constantine's changes regarded the style and space of worship, and material evidence shows the use of censers across the Roman church in the age of the Great Emperor. Even though he converted, his Roman pagan background continued to filter through his worship practices. As Christianity became legal, the previously pagan spices and censers were made available to Christian churches. By the medieval period, with Christianity well established across Europe, the Mediterranean, and beyond, incense was put to widespread use in churches, basilicas, and cathedrals.

Six centuries after Constantine, many miles to the north, Prince Vladimir of Kiev underwent his own conversion, turning from the traditional Nordic pagan rites of his homeland to the new Christian religion still unfurling across Europe and into western Asia. As he was acquiring new land, wives, and concubines, Vladimir and his forces decided to make a sacrifice to the gods. A human sacrifice. The lot fell to a young boy named Ioann, whose father, Fyodor, stood up against the sacrificers and their idolatrous actions. Fyodor was a Christian, and he openly assailed pagan ways. As might be expected, this act led to his death and his son's. According to historical reports from the time, Fyodor's accusations nonetheless left a mark on Prince Vladimir and became a turning point for his moving beyond pagan traditions. Fyodor and Ioann (Theodore and John) eventually became known as the first martyrs of the Russian Church.

Like Constantine before him, Vladimir eventually made Christianity the official state religion, but before that happened he did some crosscultural research in the form of sending envoys to neighboring countries to investigate their religious traditions. In an early act of interfaith dialogue, he encouraged his people to respect the various faiths and see what might be learned from them. (He also seemed to realize the political potential of religious alliances.) Envoys went to see the Muslim Bulgars, the Germans, and the Greeks. Somewhere along the way, Vladimir heard from a contingent of Jews as well. The historical compilation *The Russian Primary Chronicle* (attributed to the historian-monk Nestor) reports that the first two visits were not so positive: "The Bulgar bows, sits down, looks hither and thither like one possessed, and there is no happiness among them, but instead only sorrow and a dreadful stench. Their religion is not good. Then we went among the Germans, and saw them performing many ceremonies in their temples; but we beheld no glory there."[15] Since the third time's a charm, the visit to the Greeks led them to the grand city of Constantinople and to the vast expanse of the Hagia Sophia. The patriarch there knew how to put on a show, getting the clergy to assemble in their splendid garments in the resplendent space, getting the choir to sing, and incense to burn. The report of the envoys recounts this, "For on earth there is no such splendor or such beauty, and we are at a loss how to describe it. We only know that God dwells there among men, and their service is fairer than the ceremonies of other nations. For we cannot forget that beauty."[16] Here is the start of the Russian Orthodox Church and indeed modern Russia itself, born from sensual encounters with smells and spaces and singing.

"Something smells fishy about this set up." "I smell a rat." Our metaphorical language suggests we can root out problems by detecting odors—and perhaps that we might find solutions through our sense of smell. Thus, the journalist has *a nose* for a good story and the thrifty person has *a nose* for a bargain. The smells of incense in temples and churches purify, channel prayer, and change our minds, while other smells offer discernment or judgment and lead people on. Like bloodhounds we move, reverse direction, do something we didn't expect, and entire civilizations shift course from a few, well-timed whiffs.

While we can point to such linguistic examples still in use, the physical sense of smell has been downplayed in the modern world while vision has reigned supreme. The ongoing industrial and scientific "revolutions" spanning the sixteenth through the twentieth centuries were built on the sense of sight, on visual observations and optical instruments that emerged hand in hand with modern science and knowledge. Telescopes, microscopes, and printed books are three of the key objects that were developed during, and in turn created, modernity, and they are all visually engaged.

Sigmund Freud conjectured that human evolution was due in part to a shift in the senses. We used to move on all fours, close to the ground and guided by smells (anyone who has taken a dog for a walk knows what it's like to be steered by scent), but *Homo erectus* began the long revision of the primary sense organ from nose to eye, and secondarily ear. Freud even linked sexual perversions to the more primitive influences of the olfactory system. The implications are clear: smell is close to the ground, base, lowly, and primitive, but we have lost our need for those vulgar abilities as we high-minded moderns stand up straight and survey the world in front of our eyes. We now "turn up our nose" at those below us.

Since smell is attached to emotion and rationality is in opposition to feelings, there was another clear reason to revile the nose in the fetishistic rationality of the modern age. Preceding Freud were other Germanic philosophers, such as Immanuel Kant and G. W. F. Hegel, who likewise created a hierarchy of the senses, with the intimate senses of smell, touch, and taste situated below seeing and hearing. Taking what seems like a benign philosophical charting of the sensorium further, one prominent nineteenth-century naturalist, Lorenz Oken, even outlined a hierarchy of the senses based on race: the European related to the eye, the Asian to the ear, the Native American to the nose, the Melanesian to the tongue, and the African to the skin. The racist overtones later became implicated with ongoing nineteenth-century pseudoscientific practices such as physiognomy, much of which became tied to the search for the pure Aryan race, as will be discussed in the chapter on crosses.

Today as we reach the limits of what we can learn through a vision-based science, other senses are emerging as indicators of the human condition. The aromatherapy industry continues to move along, on somewhat the same fringes as the past two centuries, yet now increasing numbers of scientific studies give evidence to the efficacy of scents as healing, mood-altering, and mind-changing substances. IBM, among others, is investing millions in "cognitive computers" that can hear and see and smell. One promise suggests that computers, perhaps via smartphones or smartwatches, will one day be able to diagnose illness based on biomarkers in the breath. Meanwhile, dogs are being trained to sniff cancer cells in human bodies and are turning out to be surprisingly effective at it.

If dogs discern through the nose, gods do so even more. Several passages throughout the Jewish and Christian scriptures play this out, pulling from the intertwined roots of the Hebrew words *re'ach* and *ru'ach*. The former generally refers simply to smell. The meaning and use of the latter varies from "breath" to "wind" to "spirit," such as the *ruach elohim* that hovered over the formless void, as described at the beginning of Genesis. Physiologically, it is difficult to breathe without simultaneously smelling, and the language of scriptures plays out the bodily entanglement.

A curious, oft-quoted passage in Isaiah 11 indicates that the prophesied Messiah stems from the root of Jesse. This is the *maschiach* (in Greek, *christos*), the "anointed one," the king who will come and reign like King David before, allowing the lion and the lamb to lie down together. Isaiah prophesies that the "spirit [*ru'ach*] of the LORD shall rest on him."[17] The phrase could also be translated as the "breath of the LORD shall rest on him." This Messiah will judge the righteous not "by what he sees with his eyes, or decide by what he hears with his ears," but rather, if one translates it literally, the language here is that "he will delight in the odor of the LORD."[18] Some translators even suggested the Messiah will be "quick scented," a leader who's got a nose for things. The twelfth-century Christian mystic Hildegard of Bingen comments on this passage by suggesting, "By our *nose* God displays the wisdom that lies like a fragrant sense of order in all works of art, just as we ought to know through our ability to smell whatever wisdom has to arrange."[19]

The Christian New Testament continues in this way, as Saint Paul suggests to the followers of Jesus Christ: "Through us spreads in every place the fragrance that comes from knowing him. For we are the aroma of Christ to God."[20] Throughout Christianity until the modern period, smell has often been linked with holiness. There are accounts saying that upon the death of a saint, sweet smells wafted over the area. One of the most famous examples is Saint Teresa of Avila, who through her life was said to emit a pleasing fragrance. After her death in 1582, her body retained a particular scent for years to come and is connected with several healing miracles, especially as relics of her body were distributed across Europe, with some of these continuing to emit a sweet, healing odor.

Situated along the ancient trade routes of Arabia, the city of Mecca in the sixth century had a solid economic basis. Along with the varieties of goods passing through town came a potpourri of languages, outlooks, rituals, and myths. A young man named Muhammad was born here in 570 CE, amid the diversity, and listened to the ways of the world, the stories from afar. When, in his fortieth year, he began to hear the voice of God in the wilderness, he knew it to be the truth he had been looking for. Over the next twenty-two years of his life he listened for more divine revelations. These would eventually be collected and written down and become known as the Qur'an. As he recited the revelations in Arabic, others became convinced of their truth as well, and Islam was born of the poetic tongue of the prophet Muhammad alongside the spice route. Words and fragrances rise together.

Frankincense and myrrh were the most common types of incense that had been making its way for centuries by caravan from the southern points of the Arabian Peninsula to the Mediterranean civilizations of the ancient Egyptians, the Greeks, the Roman Empire, and Israel. There were many other scents as well, perfumed and burned, that made the journey, and Muhammad himself was clearly interested in the importance of good smells. The Prophet's collected sayings and traditions, known as the hadith, have numerous stories bespeaking the need for good smells in various matters of life. History has it that Muhammad's wife, Khadija, came from a family who traded in spices, and she is the one who recounts the story of people who came for Jummah (Friday prayer) smelling bad, presumably because they walked from afar in woolen clothes or came directly from their labors. From this experience began the emergence of ablutions, and ultimately the construction of great baths that would become incorporated into mosque complexes. It is important not to smell bad when praying.

With all that smell in the background, Islam nonetheless established itself without recourse to external accessories of worship such as icons and incense. Like the fledgling Christian religion of a few centuries earlier, it attempted to focus inward.

Clearly established rituals of cleanliness permeate the Qur'an and the sayings and actions of the Prophet collected in the hadith, but little space is devoted to seeking pleasant smells in everyday rituals. Those seem to be reserved for the pleasures of Paradise, a great multisensual garden awaiting the faithful. Promises are made to people that Paradise will be a nice smelling land.* Paradise has often been associated with the Garden of Eden, out of which came Adam and Eve after the Fall. Some commentaries on the Qur'an indicate that they brought with them a few things from the garden: the Black Stone, the rod of Moses, and incense.[21] Yet regardless of the Qur'an's words, incense has been part of Muslim life in many times and places, sometimes for sacred purposes, sometimes for profane.

Some miles from Muhammad's home lies the land of the nomadic Tuareg. Traversing some of the harsher ecosystems on earth, these Berber people have existed for centuries in and around the western parts of the Sahara Desert, practicing a religion that combines ancient animistic activities with Islamic motivations and interests. Over the past couple of decades, the American anthropologist Susan Rasmussen has spent significant time with them in Niger and Mali. One dimension of their cultural life that has become intriguing to Rasmussen is the central role of the Tuareg "smellscape." Scents become medicinally therapeutic, serve as mediums to the spirit world, offer protection, and denote space, while they also mark fear and danger and can become taboo. There is a scented social code, with established uses of perfumes and incense to signify hospitality and friendship as well as courtship.

During weddings, incense becomes paramount for the Tuareg as they mix and merge Islamic and animistic activities. Like

---

* It is interesting to note that Islam traditionally casts heaven as a garden, while Christianity sees it as a city; indeed the word *paradise* stems from an ancient Persian word meaning a "walled enclosure" like a garden or park.

all rites of passage, weddings indicate a change in social status for the initiates. The anthropologists Arnold van Gennep and Victor and Edith Turner have discussed this aspect as the *liminal stage*, a threshold arena betwixt and between regular time and space. I've heard rites of passage likened to a ligament, whose primary function is to bind bones together—as many of us who have had knee, ankle, and wrist problems can attest, the joints are weak points in the body. The bones on this metaphor represent the stable stages of life. Like the ligament, the initiate at this in-between stage is vulnerable and in need of protection; he or she needs a brace. This is given in the form of amulets, prayers, spells, and other symbolic gestures and performances enacted with communal support to enable the transition from one stage of life to another. Rituals around the world provide many examples of the use of fumigants, perfumes, and incense in transitional life passages.[22]

Along with the amulets that keep vigil over Tuareg bride and groom, but especially bride, is a constant burning of incense during the eight-day wedding ceremony. While the bride is the central focus of protection, many around her also become permeated with the smoke, absorbing it into their hair and clothing, thereby enhancing their immunity. Through these observations, Rasmussen finds that "scent is a metaphor for the evaporation and regeneration of the social and physical body, in addition to envelopment of the person to protect him or her against danger. . . . Maintaining oneself in good aroma (and, for that matter, sharing it with others) is not simply a means of being personally attractive or socially nice. It is a matter of sanctity and sin, life and death."[23] The metaphor is thoroughly situated within the lived social exchanges of the people; it is not mere ornamental flourish. Scents like those given off by incense construct the lives of those who come into contact with them and provide access and protection in light of new responsibilities in life and in the face of death.

———

On a late summer day, sticky and sweaty, I arrived in Vrindivan, India, shoulder to shoulder and nose to nose with a million other temporary residents. Unlike them, I was not on a pilgrimage, or I don't think I was. They had come for Janmashtami, Krishna's birthday, much like Christians cluster in Bethlehem at Christmas. The much-loved deity, praised for his mischievous youth as much as his cosmic power, is celebrated here in the land of his mythical birth, the area known as Vraj.

Diana Eck, Harvard scholar of Indian religious traditions, once claimed that "India must be seen to be known," and so I had come to watch them watching Krishna, to experience something of this curious religious devotion that I had only read about in Eck's book *Darshan*.[24] She tells of visual exchanges between Hindu deities and worshipers, how the enlarged eyes of the sacred icons stare back at their viewers to enact a mutual gaze. Onlookers gain a blessing by going to the temple and being looked at by the deities, in this case by a statue of the Lord Krishna. And in this case as part of a throng of thousands of others slowly passing before the center of the temple's altar. I was new to India, and my landing in this place and this time merely coincidental. I had no idea it was the time for celebrating Krishna's birthday, but perhaps that was auspicious in itself. I heard bells and yells echoing through alleys and across the Yamuna River, I saw people and animals and buildings spectacularly old and astonishingly new, and I smelled smoke from burning things I didn't recognize.

Certainly India must be seen to be known, but it must also be touched and tasted and heard, and most definitely smelled: not only in worship but also throughout everyday life. India is sensed from the bright-colored *kumkum*, vermilion, and fresh flowers set out along outdoor markets, from the street food known as *chaat*, from the constant bells and buzzing and beeping across roads and fields, from the perpetual smoke of burning incense. On one level, the encounter with any new place is a shock to our senses, which become somewhat dulled by the daily habits of home. But for those of us outsiders who have been inside India, there seems to be something unique that piques the senses in ways unlike most anywhere else. This led one scholar to suggest that "no account of India, from Kipling to the recent popular novels of M. M. Kaye and the accounts of Geoffery Moorhouse, fails to evoke the peculiar smell of that subcontinent, half corrupt, half aromatic, a mixture of dung, sweat, heat, dust, rotting vegetation and spices. The intimate relationship between smell and the exotic."[25] Strongly mixed with the aromatic smellscapes of rural and urban sites across the subcontinent is the wafting smoke from *agarbatti* (*agar* meaning "aloeswood" and *bathi* meaning "stick"). Storeowners burn it in the mornings as they open their shops, taxi drivers burn it in front of their taxies, and the devout in temples all over wave burning incense as they perform their devotional *puja* to the deities.

This creates an environment in many ways diametrically opposed to the strictures of the Jewish temple incense offering. Confined to the temple, with a protected secret recipe, the sacred smells of the ancient Israelites were legitimated and regulated by religious authorities, keeping the sacred—and their own social status—safe and secure. This confinement was certainly buttressed by the costly price of incense, meaning that the average household could not afford to burn a substance valued at the level of gold. Nowadays, due to agricultural and industrial revolutions, the making and marketing of incense has reached the level of the mundane, accessible to all for a small price. All that brings up a curious point about the ways incense gets us in the mood for worship, for special times and places. If we smell it everywhere, is everything holy? Hazy can be the line between sacred and profane.

A revealing account of this obscuring can be read in an online catalog for the Indian company Tiranga, which sells various joss sticks, including that of gulab (rose):

> This meditation scent is most popularly used in the Indian rituals. It has been appreciated for decades as exceptional quality incense for deep calming meditation and for creating sacred spaces. Powerfully fragrant and long lasting, the scent will linger in your rooms for hours. It evokes the feel of the tropical and evokes a warm, melodious scent. This unique scent is reminiscent of a warm summer evening.[26]

Tiranga knows that smells evoke and produce feeling: they calm us, create space, and place our lives within a sacred continuum. The catalog description unintentionally shows the historical trajectory of religious devotion into modern life and the continued use of sensual objects within that. Beginning with the traditional, more public setting of rituals and sacred spaces, the description shifts to one's own private rooms, and ultimately to that most private of spaces, one's own memories and experiences. On the other hand, the description can be read backward to understand how one's life is situated within a grander, mythical narrative. I myself can buy and use this product and legitimate my purchase by positioning my personal reminiscences within the collective, longstanding tradition. The sacred is not erased so much as displaced, moved and multiplied to places beyond the temple. The formerly profane takes on an air of sanctity. The question remains, however, as to how far the "sacred capital" (as my friend and colleague Timothy Beal might phrase it) is spent down.[27] Is the sacred worth as much in a living room as in a temple? Does it matter?

As with the Tuareg, the uses of scents and incense in South Asia do not necessarily connect people with the time of the past—modern marketing blurbs aside—so much as the space of the present. That modern Westerners make much of the rela-

tion of scent and memory tells us something about our understanding of ourselves, but as the religious studies scholar James
McHugh has argued, smell in the history of South Asian religion
and culture, is "social, connecting people to other people and to
the things in the world."[28] There is a social life of scent, establishing relations between people, within space, in the here and
now. There are good and bad, appropriate and inappropriate,
auspicious and inauspicious fragrances. Of course, scents also
connect humans with the gods, but for that we have to get the
recipe right.

In one of the most popular books in Indian history, the *Ma-
habharata*, a Brahmin ascetic named Suvarna gives an answer to
the question of just why *devas* (gods) desire flowers and incense.
There is a simple answer of course: that they (like the Hebrew
Bible's God) are pleased with and gratified by the smells. Good
smells increase joy, and that joy is then shared with the giver
of offerings. Yet here too is a code for giving, and distinctions
between smells become crucial to understand, lest one offend
the divine. Suvarna tells that when selecting incense, resins are
the best for the *devas*, while *guggul* is of the highest order. Also
known as bdellium, *guggul* comes from the resin of a small tree
in the myrrh family. Curiously, the only exception to the good
resins is *sallaki*, from the *Boswellia serrata* tree of the frankincense genus. Frankincense is to be used for the *daityas*, the
enemies of the gods. One god's pleasure is another god's enemy.

The Vedic tradition links *guggul* to Agni (the god of fire, naturally). In those much older, authoritative texts, it is not so much
a sacrifice or offering as it is linked to the very body of Agni; the
burning of *guggul* ritualistically reconstitutes the god's body,
which had been dismembered, according to the ancient myths.
As Agni's popularity diminished over time and other deities like
Shiva, Vishnu, and the great traditions of the goddesses (the *devis* such as Durga, Parvati, and Kali) came to prominence among
the devout, they too had their likes and dislikes. Medieval texts

tell of Shiva's love of a specific type of *guggul* called *mahishaksa*, while camphor and aloeswood are also highly praised.

Guggul had been prominent across northern India for millennia, but due to massive harvesting it is now a threatened species and the Indian government has banned its export. The impetus for much of the overharvesting seems to have been some studies that suggest the active compounds in it reduce cholesterol, though other studies disprove this. Along with the fads surrounding so-called ayurvedic medicine—some legitimate, some not—worldwide interest in the old shrubbery could spell its demise. The gods cannot be pleased.

In Vrindavan I was connected to these other people who had come to the city because of ancient stories told about Krishna and his life in the area, many of which are found in the *Bhagavad Purana*. Among other tales about the god Vishnu, and especially his avatar Krishna, we learn in these sacred texts about the evil demon Putana (whose name literally means "Stinker"), who sets out to destroy the infant Krishna by poisoning her breast and getting him to nurse from it. Krishna, great god that he is, literally sucks the life out of her, and her monstrous dead body is dismembered and burned. As the smoke rises, the stinker's body transforms into the pleasing smell of aloeswood. People from around the area of Vraj were drawn to its bouquet and ultimately to the Lord Krishna, to whom they offered blessings (*puja*).

Besides the scented offerings, and because Vraj is an area that has historically been a place of cow herding, Krishna is especially fond of offerings of dairy products like ghee, curds, and yogurt (and was infamously caught as a child stealing butter—a scene often depicted in devotional imagery). At Janmashtami, I watched the priests at a local temple pour liters and liters of spiced yogurt and ghee over a small black statue of Lord Krishna, the liquid running over the slick stone body and draining off somewhere I couldn't see. When I returned to the ashram where I was staying, I found one of the priests with a keg of the liquid from the ritual offerings. He set it up in an open space and the community anxiously lined up to partake of the *prasad*, the holy leftovers given back to us humans by the gods. This is consecrated food, but unlike the transubstantiation of Holy Communion in the Roman Catholic Church, nobody seemed to mind its sloshing and spilling around. I too took, drank, and, later, ate. I left with a sweet taste in my mouth that eventually disappeared, vivid images that stayed in my mind and camera for a long time, echoes of ringing bells and chants that became confused. But today I cannot recollect the smells.

In Sir Arthur Conan Doyle's story "The Red-Headed League" Sherlock Holmes is working out a mystery, as he does, back at his Baker Street digs. He tells his friend and assistant Doctor Watson that he needs to think about the details of the evidence surrounding their current conundrum. As usual, Holmes confounds his friend by doing what seems to be nothing, sitting in a chair with his eyes closed. "It is quite a three pipe problem," Holmes tells his quizzical companion, "and I beg that you won't speak to me for fifty minutes."

Doyle's story indicates another way that incense relates to time. Not in a remembrance of time past but in a present way of structuring chronology. Burning takes time. With practice and observation, the timing can be predicted. In turn, burning *makes* time. Holmes knows that it takes about fifty minutes to burn through three pipes' worth of tobacco (which is an interesting number in the story, since fifty is not easily divisible by three). When working on a mystery, Holmes is collecting his thoughts in the present instead of recollecting them from the past.

Centuries ago Buddhist monks in China made similar observations about the burning of incense. In China and on into Korea, Japan, and the Indochinese peninsula, incense began to be used to mark time. This occurred in political, economic, and social realms, as well as religious ones. The visual, tangible, olfactory, spatial, and protective dimensions are not erased, but sometimes took a back seat to this other function. In many contexts the type of incense is key; in others the variety doesn't matter.

Many types of incense have been used across Southeast Asia. Prominent among them are aloeswood and camphor, both of which can be derived from native plants in the region. Frankincense appears in many places, though it is rarer because it must be imported from the Middle East. For Buddhist traditions, the most popular ingredient is sandalwood, native to India, but imported and used extensively in many forms in medieval and modern Chinese rituals. Tradition suggests that the first statue of the Buddha was carved out of white sandalwood and brought from India with Buddhist texts. Rosaries and other carvings are made from sandalwood, because it is a fragrant material even without incineration.

A mechanical clock ticks. An incense clock sizzles, consuming oxygen and resinous powder as it burns off seconds, minutes, and hours. Some accounts tell of messengers who had limited amounts of time to sleep on their journeys. To ensure that they woke up on time, the messengers would put an incense cord or stick between their toes, light it, and fall asleep: one can imagine the shock of the alarm. In agricultural settings, a particular length of burning incense would indicate the amount of water to be used for irrigation: open the sluice and light the fire; when the incense is burned up, close the sluice. And on ships, incense was used to mark the times of sailors keeping watch and was as important as the compass.

Based on the preceding, one might easily deduce how incense was used in sacred settings. Monastic Buddhist services occur at regular intervals throughout the day, much like prayers in Islam and Judaism, and *puja* in Hinduism. Before mechanical clocks and without simply resorting to the sun, people needed a way to mark time, and so precisely measured formations of incense were burned to indicate the time between meditation and other activities. Incense was sometimes formed into sticks or cords, but the pulverized material was also laid out in trails on a flat template (think of those cartoons with a trail of gunpowder leading to a keg of explosives), and carefully calculated to burn out in a specified time. There are many designs for these trails—one is called the winding river incense, for obvious reasons—and hence the visual dimension of incense use cannot be overlooked here either.

The time-keeping functions likely developed after an earlier use of incense that connected its pragmatic purposes with spiritual resonances. One export that Buddhist monks, texts, and traditions took to China was the variety known as Tantric Buddhism, an esoteric set of practices and principles that regularly verge into mystical experiences. One practice came from a piece of Tantric scripture called "The Incense Seal of Avalokiteshvara Bodhisattva." Avalokiteshvara (meaning the "one who looks down at the world") is a popular figure, highly revered in Buddhist communities. Often a male but sometimes also female, the being is a bodhisattva, a "Buddha to be," one who has renounced the final entry into nirvana and out of compassion stays around to aid others out of the cycle of *samsara* (the birth and rebirth cycles of reincarnation). One story tells of his having a thousand arms, each of which aids the suffering of the world. Avalokiteshvara became synthesized with the Chinese goddess Guan Yin, and in Japan took on the form of the Amida Buddha, or the Kannon Bosatsu.

In the ritual of the Incense Seal, powdered incense is laid out on a template (a seal) that takes the form of the verbal characters of a mantra, in Siddham script. (If you've seen the stylized characters of the Hindu sacred syllable for *aum*, you might be able to imagine this.) The trail of incense is burned, and as the powder burns mantras are chanted; the experience brings the

practitioner through several stages toward deeper enlightenment. The text ends thus:

> Use sandalwood, lotus, or other fine incense in such a burner,
> and every day the Diamond Realm [of Tantric realization]
> will shine brighter and brighter. . . . The incense burner pat-
> tern truly manifests [the Tantric teaching]. Perform the vari-
> ous *mudra* [symbolic hand gestures] and recite the *mantra*:
> *om va jra dharma hrih*! [Hail to the Adamantine Dharma
> of Thousand-Armed Kannon!] If one utilizes this *mantra* all
> calamity and sickness will be avoided; one will be reborn in
> the highest paradise after death and be a facilitator of the
> liberation of all. Rely on this teaching, practice it, and per-
> fect enlightenment will quickly be attained.[29]

Note here that the type of incense is not as important as the
pattern in which it is laid out and the connection between the
burning and bodily performances of hand gestures and spoken
words. This rite is not an offering as much as an incantation.
Avalokiteshvara is invoked, but unlike the Hebrew Jehovah,
Hindu Shiva, or Taoist Li Tiegual, this being does not require
sacrifice and offering. Incense is used as a basic time marker but
can also be used to attain enlightenment. That incense is used in
pragmatic as well as mystical ways indicates how incense permeates many layers of religious life. One is not more important
than the other. The sacred and profane mix and merge in strange
ways among the senses.

Along with the seeds of Buddhism and garden design, basic
practices and accoutrements of incense rites came to Japan in
the sixth century. In general, incense was burned as a way to
invoke the Buddha's presence and as an act of purifying a ritual
space. Several types of aromatic plant matter were initially used,
such as sandalwood, cloves, and camphor, while unique com-
binations of materials were created among differing sects and

monasteries. Incense use reached a new level of refinement when the Chinese priest Ganjin traveled to Japan in the eighth century, bringing both Buddhist doctrines and fresh incense blends and recipes, imports that had significant effect on the Japanese use of incense for centuries to come.

By the Heian period, an aristocratic industry and culture emerged around incense. Its secularized use in Japan became known as *soradaki* (empty burning), which was distinguished from *sonae-koh* (offering to the Buddha). In the ninth century, one Prince Kaya took on incense as his personal royal hobby, becoming a master blender, codifying the "Six Scents," and helping to usher in what came to be called the golden age of incense. We know something of these six scents today because they were defined by the Buddhist poet-priest Jakuren in his twelfth-century work *Selections from the Incense Anthologies (Kunshu Ruisho)*. The blends were called Plum Blossom, Lotus Leaf, Royal Steward, Chrysanthemum Flower, Fallen Leaves, and Black. The names were meant to be evocative and did not indicate that these substances were actually the ones used. Jakuren's anthologies contain extensive recipes for blending, and we learn, for example, that Prince Naya's version of Plum Blossom contained aloe, seashells, spikenard, sandalwood, cloves, musk, and amber. The amount of each ingredient and the process of blending were crucial, while the final creation might also entail burying the mixture in the ground for days or weeks, allowing it to age.

Prince Kaya himself was an ancestor of Murasaki Shikibu, famous for writing what is called the world's first novel, *The Tale of Genji*, in the eleventh century. The story of Prince Genji describes both everyday life and the complexities of social etiquette during the period, referring frequently to the scents of incense, which were used within particular places and as a perfume. Clothes were often hung over a special rack with an incense holder sitting below it. Cooking the incense would enfume the fabrics. *The Tale of Genji* also indicates how courtship and other interpersonal dynamics were mediated through scent, at the expense of seeing and hearing. People came to be known for their scents, and characters such as Kaoru Chujo ("The Fragrant Captain") and Niou Miya ("His Perfumed Highness") appear at points in the story.[30] The praise and parsing of incense became so heightened that there developed a "way of incense" (*ko-do*) that mirrored the now more remembered "way of tea" (*cha-do*). Scented media is social media.

Perhaps you have visited the grand spaces of Chartres Cathedral, the Blue Mosque of Istanbul, Saint John of the Divine in New York City, or one of the many temples of Orissa, Beijing, or Los Angeles. Recall for a moment the vast space and the sensual encounters that brought you more fully into that place. It may have been the diagonal streams of sunlight pouring through colored glass, dust motes floating, caught in the light's gleam. Prayers, chants, or music may have been heard, while the sound of shuffling feet alerted you to the presence of others. Now imagine not just the images and echoes of this holy space but also the smells—the frankincense, sweet yet pungent, washing away the pollution of the vehicles, the odors of the vendors, and sweaty bodies on the streets outside. The latter sense is somewhat more difficult to reimagine, for several reasons, not just because smells can be fleeting.

When I visited but a few of the three thousand mosques of Istanbul, I was fortunate to have a guide to fill in the sensual details that are missing from these spaces in modern life. Architectural historian Nina Ergin has been studying the mosques of Istanbul created during the Ottoman period (1453–1922), and she showed me several of the mosques, noting their visual designs but also pointing out the ways they might have been sensually apprehended before the secularization of Turkey disbanded many larger mosque operations. During the Ottoman period, many of the taxes and spoils of war went toward the maintenance of mosque life. Although strictly speaking a mosque (*masjid*) is simply a "place of prostration," and there are no strict requirements as to how the building should be constructed—it's the activity inside that counts—Ottoman mosques were community-wide complexes that incorporated *madrasas* (schools), baths, gardens, and mausoleums, as well as the various infrastructures necessary to maintain all that, including kitchens and places for workers to do their tasks.

The great mosques designed by Mimar Sinan (chief Ottoman architect in the sixteenth century) are still in use today, along with many small mosques tucked away among the ambling streets of the city. Sinan's mosques include the Suleymaniye, Rustem Pasha, and Shehzade mosques, though today they are each sensually apprehended in ways unlike that intended by Sinan. Master architect that he was, the designs were created to be not only visually spectacular but also acoustically resonant and aromatically evocative. A number of the mosques even employed a person responsible for scenting the place. Known as a *buhurcu*, this person, as well as the Qur'an reciters, lamplighters, and cooks, helped create sensual ambience.* As Qur'anic passages were recited from prominently placed platforms, incense would burn and drift with the words across the open space of the prayer hall. The Word of Allah became tangible, audible, visible, and fragrant, synesthetically drawing the devout into relation with the divine.

With the demise of the Ottoman Empire and the secularization of the state, funds for these types of services dried up. The soup kitchen at the Suleymaniye mosque is now a restaurant that caters to tourists, and some of the baths connected to mosques are also oriented to bring outsiders' money in. All that is to say

---

* Similarly, in Christian and Buddhist traditions, particular groups of people, artisans as well as custodians, have been employed with the primary purpose of creating and maintaining incense for use in churches and temples.

our understanding of sacred architecture in the present age is primarily one of vision, missing much of the smell and sound of the spaces. Visiting and analyzing buildings, we discuss columns and arches, windows and aisles. Every once in a while we notice the ways sound bounces off the walls, but these examples pale in comparison to the places' full uses in their past.

A larger issue is at stake with these historical memories of Heian Japan and Ottoman Turkey. As we reconstruct the past we would be well advised to attend to the senses of the ages. Not only has the smell of incense (and perfume and other aromatics) drifted from our memories, it has also vanished from our histories. A particular scent may take us back to a particular time and place, but we cannot, willy-nilly, conjure up the way something smelled in the past. Processes of globalization, colonization, and secularization, mixed with ever-new technologies, have remade the world, connecting groups never before connected, producing a global village of sorts. These same processes have simultaneously remade our sense perception. We simply don't smell like we used to, and flashing neon signs no longer capture our attention as they might have a half century ago. But to say we live in a media-saturated world is not quite accurate; we live in an *audiovisual* media saturated world. Our media attends to, and bombards, primarily only two of our senses: hearing and seeing.

Leave it to the mad men of Madison Avenue, where advertising must conjure new spells to lead the masses into new conversions. They know we need new triggers to outpace the old audiovisual tricks, and so one emerging area is *scent branding*. Entire companies have shot up based on this principle, and the magazine *AdWeek* recently called it "branding's final frontier."[31] Major corporations are buying in. At the heart of the new frontier is creating signature scents, special mixtures designed for specific settings. Taking into account demographics like race, age, and gender (Sony has toyed with scents to allure women toward their mostly male-purchased electronics), along with the product being sold (the pleasant scent of, say, cut grass doesn't go over well in Victoria's Secret), research and development facilities consider a range of variables as they develop new recipes. The Mandarin Oriental Hotel in New York City has a scent called Sequoia that glides through the lobby, greeting visitors who have just walked in off Columbus Circle. Walking through most any shopping mall in North America or the rest of the postindustrial, consumer-driven world, you've already had a similar experience: passing an Abercrombie and Fitch, subtle muscular scents waft out the door, while Cinnabon's aromas are more overstated.

One new company called ScentAir, based in North Carolina, explains its big idea on its website: "By targeting the senses, brands establish a stronger and enduring emotional connection with their customers." The sleek audiovisual site gives some interesting world history on the use of odors, while eliding any direct religious references. In the end they suggest, "Experiences matter. Our sense of smell is the strongest way to add more to the customer experience."[32] Donna Sturgess, president of a neurological marketing firm called Buyology, similarly says in ways that might stir the bones of Maimonides, "Pleasant, subtle scents lift our moods and impact buying behavior."[33] Multiple studies have shown strong correlates between pleasant smells, happy feelings, and thus people lingering longer in those places.

Neural marketing. Scent branding. The power of contrived sensual experience to make us happy and comfortable, to connect, linger, and ultimately buy. Is this the new age? Or is it entirely old? Rather than simply and cynically reacting against advertising's seemingly more intrusive tactics (after all, they are just doing what advertising does in a capitalist economy), might we rethink religious history itself and wonder how particular mosques, sects, and even new religious movements *branded* themselves? Perhaps a history of incense in sacred spaces is a history of scent branding, of creating an experience that lifts moods and affects behavior, of distinguishing one's space, and thus one's self, from another.

There is one final consideration. That incense (or tobacco, or wood logs, or houses) takes time to burn also entails an end to the burning. The substance gets used up and can no longer be used as fuel for the fire. This fact provides a characteristic of incense unlike what we have seen so far. Stones are marked by their relative permanence, their unchanging nature in the span of a human life, while incense is temporary, ephemeral. The English poet Walter Savage Landor once said, "No ashes are lighter than those of incense, and few things burn out sooner."[34]

Religious traditions, seen historically, might appear solid, staunch, set in their ways. Indeed, part of the authority of churches and temples stems from their abilities to create an aura of eternity, of having lasted, unchanging over time. We recite creeds from a millennium and a half ago, read sacred scriptures from three millennia ago, and conduct, or so we believe, rituals to the deities the same way we always have. It is as it was.

Wedged within these mythical creations of solid history are the passing, fleeting, fading. Poet William Wordsworth ably gets at the transitory temperament of life in "Intimations of Immortality." Everything in life, at a younger age, seemed "Apparell'd in celestial light." But over time "the rainbow comes and goes, / and lovely is the rose; . . . But yet I know, where'er I go, / That there hath pass'd away a glory from the earth." Beauty and grace, presence and light are not permanent states of experience on this earth. We grow older and ultimately are able to see only the trails of glory that passed before our eyes. C. S. Lewis likewise locates fleeting glimpses of glory within the natural world. Lewis knows the senses guide us, and through such experiences people desire something that transcends the here-and-now experience—at least for those predisposed to do so. Lewis outlines this yearning, this longing, in deeply multisensate language: "That unnameable something, desire for which pierces us like a rapier at the smell of bonfire, the sound of wild ducks flying overhead, the title of *The Well at the World's End*, the opening lines of 'Kubla Khan,' the morning cobwebs in late summer, or the noise of falling waves."[35] In the end, we are left with the possibilities of paying attention, of sensing with a kind of divine perception in order to capture those moments in the blink of an eye.

Religious traditions operate with the ephemeral. And in many instances it becomes a reminder of our own fleeting, changing nature. At other times, the fleeting experiences are glimpses of glory, of Paradise, Heaven, or the Pure Land, reminders that this life may be fluctuating but there is another life with more surety, more lasting harmony. The religious point is to pay attention, to feel, now. Incense reminds us not merely of our own selves, Proust-like, but about the passing nature of our lives, and how that might itself be something holy. Poet Diane Ackerman brings the ephemeral and the holy together through the sense of smell:

> It may be, too, that smells move us so profoundly, in part, because we cannot utter their names. In a world sayable and lush, where marvels offer themselves up readily for verbal dissection, smells are often right on the tip of our tongues— but no closer—and it gives them a kind of magical distance, a mystery, a power without a name, a sacredness.[36]

If frankincense was given as a gift alongside gold and precious stones, the key difference is that gold and stones are of a substance built to last. Their value lies in their solidity. The value of incense derives from its disappearance. To get what is desired from this object means that it must be eliminated, burned up. Such holy frivolousness!

DRUMS

*The drums were still beating, persistent and
unchanging. Their sound was no longer a separate
thing from the living village. It was like the pulsation of
its heart. It throbbed in the air, in the sunshine, and even
in the trees and filled the village with excitement.*

—from Chinua Achebe, *Things Fall Apart*[1]

The heart is a drum. Its beating is the rhythm of life. Its pulsing provides memories stretching back to our embryonic state:
sounds that shaped and soothed us before seeing or speaking. In
the womb we are woven into a sensual soundscape that persists
deep within matured bodies, surfacing on occasion to connect us
to other beings, to the world around, to the flow of life's cosmic
dances. Constant, steady tempos indicate a good life; erratic,
rushing rhythms a cause for concern. No pulse indicates an end.
To be is to beat.

Charles Darwin surmised that the beats, tones, and cadences of music preceded language on an evolutionary scale and
brought beings together: "The suspicion does not appear im-
probable that the progenitors of man, either the males or females,
or both sexes, before they had acquired the power of expressing
their mutual love in articulate language, endeavored to charm
each other with musical notes and rhythm."[2] Birds do it. Bees

do it. Fact is, Homo sapiens does it too; prancing and preening, and dancing and singing, we supply rhythms and melodies and harmonies that bring us closer. We make music for attraction, to draw others to us, which paradoxically gets us beyond ourselves, losing ourselves in the process, if only to find something of our true selves remade. The "profound meaning of music and its essential aim," composer and music theorist Igor Stravinsky says, "is to promote a communion, a union of man with his fellow man and with the Supreme Being."³ By all means, "It don't mean a thing if you ain't got that swing," as the song goes.

Even on a vast cosmic scale—which we tend to think about in primarily visual terms, seen through telescopes—the universe itself beats. Astrophysicist Janna Levin has been working on documenting the sounds of space, particularly black holes. As she puts it, outer space wobbles and rings out; black holes, those scientific wonders of curved space and sucked-up light, pound and pulse. And that primary mythical metaphor of the beginnings of it all, the big bang, is nothing if not percussive. We are part of a vibrating, rumbling galaxy that we cannot always consciously hear, but that undergirds our comings and goings nonetheless.⁴

Perhaps this is why the drum is one of the most essential and widespread musical instruments in the history of human cultures. Drumbeats knit us into the cosmic fabric of the universe, into the social fabric of families and lovers, and into the rich textures of religious traditions. The sound of the drum reaches our eardrums, sonic percussions that draw people together in space just as it pulsates in time, cocreating melody, harmony, rhythm, and tone. The drum measures time, providing a sonic backbone for the jazz trumpeter and sutra-reciting monk alike. But it is not merely a metronome, some constant presence relegated to the background to help us keep on the path. Across religious traditions, drums invoke the gods, protect people, create rain, unite communities, and bring us to the point of ecstasy. They also conjure division and destruction, stir wrath, and start war. Drums can be living beings themselves, with or without their sound, and so one persistent question is whether it is the object itself (the drum) or the object that is produced (the sound)* that is most central.

Rhythm is deeply rooted in human bodies, and thus in consciousness itself. Which may go some way to understanding why drums figure prominently among the creation stories of peoples around the world. Drums are divine gifts, and the object itself possesses powers, as does the sound produced from it. The drum and the beat are intimately intertwined, and as the drumbeat reaches the human body, the body begins to move, dancing, grooving, tapping, praising.

Of the thousands of iconic images from South Asia, one of the best known is Shiva Nataraja, the Lord of the Dance. In these typically bronze forms, the dancing *deva* is caught midjig, one leg down trouncing the demon of ignorance, the other slightly crossed over and suspended midair; his four arms displaying gestures (*mudras*) of blessings. In one hand he holds a consuming flame. His matted locks sprawl outward, catching the Ganges River within the weaves. Surrounding the great god is a circle of fire, spinning as if Shiva is dancing across a cosmic treadmill, revolving the universe through his two steps. One step and the world is created, the next it is destroyed, and so on and so on, as another of his hands holds a small, hourglass-shaped *damaru* that carries the cadenced cycles of death and rebirth. For devotees of Shiva, this drum makes the sound from which all things come, setting the stage for the rhythmic dance that maintains our existence in a tensed balance. Sounds of creation in one hand

---

* It should be made clear up front: hearing is a *material process*. Just because we cannot see the sound waves vibrating off the drum skin and heading toward our ears does not mean it is immaterial.

and fires of destruction in another: the Dance of Bliss. A dance creative and destructive, erotic and spiritual, all at once.

In the creation story of the Dogon of present day Mali, the great god Amma creates the earth and sky, spirits and animals, and ultimately people. To aid in human work, Amma sends a blacksmith down to earth (divine blacksmiths are prevalent in many of these stories, because the sparks from their anvils can be seen during thunderstorms on earth). At one point a terrible drought threatens life, and so the blacksmith beats his anvil, as does a leather worker who made and plays a drum. Pleased by the percussion, Amma releases the rains.

Among the Mataco people of Argentina, the story is told of a great cosmic fire that destroyed the world. Out of the ashes fly two birdlike creatures, Icanchu and Chuña. Icanchu seeks a place to create a homeland and comes across a burned-down tree. He bangs on the remaining stump like a drum, chants, and dances all through the night. When the next day dawns a small shoot has sprung up from the charcoaled drum. The shoot becomes the first tree of the re-creation, the cosmic center of the world, and the birth of life for the new world.

In Chinese Taoist stories, the Jade Emperor—the sky god— rules over a number of lesser gods who interact with human life. One time one of these lesser gods, the rain god, abandoned his duties, leaving the land in drought. Animals and people died. So toad, fox, bear, and tiger went to the heavens to ask for rain. The gates of the heavens were closed, so toad beat a drum, which only annoyed the Jade Emperor, who then sent his forces against him. Somehow toad overpowered them, causing the king to admit toad into the palace and listen to his grievances. Toad asked for rain, and got it, and since then has been commissioned to be the one who announces the coming rains with his thunderous drums.

At the northeastern edges of Siberia, the Koryak share mythologies in common with Native American peoples along the

Pacific Coast of North America. The supreme being in the Koryak tradition has an assistant named Big Raven, who is the
first man and the ancestor of the people, serving to establish
harmony in the universe. As such Big Raven has given gifts to
humans to help them along in their humanly travails. Among
the gifts are reindeer, light, instructions on how to hunt, ritual
directions, and a drum. In one story, rain has not come to earth
yet. It arrives only when another deity named Universe attaches
his consort's vulva to a drum and beats it with his penis until
liquid squirts out and onto the earth as rain. The rains don't
stop—godly stamina being what it is—floods threaten life, and
so Big Raven and his son fly to the heavens, cause Universe and
his wife to fall asleep, and dry out their genitals by a fire so that
the drum beating (rain making) will cease.

Precipitation and percussion are matters of life and death. As
the gods bang their booming drums, rains beat down to create
fertile fields. Without rain we get fires, drought, and death. Too
much and we get floods, and death. That contemporary modern
people often believe the religious symbolism of water (as read
about in scriptures or practiced in rituals like baptism or mikveh
immersions) is simply a pleasant "cleansing" substance indicates
something of our distance from nature. Throughout mythologies around the world, water erupts as a powerful, chaotic force
that sustains just as it may destroy. Entire rivers, like the Ganges
or Yamuna, are themselves deities with sovereign authority, or
like Hapi, the ancient god of the Nile who caused the flooding
that ultimately made the banks fertile. We have to know how
to be in synch with water. We've got to get our rhythms right to
call down the correct amount of rain; Goldilocks-like, it cannot
be too much or too little, but just right, the proper pulse.

Sex, violence, and rock and roll. They are all there, in the
beginning. Such is the stuff of mythology. Joseph Campbell
once suggested "mythology is the womb of mankind's initia-
tion to life and death."[5] Among the deep truths of these ancient

stories, humans, deities, and animals beat drums, and through this beating cause supernatural action, changing the course of worldly events and giving humans a tempo with which to walk the earth. The great violinist Yehudi Menuhin similarly evokes such a profound mythological creation when he suggests, "Music creates order out of chaos; for rhythm imposes unanimity upon the divergent."[6] Bound to the creation and maintenance of the religious worlds in which we live, drums play a vital role in the existence of people. Their sounds form a sonic structure within which our bodies collectively subside.

In the contemporary Euro-American imagination, the image of drums is likely to be a drum set, with several variously sized drums—kick, bass, snare, toms—arranged in a precise way, with perhaps a top hat and cymbal attached. Even the new electronic versions keep a similar layout. That same set could be found at the center rear of a rock concert stage, in an elementary school music room, in the corner of a jazz club, or on the platform of a Christian megachurch. But in most cultures individual drums have had single purposes: a cylindrical hand drum would be used for one type of ritual while a large kettle drum would be played in another time and place, for another purpose. Often, the drums are housed in special spaces and taken out and used only for specific occasions. Not all traditional uses of drums are for religious purposes, but a great many of them are.

When we think of drums we tend to think of membranophones, consisting of a hollow body and a stretched-taut top that is tapped, hit, banged, or otherwise struck with hands or sticks. Sometimes they are even plucked. They can be quite large and played only when propped up on scaffolds, or they can be held in the palm of a hand. They can be square or oval, fat or skinny, one sided or two, decorated and painted or left plain. Their purpose is to create a sonic snap, a quick but forceful tone that sends vibrations through space, sometimes accompanied by other musical instruments or voice, sometimes not. The reverberations are felt all along our skin, our central nervous system, and channeled most centrally through our ear canal. Drums can be tuned to various pitches, and are beat during war making, ritual making, and lovemaking.

Throughout history, drums have been made with natural materials remade as thoroughly cultured objects. Louise Erdrich's beautiful novel *The Painted Drum* tells of an Ojibwe Dance Drum found in New Hampshire, and stories of it are linked back across time and space to the Great Lakes region and ultimately to its creator. One of the novel's narrators tells the story of how his grandfather made the drum. In the midst of family turmoil, the grandfather camped out in a forest to find the right section of the right tree in the right grove to use as the drum body, examining the trees for rot, carefully marking and cutting and hollowing out the chosen section. He then used the hide of a freshly killed moose for the drumheads, top and bottom. He clearly knew what he was doing, he had know-how. But he still needed a dream, a visit from the spirits who would tell him how to decorate it, how to finish it. We'll see more on the Ojibwe Dance Drum later in this chapter, and by no means are all drums created in such a deliberate manner, but the story reminds us here of the ever-so-thin line between nature and culture, our human evolutionary and historical reliance on the things of the earth.

Traditionally, trees have been cut to form drum bodies, animals skinned to form the membrane: death being the necessary prerequisite to the life of the drum. In fact, in the longstanding caste system of South Asia, the outcastes have been charged with handling corpses and animal hides, because those remains are seen as polluting. In many cases, their charge has included drums. The word *pariah*, for instance, has ancient Tamil roots that literally means "drummer" (not all "pariahs," in the strict sense of this term, are drummers, however). A *parai* is a drum played by Dalits (the outcastes or untouchables) for funeral and other ceremonies in Tamil Nadu. Elsewhere in South India, one radical Christian Dalit pastor named Parattai has used the traditional drumming, dance, and song of the people as an activist weapon, to overcome the oppression that is still experienced in spite of the caste system being outlawed.

As with the stones that provided *Homo sapiens* with advanced technologies for living, beating and banging sounds have been with us since the beginnings of culture, ritual, and human society. Perhaps it was the rhythmic scraping and brushing and honing of stones and sticks that produced a pleasing sound—it's hard to sharpen your tools without a tempo. Yet, while it would be easy to suggest some deep and clear connection to nature occurs when drums are banged, there are also practical matters to attend to, and these cannot readily be overlooked. In the absence of good wood (and presumably people who know how to fashion a drum body), an old radio speaker with skin stretched across it has been used by the Flathead tribe of Montana, and performers in New York City subways set up a series of plastic buckets and bang on them with pieces of steel pipe. Which leads us again to wonder whether it is the sound that is central or the thing itself, inseparable though those are.

I was telling a friend about writing this chapter, and he told me of a drumming circle he experienced once at an arts fair. All these guys (apparently they were all just that) sat around in a section of forest on the edge of the festival and beat their drums. There was no leader, no preplanned musical notations, just the ins and outs of drummers playing together and contraposed to each other. The trancelike state that emerged on the part of the players was no doubt due in part to the use of other natural substances, but it also had much to do with the beat and beating itself, the interplay of the persistent, pulsing players.

Which is somewhat amazing to think about. Mystical trance experiences have been an aim of religious traditions in many times and places, the achievement of which has generally needed special objects, sage guidance, ingested substances, and an environment beyond the quotidian—deserts, mountains, and forests figure large. But the thing that facile views of religion miss is this: religions are not against experiences of trance, inebriation, intoxication, or other ecstatic states of being. Priests, authorities, and artists realize the power of these experiences, their potential for transcending the here and now, and thus regulate such experience just as they simultaneously encourage it. It's good to have those extra glasses of wine . . . on this one night of the year that is different from all other nights. It's okay to dance and drink and be merry on Tuesday . . . for Wednesday begins forty days of penance. Take the peyote, for it provides insight . . . during a crucial period of life when one must take on further responsibilities of adulthood. Religions set boundaries, they maintain an order that adherents believe is paralleled by the ultimate order of the cosmos. But to do this well, certain chaotic domains must be broached. Deep and mysterious forces fill the universe, and they must be properly handled. Intoxication, ecstasy, and mystical trances are ways to find connections to these forces, and so they are not shunned so much as put within the correct context, and drums are one tool used for creating such experiences.*

The Sami people (sometimes called the Lapps) of the Arctic regions of far northern Scandinavia and Western Siberia have traditionally practiced what scholars have labeled shamanism. This term has been used in a variety of settings, not all of which ascribe the same meaning to it, but the term and concept are thought to originate within the Uralic traditions, of which the Sami are a part. In general, shamans heal, protect, act as guides for the souls of the departed, and serve as mediators between the earthly realm and world of spirits. By altering our sense

---

* Timothy Leary famously promoted the use of LSD, but he was also clear that it be taken in a proper, responsible setting.

perceptions (whether through ingesting, hearing, or otherwise), spirits can be embodied and made to serve human uses. A shaman is not so much possessed by the spirits as he or she *uses* the spirits as extensions of themselves, as a powerful tool to better the lives of the community.

For the Sami, the shaman is often brought to an ecstatic state by playing a drum (*runebomme*). Sami drums, typically egg-shaped and handheld, are the key medium of communication with the divine, and the skins are painted with various representations of the gods, animals, and people. Some of them depict a three-tiered cosmos with the gods above, the earthly realm in the middle, and the underworld at the bottom. Decorated with dangling animal bones and teeth, their rattling accompanies the beat. When properly played, drums, drummers, and listeners can transcend the three realms, mystically unifying what was once separate, divining the future, and protecting life in the present.

Elsewhere, one of the great annual festivals for the Sherpas of Nepal is known as Mani Rimdu. It celebrates Guru Rinpoche, the eighth-century missionary who brought Buddhism to the Himalayan regions of Tibet, Bhutan, and Nepal. It is also a time of offering propitiation to the gods for rain, long life, and the ongoing battle against evil. As such, Sherpa religious practices and beliefs mix Tantric Buddhism with indigenous ways of understanding, the result being that many of the rituals might seem strange to other Buddhist traditions such as the Theravada aspects found in Sri Lanka and elsewhere. The old pre-Buddhist deities of the mountain people were reincorporated into a new pantheon of gods and goddesses, and these remain specific to Himalayan practices. While the Mani Rimdu ritual has evolved over the centuries in various monasteries, since the 1920s it has emerged as an increasingly significant event at the Tengboche Monastery. In more recent years it has become a large tourist draw, especially as it corresponds with the peak mountain-climbing season that bring Westerners to the high altitudes.

Mani Rimdu is three days of dance, drama, and offerings. Over the period, thirteen acts of a sacred play take place. Dressed in symbolic, ceremonial garb, dancers and actors perform cosmic dramas of good and evil, acting out deities and demons, and ultimately Buddhist dharma (teachings and doctrine). During the fourth act, four drum dancers (*Rnga-'cham*) emerge amid the playing of thigh-bone trumpets and cymbals, performing what one abbot of the monastery called "the eternal beat of the heavenly drum which vibrates in the world as life and death vibrates."[7] This, ultimately, is the Buddha's message of truth to the world. In Tibetan versions of Buddhism, truth exists along a wavelength. Life and death operate along an oscillating wave of existence—not so much an on-off switch, an either-or, as many Western traditions might see it, but a fluctuation of a continuous, interconnected process. The skin head of the drum is struck, sending out vibrations to the immediate vicinity, allowing its hearers to tap into that reverberating truth. The drums not only symbolize this connection to the life-death oscillation but also are felt and experienced as that rippling current itself. Truth vibrates. We vibrate with it, losing the illusion of our selves along the way, and going deeper into the dharma.

Meanwhile, the Yoruba of West Africa (present-day Nigeria and Benin) have used drums in a variety of ways, one of the most important being communication between humans and the *orishas* (deities). Key here are the drums known as the *batá*, relatively small, two sided, and put together in groups of three, four, or five. As Yorubans were enslaved and brought to the Americas, they brought musical and ritual traditions as well, which is how the *batá* traveled to Cuba. A few things about the drums and drumming ceremonies were changed in processes the Cuban ethnographer Fernando Ortiz would call *transculturation*. The African traditions mixed and merged with Roman Catholicism and some indigenous traditions on the island, and the new tradition became known as Santería (or Regla de Ocha, or Lucumi).* In the Santería tradition, there are typically only three drums: a large drum (*iyá*, the "mother"), a small drum (*okónkolo*, the "baby"), and a medium-sized drum (*itólele*, a word meaning a "completed action").

In Afro-Cuban drumming rituals, the *iyá* player begins with a deep cadence while the higher-pitched *itólele* responds to it. Meanwhile the *okónkolo* holds the beat steady. Drummers sit with the instruments across their laps and create various rhythms, evoking different deities with different rhythms and melodies, as the three drums interact with each other, with a singer, and with dancers. In a ceremony called *toque de santo*, drumming brings an *orisha* into the community, and a select person becomes possessed by the specific *orisha*. The term often used is that the *orisha* "mounts" the person, riding them as if on a horse. The possession occurs for purposes of healing and guidance for both individuals and communities at large. They are always means to an end, and never intended for the ecstatic experience alone.

Embryonic-like, persistent tempos lead to trance, to posses-sion, to a time out of time, a place out of place, upside down and inside out, a mystical *at-one-ment* with the universe. Pounded time and repeated rhythm at a drumming circle, a rave, a high mountain monastery, or a disco create space through sound, a place where throbbing mobs coalesce. People who hear the sound are im*pressed* by the sonic waves and as the beat surges into the autonomic nervous system, the body uncontrollably begins to dance, sway, move. The sensual bodies of the par-

---

* Outside of Cuba, it is typically known as Santería, which is a Spanish construc-tion referring to the "saints" (*santo* = saint). Early contact between Catholics and Yoruba resulted in both sides identifying the many *orishas* of the Yoruba with the many saints of Catholicism. For a variety of strategic reasons, the Yorubans would hide in plain sight their worship of their own deities by merging them with the Catholic saints: Chango merged with Saint Barbara in part because they both were associated with the color red; Orula with Saint Francis, etc.

ticipants are transformed, sandwiched layers of the cosmos are merged into one. And yet, the mystical sounds that eliminate boundaries work only by the fact that they are highly structured and organized. The paradox is that trance comes about at particular times and places, structured precisely so as to eliminate structure.

Is music universal? If we ask whether cultures around the world today use voices and instruments that are played with organized rhythm and harmony and melody, whether people gather to hear their sounds, and whether the voices and instruments induce bodily based emotional responses, then, yes. But if we quickly fall into language that asserts music *transcends* all difference and can be universally *understood*, we have missed much. Surely this notion is the stuff of Hollywood or well-intentioned people determined to find commonalities. Music has undoubtedly bridged cultures, but if I ask the students in my class, who generally hail from the northeastern United States, to listen to Chinese opera and to tell me what emotions are being expressed, they have no idea. What they believe to be sadness can be a point of joy. To my rock and roll–cultivated ears, desire sounds like vengeance in the Chinese opera, triumph like defeat. Music and emotions may be linked on a primal level—our hearts all beat, songbirds attract mates—yet it is in playing notes and beats and pauses that the emotional and intellectual differences become apparent across cultures. The muses of music would seem to speak in strange tongues.

Related questions emerge. Is banging a can with a stick music? A monotonous solo beat an anthem? Musicologists and philosophers will answer resoundingly no. Igor Stravinsky, in his Charles Eliot Norton Lectures at Harvard University in 1939–40 said quite matter of factly, "I conclude that tonal elements become music only by virtue of their being organized, and that such organization presupposes a conscious human act."[8]

Nature is not culture. Humans use instruments, born of natural materials like wood and skin, or even their own voice and body, to recapture something of organic life. In so doing, the sounds are transformed, cultured, and organized so as to have an effect on people. Drums, as musical instruments, contribute to our quality of life.

Researchers at the Auditory Neuroscience Laboratory at Northwestern University have been investigating the role of music on brain functions. Learning to hear, play, and create music (taking piano or voice lessons, for example) improves our lives far beyond becoming a better drummer. Music, their studies suggest, provides a workout for our brains and gets many of our auditory abilities in shape. Which is not far from Socrates's take on it twenty-four hundred years ago. Regarding the subject of how to create the great Republic, he states, "Musical training is a more potent instrument than any other, because rhythm and harmony find their way into the inward places of the soul, on which they mightily fasten, imparting grace, and making the soul of him who is rightly educated graceful."[9] Just as going to an aerobics class can help us feel more energetic at our job, we become better listeners to our significant others when we practice our scales. Even our boss's instructions might make more sense because we spent an hour on the back porch last night listening to the cadences of Coltrane's *Blue Train.*

One reason this happens is because musical training entails learning how to translate "mere" sounds into meaningful sounds. Listening is not passive—with sound waves striking our waiting eardrums—but active. Researchers are clear that the training they are talking about goes far beyond simply turning on the radio while we're driving down the street, which probably actually decreases our abilities to listen well. Musical training entails the ability to analyze musical sounds in terms of pitch, tempo, and timbre; to distinguish one instrument from another; and to use memory to link earlier parts of a musical piece to later parts.

Children with musical training have been shown to have better vocabularies and reading abilities than those without, and music training seems to be linked to a greater ability to learn foreign languages. Of note too are studies showing that children with learning disabilities, including dyslexia, can benefit from music training, because the practice helps develop regions of the brain that allow us to distinguish "noise" from meaningful sounds.

A meta-analysis published in 2013 confirms what many of us have experienced already, that certain types of music act on the nervous system and help us sleep better.[10] Some of the studies came from Asia and used music from that continent, and others from European-based musical cultures. In all cases, the music must have low-frequency tones and a slow, stable rhythm of sixty to eighty beats per minute (bpm).* Quick beats and erratic rhythm quicken our pulse and don't let us rest; instead, they revive the body and prompt activity, which is useful for short, temporary actions. A slow and steady tempo is good for activities over the long haul: chewing, walking, pumping blood, having sex, or breathing. If we lose the beat (choking, tripping, arrhythmic palpitation, coitus interruptus, apnea), our actions become convoluted and confused, sometimes even dangerous.

That music is both enjoyable and practical tells us something about why it is so widespread, why so many cultures have valued it, and why it is so often linked to religious practices. Rituals rely on repeated performances, on knowing what to expect, and through that, to be affected emotionally, physiologically, and ultimately spiritually. Researchers are now empirically charting what religious traditions have long known, that particular types of music create particular types of responses in the bodies of the ritual participants. Within this, emotions and states of living are conjured by thumping sticks on drums: the deep pounding of a

---

* *Adagio* is between 55–65 bpm; the term literally means "at ease," as if old Italian musicians have long known what neuroscientists are just now quantifying.

do-daiko, the triumphal, percussion-heavy John Williams music at the beginning of *Star Wars*, the discordant beat of Stravinsky's *Rite of Spring*, the interactive *batá* in a Cuban house, the long drum solos that became a staple of rock concerts in the seventies. Musical instruments change our lives, and not just for the duration of the song. It all depends on our playlist. And how our list plays us.

Jazz giant Art Blakey grew up playing piano in his Seventh-Day Adventist church in Pittsburgh while he was learning his Bible at the same time. His talents got him jamming at clubs, and as a young teenager he was playing piano at the Democratic Club in Pittsburgh when the club's owner purportedly forced him at gunpoint off the keyboard and onto the drums. (At least that's the way he's told the story.) There Blakey remained for the next fifty years, holding down the beat for many of the jazz greats like Horace Silver, Miles Davis, Charlie Parker, Sonny Rollins, Dizzy Gillespie, and Thelonious Monk.

In 1947 he went to West Africa for two years. Musical biographical accounts say it was there he learned something of polyrhythmic drumming and his style changed significantly. But according to Blakey, his visit had nothing to do with music: "I was into religion, studying religions. I wanted to find out about it because religion isn't a figment of man's imagination . . . It's a way of life for the majority of people in the world, so you have to understand it to understand the people."[11] Over time he checked out eleven religions of the world, saying, "He that knoweth only one religion knows nothing at all about religion," paraphrasing Max Müller, the nineteenth-century German philologist and father of comparative religions (who was rephrasing Goethe on languages). Oddly enough, at a time when jazz was ascending as a premiere, quasi-indigenous art form of the United States, and as African American groups were linking back to African roots, Blakey somewhat famously denied the African connection.

More confounding is the fact that around that time he

changed his name to Abdullah ibn Buhaina and is believed to have converted to Islam, though he later denied this too. Dizzy Gillespie has noted that many New York jazz musicians in the forties and fifties did convert to Islam, though there are no public records of Blakey's conversion. He also founded the Jazz Messengers at this time. The term *messenger* has Muslim connotations, as Muhammad, that great seventh-century reciter of the Word of God, was the last and greatest messenger of Allah. This doesn't mean that's what the band name necessarily implies, only that several pieces of evidence indicate an interest in and possible conversion to Islam. Indeed, much of orthodox Islam historically has not included the playing of instruments in ritual settings, and imams and muezzins chant a cappella. Then again, drums are prevalent in many African Islamic settings.

Musicologists and others have been careful not to take Blakey's word for it. Verbal utterances are one thing, but the beat doesn't lie, and a marked shift in his post-Africa style has been noted. Ingrid Monson has suggested that Blakey's recordings through the 1950s, with their African and Afro-Caribbean inflections, helped shape many jazz rhythm sections throughout the 1960s. In Blakey's 1957 piece "Ritual," the invocation of African traditions becomes clear as "he tells a story about the Ijaw people, combines a Brazilian and an Afro-Cuban rhythm to create a hybrid groove, and solos almost exclusively in the lower register on toms and bass drums as an Ewe master drummer might do."[12] Monson sees Blakey's shifting accounts of his own life and intentions to be that of the mythical trickster, the clever being that can morph into different identities based on the context—which can certainly be said for Blakey's drumming.

Like all great jazz musicians, Blakey *improvised*. Improvisation is not unique to jazz, even though this music form raised it to dizzying heights. He grew up in a Christian Adventist tradition, learned something about West African versions of Islam, indigenous Yoruban practices, and Afro-Caribbean mixtures, as well as the blues, gospel, and jazz that were emerging on the scene in and around New York City. This creates a hybrid style (and religious faith) that mixes and merges, but more important, each of the culturally based styles can be drawn on at various times, and an extended improvised set might be seen as a tour of world music. In and through improvisation, the African past continues into the African American present, prominently including the ritualistic dance-possessions that occur across West African cultures and have been carried to the Americas. The call and response embedded in jazz traditions, the mix of individual playing that becomes absorbed into the larger group, and the repetitive phrases all mark the relations between a contemporary jazz set in Manhattan and a ritual practice of contemporary Mali.[13]

People travel, as do drums. In London's British Museum is a drum whose label states its provenance as "Virginia, USA." It is part of the original eighteenth-century collection of the museum, much of which came from the accumulations of an Irish doctor named Sir Hans Sloane. Initially it was thought to be an "American Indian" drum and labeled as such. Almost two hundred years later a curator looked at it and realized it could be no such thing, as its style was similar to that of drums found in West Africa. Seventy years after that, the British Museum undertook a scientific assessment of the drum and found that its wood comes from *Cordida africana*, a small evergreen tree native to West and East Africa. Further research revealed that the Akan people must have constructed the drum, perhaps in the seventeenth century.

This Akan drum is an object carved from a tree and covered with cured animal skin to make a sound. Originally used as a central component of Akan religious-political ceremonies, it has fallen silent over the centuries, no longer creating cadence. Nonetheless, there is a pulse. In the last four centuries, the drum has traveled from Africa to America and then to England, taking on new meanings along the way while retaining its own story.

Playwright Bonnie Greer reflects on the activities and travels of this drum: "The thing that's remarkable about these objects, for us who were taken—and forcibly—from our environment, is that these objects have traveled with us, and they've actually become what we have become, and they have accompanied us here to live in this place, and to thrive in this place."[14]

No one knows, or likely will ever know, how the drum made its first oceanic voyage. Clearly, it came as part of the slave trade alongside the estimated twelve million Africans who were forcibly brought to the Americas for labor. People were stripped of their possessions, removed to a land far away, and ultimately stripped of their identity. But identities and objects have a curiously resilient force and find their ways across dehumanizing conditions. Myths, rituals, and symbols survive in the bodies and minds of humans, and sometimes are reconnected with those objects that comprise the knowledge and know-how of the myths, ritual, and symbols.

As enslaved Africans began their lives on another continent, they carried the sounds and prayers and dances of their former lives, creating communities and sometimes political upheaval. At the center of these activities was often a drum. European and American slave-ship captains had understood this power, and so would have drums played as their captives were made to dance during the Middle Passage. Though done in the midst of deep cruelty, this was seen to keep health and stave off depression, which it probably did. But when the Africans got to America, they found ways to make their own music, and drums brought people together. The drumbeat's powerful qualities lifted spirits and fostered community. So much so that their beating could subtly shift from ritual to revolt, and many places in the Americas began to outlaw and confiscate drums from African Americans. The South Carolina Stono Rebellion of 1739 began with a drummed call to arms and cries of "Liberty!" gathering dozens of slaves who burned plantations and killed many whites. This was the largest uprising before the Revolutionary War, leading to the Negro Act of 1740, which imposed many strict regulations about slaves gathering, raising food, and moving. In addition to prohibitions against carrying various weapons, the act also made illegal "using or keeping of drums."

The British Museum drum's journey mirrors the trans-Atlantic journeys of Art Blakey, who "returned" to his ancestral roots in Africa only to find a new sound that propelled him forward. The Akan drum today stands at the heart of the former British Empire, motionless on its pedestal. From there it serves witness to ghastly human activities and preserves identities even as they become fluid. Objects and sounds accumulate, collecting accounts of lives lived and lives lost. Blakey's hybrid drumming style came from his travels, his listening, his playing. He carried his bodily know-how with him. And drums themselves travel, picking up adaptations, styles, and sounds; creating communities, feelings, revolt, and memories.

In my childhood church, a man once came to speak out against rock music. This was in the 1970s, at the advent of the contemporary Christian music (CCM) scene, an emerging genre (and later mega mass market) that included heavy metal acts such as the Resurrection Band, gospel-based musicians such as Mylon Le Fevre, and folk-rock singer-songwriters such as Larry Norman and Keith Green. The beginning of CCM was not without its critics. Yet, unlike the many moralists who railed against rock and roll's raunchy lyrics, its associations with sex, drugs, and rebellion in general, this particular preacher at our church went for the jugular. The real reason rock and roll is wrong is because of its beat: the rock beat is antithetical to the beating of the human heart, and thus against God's own rhythmic creation—even if you are singing praises to God at 120 beats per minute. On one hand, this preacher's ideas paralleled contemporary neuroresearchers' findings about styles of music and the ways beats per minute affects the body. On the other hand, there is much missing from the argument, as it would seem this line of logic might quickly have to discount any aerobic exercise that gets the heart rate up.

Other theologically conservative Christian groups have followed suit. They have created extensive studies suggesting that while the Bible is filled with admonitions to play *music*, it does not mention drums—at least as certain translations of the Bible have it—and thus Christians should not play them. In general, concerns raised include the understanding that singing is central and instruments should not overtake vocals; that drums (and rock music in general) make *entertainment*, which directs attention to the players, and not *worship*, which directs attention to God; and, ultimately, that drums are linked to demonic ritual activities, which generally encompasses everything from African rituals to Vodun to shamanism to Islam. Manipulation comes from pulsation.

There is something powerful in the simple act of banging a drum that has frightened people. It is not simply about any anarchy of rock and roll but about the sound itself, and especially the drumbeat and the effects this might have on the body (particularly when it might be provoked to move and sway to the beat: to dance). The nineteenth-century English writer, reverend, and hymnist Hugh Reginald Haweis published a popular book called *Music and Morals* in 1871. There he states, "The drum is a terrible instrument of vengeance, and is often a terror to the drummer himself, as well as to his less emphatic companions." A century later, quasi New Ager David Tame wrote *The Secret Power of Music*, which is blatant in its dislike for drums and for any music that has roots in Africa, going so far as to suggest that "as the rhythmic accompaniment to satanic rituals and orgies, voodoo is the quintessence of tonal evil. . . . It is a global phenomenon; a pounding, pounding destructive beat which is heard from America and Western Europe to Africa and Asia. Its effect

upon the soul is to make nigh-impossible the true inner silence
and peace necessary for the contemplation of eternal verities."[15]
Arguments against drums consistently stem from a theological
outlook that believes religion is quiet, interior, and calm, which
in the grand scope of things is very much the minority view.

The demon-drum argument is also a key juggernaut of Terry
Watkins, founder of Dial-the-Truth Ministries. In his tracts—
now mainly online—Watkins and his ministry are the sort that
becomes the grist for liberal parody with their insistence not only
on the authority of the King James Bible of 1611 (a movement
self-described as King James Onlyism—even other contemporary conservative translations like the NIV—New International
Version—are considered "perversions") but also in their claims
that Santa Claus is an imposter who is actually Satan, that hell
is a real place, that tattoos are evil, and so forth. Watkins has
written about his own background as a rock music guitarist, and
while he still plays guitar, he is strongly against rock and roll,
and especially drums. Stringed instruments *are* mentioned in the
King James Version as pleasing to God, but not drums. His web-
sites even make an I-told-you-so link to a *New Scientist* article
that suggests a connection between listening to fast music while
driving and an increased propensity to end up in a car crash.

Some Christian reticence is braced by a reading of several
biblical passages that mention a place called Tophet in the Hin-
nom Valley (2 Kings 23; Jeremiah 7 and 19). There, ancient
Phoenician and Canaanite devotees of Moloch, god of fire, and
Baal, god of thunder, burned their children alive to appease the
deities. Drums were played to drown out the young screams.
The Hebrew word *toph*, means "drum," thus Tophet refers to
the place of the drum. Along with the burning fires of Gehenna,
Tophet became associated in later Christian theology with hell.
Fire, drums, and hell itself become entangled in Christian consciousness. This has given rise to many accounts around the
world of cultural groups who have used and valued drums but

had them taken away or destroyed when Christians came to conquer people and land.* A number of missionary, military, and anthropological accounts detailing the "discovery" of new people would refer to the groups use of a *tom-tom* drum, an onomatopoeic term originating in South Asia and picked up by English speakers to pejoratively refer to the drums of barbarous, uncivilized people.

Speaking to this situation, Nigerian poet Gabriel Okara's "Mystic Drum" bespeaks a drumbeat; the drum in his poem seems to be both an interior and an exterior instrument. With its entrancing rhythm, the dead dance and sing with their shadows, fishes turn to men, and even "the gods and the trees begin to dance." Ultimately, Okara's poem is a message of colonization, as outsiders—in the form of an Eve-like character lurking at the edge of the forest—effectively silence the beat. The compelling drumbeat is replaced by the woman's mouth, a "cavity belching darkness." Okara hypnotically hints at the merging of things, the topsy-turvy mystical world of animals, humans, gods, and nature playfully performing in ways they are not normally disposed to do. Colonization, and hence Christianization, then imposes a new order, and the mystical ties of the beating drum are broken.[16]

Okara poeticizes what historical reports also evidence. One missionary account of the White Earth Reservation tells of how the Ojibwe had to give up their "heathen dance" after they converted, since this is opposed to Christian life. A missionary who speaks of encounters with the Ojibwe yet sensed, "there seems to be a chord that carries the throbbing of the drum into the Indian's heart."[17] Even so, that chord had to be cut according to this brand of Christianity and many drums were confiscated

---

* A curious side note: while we use the term *iconoclasm* to name the pious activity of destroying visual icons, we have no similar word for the pious destruction of sound instruments.

from Native Americans. And the Sami people mentioned earlier even mark the time before and after Christian contact. The time before is called "drum time" and the time after is called "the time when one had to hide the drums."[18] The drum was so central in their culture that one description tells of a Sami complaining to a Christian authority, "Taking away our drums is like depriving you of your compasses."[19] Drums orient lives and are present at the depths of the beating body. Missionaries have understood that conversion is not simply an act of ticking a different box on a census form but has to do with the core of identity, and sensual objects lie at the heart of this.

There is a seventeenth-century story about the Drummer of Tedworth, one of the most widely disseminated accounts of demon possession known in Christian lands. The story is best known due to its centrality in Joseph Glanvill's 1668 book *Saducismus triumphatus* ("Triumph over the Sadducees")—the Sadducees here connoting the ancient Jewish sect of Jesus's day who did not believe in an eternal soul, just like the proto-Enlightenment skeptics of Glanvill's day. To counteract accounts of the empirical doubters, Glanvill gives evidence for various supernatural disturbances, witchcraft, and poltergeists. In the 1660s, as he tells it, a drummer in England named William Drury was imprisoned on forgery charges brought up by one John Mompesson. While Drury was in prison, and his drum confiscated, Mompesson became victim to midnight thumpings echoing through his house, drumrolls, and furniture thrown about—all the classic stuff of poltergeists, only here with a strong emphasis on the drum sounds. According to Glanvill, these occurrences happened over months, allowing numerous people to observe them. Glanvill's account became widely known, with some, like Methodism's founder John Wesley, seeing it as a truthful account of demon activity, and skeptics, like the illustrator William Hogarth, showing the silliness of it all. Within two decades *Saducismus Triumphatus* had crossed the Atlantic and influenced the outlook of New England Puritan minister Cotton Mather, who would write his own works that had a dramatic effect on his land, including the 1692 Salem witch trials.

Like all things sacred, the beating drum has the potential to create and destroy, to join together and break apart. We have to be careful in our connections to these muses, for in the wrong hands, awesome forces can be unleashed. The drummer Terl Bryant knows this well. Once while playing his drums a woman came up to him, doused him with water, and commanded the "evil spirit of drumming" to come out of him. As it turns out, Bryant himself is a committed Christian who has played with secular and religious musicians around the world, while retaining a strident faith. He founded the network Psalm Drummers, in which Christians gather to play drums collectively. In his book *A Heart to Drum*, he outlines the reasons, biblical and other, why drumming is pleasing to God, and he encourages others to join in. Having played and thought about and felt the drums through his entire life, Bryant taps into the power of the rhythm, "because it's quite threatening and potentially quite freeing. In the wrong hands it isn't helpful. But with a heart after God it can be a powerful tool."[20]

Many of the preceding stories, save the brief note about Terl Bryant, would suggest that drums have no place in proper Christian rituals. Christians seem to take drums away from people, count them as demonic, heathen, a sign of primitive peoples. But if we look to one of the oldest and most consistent Christian cultures in the history of the world, a different story emerges, with drums playing one of the most central roles in the services.

Ethiopia is the birthplace of humanity as we know it, with the first beating of the Homo sapiens heart occurring almost two hundred thousand years ago along the Omo River in the southwestern portion of the country. Ethiopia is also one of the world's oldest nations, with rich religious and cultural traditions dating back several millennia. And it is also one of the world's oldest Christian nations. Before the Edict of Thessalonica in 380 CE made Christianity the state religion of the Roman Empire, and long before Russia made its mark on the globe after Vladimir's conversion to Christianity, Ethiopian King Ezana's early fourth-century conversion (brought about by the missionary Frumentius) prompted him to declare Christianity the religion of his nation. Eighteen hundred years later Christianity is still professed by close to two-thirds of the people. Sometimes called Coptic (which simply means "Egyptian"), the Ethiopian Church is actually distinct from the Coptic Church of Egypt, even as they have retained ties. Theologically, the Egyptian and Ethiopian churches think of themselves as the true church, since they each rejected the Council of Chalcedon's decree in 451 CE that Jesus was of two natures: human and divine. The Ethiopian Orthodox Church is theologically known as a Monophysite tradition, as Jesus had only one nature—divine. Which makes for some fascinating views of the Trinity: in many Ethiopian images the Father, Son, and Holy Spirit are depicted as identical-looking beings—three old men with beards.

Within the Ethiopian Orthodox Church, one prime reference point for the liturgy, and thus for connecting with the community and God, is through a drum called the *kabaro*. There are two varieties of this drum, one generally smaller and used in secular settings while the other is larger and used only for religious services. Large *kabaro* are typically left in the treasure house of the church building and used only on Sundays and feast days. On such days they are taken out and played at either end of a line of chanters, called *debtaras*, during the key worship services, accompanied by chanting and pounding of prayer sticks on the floor in unison.[21]

The song and dance that provides the heartbeat of Ethiopian Christianity arises from the pre-Christian Hebraic tradition, a tradition thought to stem from the Queen of Sheba, who bore one of Solomon's sons, Menelik. When Menelik grew up he went to visit Solomon, and he returned with the Ark of the Covenant and established the Solomonic Dynasty in Ethiopia. The chants, the dance, and the beating of the drum all demonstrate strong ties to ancient Jewish liturgical traditions. And some suggest that the *kabaro* itself has roots in Turkish Muslim environments and came to eastern Africa with Muslim movements southward.

The *debtara* is the key person in church services and is on a level with the priests. While *debtara* literally means "scribe," it generally denotes something more like a cantor, and they trace their roots back to Saint Yared, the sixth-century musician credited with creating the sacred music tradition of Ethiopia. Training to become a *debtara* is extensive, beginning around age five with schooling in the syllables in both written and oral forms, then moving to a mastery of liturgical texts, and eventually joining the *Zema Bet* ("House of Chant"). In the *Zema Bet* they learn the musical training necessary to sing, play the requisite instruments, and lead services. Those who complete the training go on to establish the liturgical elements of Christian worship through the year.

One of the biggest festivals of the year is *Timket* (Epiphany or Three Kings Day). As in most Eastern churches, this is much more highly regarded than Christmas. On *Timket* eve, processions of people, led by a *kabaro* player, emerge from various churches, followed by a priest carrying the ark, and accompanied by chanters and others who eventually congregate in a field under a tent. At daybreak the rituals begin again with white-gowned, turbaned *debtaras* forming two long lines facing each other, sistrum in one hand, prayer stick in another. Two or three drummers fill out the *debtara* lines and they all begin to sway in rhythm. The beat picks up volume, prayer sticks rise and fall, sistrums shake, and chanting becomes higher and louder, reaching a great crescendo. And then it abruptly stops. The ritual is over.

Perhaps most intriguing is that the *kabaro* has been inter-preted within the church's liturgies as a symbol for Christ him-self. (One account suggests the beating of the drum symbolizes the beating of Jesus at the hands of the Romans, though that is difficult to corroborate.) The drum and its sounds signal the presence of the Word of God, Jesus Christ. The Word is heard, just as the New Testament book of 1 John 1, testifies, "That which was from the beginning, which we have heard, which we have seen with our eyes, which we have looked upon and touched with our hands, concerning the word of life." Support-ers of visual icons ("Iconodules") in the Christian church have used this biblical passage to justify the ongoing visual artistic creations possible through the Christian doctrine of incarna-tion. In the Ethiopian Church we find a strong symbolic repre-sentation of the heard Word.

If drums have sustained tradition, they have also resurrected it. The Ojibwe (Anishinaabe) people live in the lands now com-monly known as Michigan, Wisconsin, Minnesota, and On-tario. Like all Native American groups, the westward expansion of white settlers in the nineteenth century forced them off their land, decimated their populations through war and disease, and had the effect of stripping them of religious and cultural tradi-tions, including the demise of drum playing that had been so central to their life. Drums were longtime staple instruments of the indigenous people across the Americas, and the Ojibwe used a variety of them in their ceremonies, as they did rattles, singing, and dance, all of which operated as forms of prayer. Drums accompany a person through their life. They are there at birth rites, through the highs and lows of growth, and present at death: a drum was often placed in a grave alongside the deceased to accompany them on a four-day journey to the village of souls. Yet, as the Ojibwe adapted to new ways of life, and struggled to survive, many of the drum traditions were forgotten. By the beginning of the twentieth century, living on a few reservations and with few prospects, a startling thing occurred, the Drum Dance was born.[22]

Sometime in the last decades of the nineteenth century, a Dakota woman had a vision. She became known as Tailfeather Woman, and her visionary story is a creation story.* The story was told in response to political turmoil, which is often when stories of creation come about. In the midst of ongoing war with the US Cavalry (possibly including General Custer), who had massacred great numbers of Native Americans including the woman's four sons, Tailfeather Woman escaped and hid under the lily pads of a lake, breathing through a reed. While in hiding the Great Spirit spoke to her and continued to speak over four days' time, giving her songs and instructions for making and playing a great drum, saying that the pounding of the drum would bring healing and unity for her people. If the instructions are followed, the Great Spirit said, the soldiers would stop killing her people. She got up out of the water, told the survivors what she had heard, went about making and playing the drum, and singing and carrying out the proscribed ceremony. Sure enough, the white soldiers heard the sounds and stopped their killing and began to listen. Sometime after, peace agreements were made between the US government and the Indians. The drum and songs traveled from Tailfeather Woman's Dakota land to other Native American people in the Great Lakes region such as the Ojibwe, and during the ceremonies some version of the woman's story is told.

The drum is itself large and round (Ojibwe refer to it as "The Big Drum"), not unlike its predecessor used in the Grass Dance of various Northern Plains tribes (Omaha, Dakota-Sioux). The

---

* Her name, Tailfeather Woman, refers to the eagle feathers that are necessary and sacred for ceremonial rites among many Native Americans.

Ojibwe historically used small hand drums for healing ceremonies, warfare, and games, so the introduction of this large drum from the Tailfeather Woman's vision was an adaptation. Needing several people with the know-how to build the drum, it quickly became a sacred object: decorated with beads, painted, cared for, and cleaned. This drum is a living being, sometimes referred to as "our grandfather," the same term used to note the guiding spirit among the Ojibwe. As such, many people have been reluctant to have the big drum photographed, as it has medicine powers; stories are told of people trying to harm the drum and having great misfortune come upon them. It is protected and cannot touch the ground; it rests in a bed in its owner's house; and it is ritually fed and presented with gifts like tobacco. The drum became so central to the life of many communities that groups would congregate around drums and identify themselves by the particular drum to which they belonged, even while understanding there is only one drum in the world: all the individual drums are part of the same whole. In the Drum Dance ceremonies, the drum stands in for the Great Spirit, just as the songs, drumbeat, and smoke from pipes are prayers to the Great Spirit. During the dance the story of Tailfeather Woman is reenacted. Women have played prominent roles throughout the history of the ceremony.

A half century or so after its appearance, the Drum Dance and the big drums themselves began to disappear. The elders who knew the ritual sounds and songs and dance began to die, as did those who knew how to make and decorate the drums. Younger generations did not carry on the traditions, whether due to lack of interest, assimilation into mainstream US society, or adaptation to a new religious tradition such as Christianity or the growing Peyotism movement. Meanwhile, the drums had become well known outside their immediate circles and became a commodity for collectors and museums. Many have sold for thousands of dollars.

Today, as Native American studies programs are offered at universities and various Indian groups have researched the roots of their own traditions, interest in the drum tradition has been growing. This decline and reinvestment became the narrative framework of Louise Erdrich's novel *The Painted Drum*, mentioned earlier. Erdrich uses the Drum Dance tradition, and the value of the drum itself, as a way to query issues of identity and love and her own Ojibwe past. The main protagonist of the story, Faye Travers, impulsively steals a Big Drum and begins a journey to return it to the Ojibwe. Along the way, the drum's own history and identity are fleshed out, a story laden with mourning and joy. In one of the book's many moving passages, the grandson of the drum's creator tells about its force in ways that speak to many of the concerns of this chapter:

> This drum was powerful. People searched it out. This drum was so kind that it cured people of every variety of ill. Because our family kept this drum, people came to us. All of the people who lived close to the drum and dreamed up its songs or helped the drum somehow—repaired it or gave it gifts or even helped the people who came to see it—we grew strong. That's what the drum is about—it gathers people in and holds them. It looks after them. But like a person, things can go wrong in spite of all the best care. And this drum had its own history and sorrow.[23]

With its "own history and sorrow" the drum becomes an external heart, one that can be broken. The Dance Drum, made from dried and stretched skins of dead animals, brings out the rhythms of life through its beat, evoking an intimate, womb-like existence. At the same time the drum provides a collective beat, allowing people to join together in rhythm, to follow, dance, and sing along, and do so with and for the gods. The drums, and the people around them, create a personal pulse, a communal cadence, and a cosmic reverberation, all at once.

———

Throughout religious traditions, as we have seen in this chapter, drums are a vital source of sonic sacrality. As instruments they are intimately tied to the sounds they make, even as layers of sacredness dovetail and diverge between drum, drummer, and drumbeat. While much of the preceding discussed drums for their musical qualities, they are not simply about the music. The Ojibwe Dance Drum is a divine-like being itself—even when not played it is taken care of, fed, given gifts and rest. The *batá* of Afro-Cuban Santería traditions are also consecrated instruments, meaning that the spirit, *aña*, is actually part of the drum, and not just when it is played. Similar practices occur with the Banyankole of East Africa, where a custom drum house is built for two royal drums. There they are tended to through milk and cattle offerings. And then there are the drum bodies, which can be highly decorated with religious symbolism; cosmograms, deities, buildings, people, and animals may be depicted in ways that not only reaffirm the sacredness of the represented person, place, or thing but also connect the drum to those social-sacred entities.

Other drums, like the talking drums of West Africa, communicate messages through pitch, tone, and tempo, but their sound cannot be said to be *music* in the strict sense of the term. Several ethnic groups of Nigeria and Ghana have tonal languages, meaning that a single word can take on multiple meanings depending on the tone of the voice, and this makes it possible to imitate speech through musical instruments that can change pitch. Drums used for such purposes are sometimes referred to as telephones and radios, since their objective is to transmit information across great distances—a mass medium that doesn't need batteries. Apart from their profane operations, these drums also have sacred uses. Among the Akan people, the drummer (*okyerema*) tells their creation story through the drum. The sacred "text" in this tradition is the combination of drummer, drum, and drumbeat heard by people who do not merely intellectually grasp the meaning but who also feel the rhythm of the story through their bodies.

Like smoke from incense or the spoken word, the drumbeat is ephemeral. Thus, a key component of the sacred nature of drums is fleeting, uncontainable, and unpossessable. We can feed the drum but not the drumbeat. This can have its advantages in sacred settings because it reaffirms the presence of a community in the here and now, emphasizing special times and spaces. The drumbeat is heard *here*, but not *there*. Or it can make a doctrinal point. In Tibetan Tantric Buddhist practices, for example, a relatively large, double-sided hand drum called a *chod* is used in a practice called "cutting the ego," in which the practitioner spends lengths of time alone in the wilderness accompanied only by the drum. Beyond the mystical effects of the practice, the sound of the *chod* also symbolizes the teaching of *impermanence* that lies at the heart of Buddhist traditions.

Echoing beats waft through space into the ear and body and then fade. If the sound itself disappears, the pulsing nonetheless reverberates through other creatures and objects, flowing through and connecting animal, vegetable, mineral, human, and divine. Like it says in the Chinua Achebe quote at the start of this chapter, the drumbeat "throbbed in the air, in the sunshine, and even in the trees and filled the village with excitement."[24]

To write a history then, whether of music or religion, it seems we have to stick to the hard, moderately permanent wood and skin (and the occasional written musical notations), and let the beats echo in the air and trees and in our minds. The sounds of the Akan drum in the British Museum, the Sami *runebomme*, or Shiva's *damaru* for that matter cannot be readily heard in any practical way. We might see the drum petrified in a museum, an image of it, or written descriptions of their use. On rare occasions, an audio recording is available, though then we have the reverse problem: the sound without the drum.

Another way to imagine this history is to bring the drums

back and play them again, improvising and making them sound again in new modes and spaces for a new age. Drum traditions, rooted in religious ritual and mythology, have resurfaced in contemporary cultures for folk festivals, theater performances, and tourist attractions. Tour packages for guided treks around the Himalayas, as noted above, now often include time at the Mani Rimdu festival, making the ritual tradition and entertainment package difficult to disentangle. Meanwhile, the *toque de santo* can be seen at folklore festivals in Havana, though no possessions by the *orishas* occur there.

And at one point most drums (*taiko*) of Japan were tied to Shinto shrines and Buddhist temples, where a single drum was played by a holy man on a holy occasion. They were also used in royal court gatherings and theatrical settings like Kabuki and Noh. After World War II, a new development occurred that produced an improvised and hybrid drumming style known as *kumi-daiko*, with groups of people playing various drums together. The traditional drums were used, but played in new ways for new settings. The originator of modern *kumi-daiko* playing was a jazz drummer named Daihachi Oguchi, who in the early 1950s took some old notations from a Shinto shrine and improvised their styles, joining several drums together. The style has become so popular that today an estimated eight thousand groups are now playing across Japan, with the Ondekoza and Kodo groups among the oldest and most prominent, with similar styles emerging across the Pacific.

The origin story of *kumi-daiko*'s North American incarnation is that a young man named Seiichi Tanaka went to a Spring Blossom festival in San Francisco in the late sixties but was surprised not to hear any of the drums he had heard growing up in Japan. He went to a local Buddhist temple in the Bay Area, borrowed some drums, and enlisted the help of a number of Japanese people living nearby. They founded the San Francisco Taiko Dojo, which continues to operate today with Tanaka as the Grand Master. Thousands of people have now played as part of this group, collaborating with West African, Afro-Cuban, and Japanese musicians and jazz players including Art Blakey. The San Francisco Taiko Dojo and Japanese groups like Ondekoza and Kodo tour the world, playing gigs such as Carnegie Hall, the Walt Disney Concert Hall in Los Angeles, and Le Palais des Congrès in Paris.

With such intermingling of the sacred and the spectacular, we return to Timothy Beal's questions about sacred capital, and whether that gets spent down with the mass dissemination and wide appeal of once semiprivate and ritualistically set drum use. A central concern is how much the sacred nature of drums, drumming, and drumbeats can be carried over into a modern, secular setting as drum traditions have been revived, reformed, and re-created. Cynicism is one tempting response. We might be led to believe we are missing the "authentic" traditions, that Mani Rimdu isn't real if it's played for paying tourists. But one point of a history of religion is that all these sacred rituals were, over time and space, made up. All traditions adapt and change, fitting new environments. Franz Kafka gets at this with a pithy little parable: "Leopards break into the temple and drink to the dregs what is in the sacrificial pitchers; this is repeated over and over again; finally it can be calculated in advance, and it becomes a part of the ceremony."[25] What was at first a disruption, an anomaly, becomes part of the process. History, including sacred history, is open ended, adaptable, unfinished. There are always more lurking leopards. Tradition is not the same old thing done the same old way, but a chain of changes, interlinked through memories, bodies, practices, and ever new playing.

Which leads to my final point. This is a book about objects, and thus this chapter is a story of drums and the sounds they make. These objects connect with the *half*, the desiring human body that plays the drums, just as the drums play the humans. We use the term *playing* drums, and indeed it is a form of play, that utmost activity of animal behavior. As biologists and psychologists are learning more and more, play is an essential element in human and other animal flourishing. Psychiatrist Stuart Brown has devoted his life to the study of play and published an overview of much of his work in *Play: How It Shapes the Brain, Opens the Imagination, and Invigorates the Soul.* There he states:

> Play is a profound biological process. It has evolved over eons in many animal species to promote survival. It shapes the brain and makes animals smarter and more adaptable. In higher animals, it fosters empathy and makes possible complex social groups. For us, play lies at the core of creativity and innovation. Of all animal species, humans are the biggest players of all. We are built to play and built through play. When we play, we are engaged in the purest expression of our humanity, the truest expression of our individuality.[26]

Add to this some recent investigations into the therapeutic aspects of playing drums—enabling healing, recovery from addiction and depression—and we see again why drums might be situated so firmly in sacred histories.[27] Philosophers and anthropologists from Johan Huizinga to Roger Caillois and, more recently, Robert Bellah have shown how play and ritual are deeply embedded in human consciousness and stand at the heart of religious traditions themselves. This can certainly be seen through the playing of drums. Sacred power resides in the drums, in the sounds, but also in the playing as bodies connect with the objects through play.

Above I mentioned the Christian drummer Terl Bryant, who found the force of drums as a vital component in his life and in connection with others. His mission is not far from Mickey Hart's, strange though that may seem. Hart was one of two percussionists for the Grateful Dead (a band that conservative Christians gleefully denounced) and has gone on to promote drumming as a quasi-magical force in human life. He gives a delightful nod to the ubiquity of drums by charting earth as "Planet Drum": he has spent years traveling the world in search of drums and stories, and finding ways for people to connect across cultures by playing together. He confesses to the obsessions and passions and pains that have led him through a life of drumming: "For a long time the drum took everything I had; it had all my attention. The call of the drum was the one constant in a life of such chaos that my head aches just remembering it."[28] His confession is not dissimilar to a spiritual autobiography, only here the higher power is the drum's call, the object that speaks. One result of his endeavors was the 1991 Grammy-winning recording called *Planet Drum* in which he plays with percussionists from India, Nigeria, Brazil, and Puerto Rico.

As the Art Blakey account above illustrated, it's difficult to tell the difference between one's search for the cultural-religious significance of drums and one's search for religions, and the role of drums within those. The history of drums and the religious traditions to which they are attached are inseparable. The poem "What We Do," in Stephen Cramer's collection entitled *Shiva's Drum*, looks into what many of these stories suggest: Cramer tells of a street musician banging on an aluminum bowl and wonders if the musician is playing the drum, "or if they're playing him."[29] Hart confesses that he was called by the drum, as was Blakey in Africa and thousands of others who find fulfillment and a sense of purpose in drumming. For Hart, Bryant, and Blakey, the call set them on a quest to learn of the drum's history and manifold manifestations. The results show the impossibility of creating a simply secular approach. One cannot study drums without knowing something about religions, and, as I'm arguing through this book, vice versa.

CROSSES

*The cross is
above everything else
a construction of nature's reality.*

—M. H. J. Schoenmaekers,
Dutch mathematician[1]

*Why not just think of it as a
metal T-shaped thingy?*

—Jon Stewart, anchor of
The Daily Show

Visual technologies—from telescopes and eyeglasses to digital video and medical imaging—have reshaped human societies by changing our perspectives on what we call reality. Photographic cameras are one type of visual technology, and these alone have dramatically shifted attitudes in the past two centuries of life in the United States: Matthew Brady's albumen prints of US Civil War battlefields brought the war to civilian consciousness; newsreels transported the World Wars directly into the seats of cinema audiences; Abraham Zapruder's eight millimeter movie camera unintentionally clustered the world around television sets by recording John F. Kennedy's assassination; and news commentators speaking on September 11, 2001, watched video clips of the collapsing World Trade Towers and said, "It's just like a movie." We can never again imagine the world without the preconceptions provided by pictures.

Many artists working in traditional media during this time turned their backs on realistic depictions of the world. Why try to paint and draw and sculpt realistically when the photographic medium can do it so much better and easier? But it was more than that. As painters in particular began to grow skeptical about how "natural" seeing is, seeing and believing began to go their separate ways. With Paul Cézanne as a precursor, Wassily Kandinsky, Kasimir Malevich, and Piet Mondrian reduced the visible world to color and geometric form, condensing the cosmos on canvas just as the First World War was gearing up. For his part, Mondrian began drawing trees in the early years of the twentieth century, not long after the invention of cinema—some 1906 pencil works show distinctly realistic representations and a solid sense of "natural" perspective. By 1912 his trees were abstracted into a series of crisscrossing lines, and barely a hint was given as to how to connect the composition to anything in nature; three dimensions were turned into two, flowing organic lines made straight. By the next decade he was working on the compositions for which he is best remembered today: black rectilinear lines forming a grid on a white background, with some of the quadrangles colored in yellow, red, and blue. For Mondrian, this process was not a retreat from engaging the natural world but rather a means of connecting with a more profound reality lying under the surface of appearances.

Jump ahead three decades, and we find the stirrings of the movement called minimalism in the artistry of Agnes Martin and carried on by Sol LeWitt, Ad Reinhardt, Donald Judd, and others. As Zapruder was recording political history, Martin penciled a grid of horizontal rows and vertical columns on canvas, creating hundreds of lines crossing at perpendicular angles. In one 1964 work, she lightly painted grey hues in broad horizontal stripes over the pencil lines and titled it *Trees*, even though the simple image was as far from anything arboreal as possible. "My paintings," Martin claimed, "have neither objects, nor space, nor time, not anything—no forms. They are light, lightness, about merging, about formlessness, breaking down form."[2] In Martin's artwork the minimal gives rise to the mystical, and at its heart are a series of crisscrossing lines. There was a tree, back in the mythical beginning, and the only way to connect with its reality now is through abstraction, so that it triggers an experience in the body of the viewer, rather than prompting an intellectual preconception of what a tree is. In a world of quick access to all things deemed reality, visual contemplation, taking time to see, becomes its own virtue for Martin.

A cross and a grid are not equivalent, though they work from the same visual principle. For Martin and Mondrian the image of a *grid*, a series of intersecting crosses, became the cornerstone of painting, the lowest common denominator, the most primal markings made by human hands that still might be called art. Their work is akin to that of the priests and shamans and laypeople who took the basic sounds of the thumping drum or the simple solidity of stones and turned them into highly conceptual and powerful objects at the center of religious worship. Only here, the museum becomes the temple. Visually speaking, nothing is more primeval, more fundamental to the connection between nature and culture and between human and divine than the sight of two crossed lines.

In writing about a history of religion, and then discussing crosses, it would be easy to suggest a cross is related to the Christian tradition. Indeed, it is. But it's much more than that, related to many traditions in many ways. Even the Christian tradition displays a diversity of cross uses that are not often recognizable. And so in this chapter, I want to show the deep visual evocations that crossed lines have had in a number of places in time and space. Along the way, we'll also look at the many varieties of Christian crosses and their precedents. Crosses, we'll see, evoke mystical visions, seal identity, ward off evil spirits, display truth, start wars, create connections, and stand as a basis for art.

Crosses are cosmic. They are visible points of focus that unlock deeper, often invisible forces. This is as true for Euro-American abstract artists like Mondrian and Martin as it is for Native American sacred imagery, ancient Egyptian amulets, and many others. Meditating with a yantra—a small cosmogram, often in cruciform—helps Hindus and Jains achieve meditative focus and connect with deities. Praying before a cross—in the form of the instrument of Jesus's crucifixion—gives Christians the experience of comfort and perhaps redemption. These are not identical experiences, as the intellectual, aesthetic, and theological meanings differ. Yet standing in the midst of each of them are images of crossing lines.

The cross is a piece of technology that provides a bridge and allows connection. Through that association comes transformation. We cross over, crossbreed, cross-pollinate, cross-dress, crisscross and will never be the same as a result. Mondrian says, "Vertical and horizontal lines are the expression of two opposing forces; they exist everywhere and dominate everything; their reciprocal action constitutes 'life.' I recognized that the equilibrium of any particular aspect of nature rests on the equivalence of its opposites."[3] He was influenced by a mystical mathematician by the name of M. H. J. Schoenmaekers who made comments like this one: "The cross is above everything else a construction of nature's reality. . . . The more he will meditate about the construction of the cross, the more exactly the mystic will see reality as a created fact."[4] The artist and mathematician were writing in the Protestant-dominated Netherlands, but these statements are not those of Christian theology. Instead, they are seeing this image as something that transcends specific traditions, a sign that undergirds nature, history, and culture. Modern artistic techniques attempted to strip the cross of any institutionally religious connotations, yet artists continued to see something visually primal, and thus paradoxically, potentially mystical in the rectilinear figure. This is the grid on which reality itself is built, and if we come to contemplate it, we are allowed a privileged vision.

In these cosmic connections, crosses conjure erotic relations, as is often the case with mystical perspectives. Vertical and horizontal, heaven and earth, parallel the masculine and feminine. Modern architect and theorist Adolf Loos was a key force in stripping away the ornamental, seemingly superfluous elements of buildings and art. His early treatise on the topic, provocatively titled "Ornament and Crime," suggests, "All art is erotic. The first ornament that was born, the cross, was erotic in origin. . . . A horizontal dash: the prone woman. A vertical dash: the man penetrating her."[5] The sexually aggressive, heterosexual stirrings here speak to a visual energy within the dashed lines of a cross. The cross is art, in Loos's terms, but also a basic building structure; crossed lines operate within modern architecture similar to the ways they function in modern painting, creating grand grids of buildings—and thus the modern steel and glass office buildings were born. Loos would influence other architects such as Mies van der Rohe—who proclaimed, "Less is more"—and their combined interests were in fashioning a world without ornament, one that was streamlined, ordered, and rational. Rectilinear lines stripped away the excesses and brought humans back to a "pure" state. Even so, this purity is no less sensual than any baroque extravagance.

Another cosmic bridge created through crossed lines is the link between life and death. To see this we begin by looking well beyond the workings of modern art. The ancient Egyptian ankh, two crossed lines with a loop at the top, was an object carried by people and gods alike. The word *ankh* means "life," and sometimes hints at eternal life. The object's use as an amulet, often held against a person's chest, displays its power to protect. Many hieroglyphs display Egyptian deities carrying ankhs, and people were buried with them because they served as protective devices into the afterlife. (The boy-pharaoh King Tutankhamen was buried with various images of ankhs, including one striking gold mirror box in this shape.) The ankh probably has an erotic element too, since some have surmised that the straight lines represent Osiris and the oval represents Isis.

Early Egyptian religious life was polytheistic, and families were devoted to particular deities among a pantheon. In contrast, worship of the supreme god Aten developed through the reign of the pharaoh Akhenaten (whose name is literally "The Living Spirit of Aten") in the fourteenth century BCE. Aten was a creator god, a singular being who, unlike the other deities, had no consort or offspring and was symbolized by a sun disc. Images of this sun disc at times displayed rays coming down to the earth, and at the end of the rays were ankhs, made as gifts to kings and queens such as Akhenaten and Nefertiti: the supreme god reaches to earth and offers a cross. In spite of the pharaoh's attempts to bring this monotheistic practice into the hearts of the people, devotion did not last, and Egypt became dominated again by polytheism after Akhenaten.

The appeal of this ancient symbol and its widespread location in a collective visual storehouse of memories have made it a prop for many contemporary pop culture productions, even without the artists having knowledge of Egyptian history. Ankhs have appeared in television shows like *Lost* and *Logan's Run*, in music videos and on album covers by jazz experimentalist Sun Ra and hard-rock band KISS, and in video games such as *World of Warcraft* and *Ultima*. And the ankh has been revived as a symbol across contemporary New Age and neopagan rituals, such as the modern movement called Kemetism, which seeks to restore select ancient Egyptian ways.

Christians too have seen crosses in quasi-mystical realms. Here crosses are associated with the death of Jesus and thus connected with the redemptive, life-giving dimensions of this sacrifice, but at times the image itself takes on a visionary quality of a connecting point, uniting the heavens and earth. (I remember a sketch from my childhood Sunday school depicting two sides of a great canyon. Bridging the two was the cross, representing Jesus, lying horizontally and connecting one side, fallen humanity, to the other, God.) In the late sixteenth century, theologian and poet Saint John of the Cross had a mystical vision of a crucified Christ. Nothing too unusual among the pious, but the vision prompted him to sketch what he saw: an image of the crucifixion from the top down, as if a God's-eye view, with the cross and body suspended in space. In Saint John's version, the cross hangs between heaven and earth, which provides something of a visual metaphor of the theology of the cross, a meeting point between the two realms, as Jesus becomes the sacrifice, the atonement that brings God and humans, heavens and earth, together.

The image was taken up by a latter-day Spaniard, Salvador Dalí, in his 1951 *Christ of Saint John of the Cross*. Dalí himself had a visionary dream in which he saw something similar to Saint John's vision, only taken in a new direction. Under Dalí's surrealist brush, Christ becomes wholly detached from earth, floating in the sky above Port Lligat, Catalonia, his body no longer suffering, the blood and nail holes cleared away. Dalí wanted a metaphysical Christ, something distinct from the earth-bound, suffering bodies that were prominent across the centuries in the Iberian Peninsula and in the Northern European reformation styles of Matthias Grünewald and others. While he hangs at the nexus of heaven and earth, there is little earthly left in Dalí's Jesus: the oil paint depicts a gnostic version of the gospel.

The image of crossed lines is ordinary and simple, and this is part of its power. I once heard the novelist Toni Morrison surmising that children's pencil scratchings on paper (or whatever surface children decide to write on) eventually coalesce into two lines that cross each other, and that is the first recognizable visual symbol a person might create. (Whether the child understands this is another matter.) The image of the cross as the meeting of two lines, situated, suspended, or otherwise located between the heavens and earth, between life and death, between masculine and feminine, between infancy and adulthood, weaves its way across ancient and modern traditions. Its basic visual appearance becomes the grid work on which reality is built.

Looking at a cross may stimulate a visual centripetal force that moves the eye inward to the crux of the lines, the meeting spot between vertical and horizontal. At this point we are led to conjure crossings, mixings, and mergings, as noted above: the meeting of two lines fuels metaphysical ponderings. But if our eyes follow the cross centrifugally, looking to the ends and edges, we find four points leading outward, mapping themselves onto the physical space around: a sacred geometry.

The Chinese character for the number ten (十) is a cross. The character carries connotations of perfection and completeness. Oracle bones* dating as far back as the fourteenth century BCE indicate only a vertical line for the number ten, but sometime during the Bronze Age a horizontal line was added. The etymological dictionary *Shuowen*, from around 100 CE, suggests that with the crossing lines the number is complete. That is, it combines the horizontal line that corresponds to east and west, with the vertical line for north and south, and thus comprising all four directions.

Some of the earliest Chinese cosmological conceptions about the shape of the world are seen on the oracle bones from twenty-

---

* Oracle bones were at one time referred to as dragon bones but are actually turtle shells and the shoulder blades of oxen. These are the oldest extant inscriptions in Chinese and are understood to have been used in divination rites.

five hundred years ago, during the Shang Dynasty. Found among the inscriptions are indications of the four directions (or quadrates, *si fang*) made up of the east, west, north, and south. Each of these was also the home of one of the four winds and became associated with four gods.[6] A fifth quadrate was eventually added to the conceptual framework: the center. (The center is not a direction per se, but pragmatically it makes sense: there can be no directions without a grounding point.) The cosmos, then, was cruciform, sometimes noted through the character *ya* (亞) the shape of which became the footprint for ancient temples, and the five quadrates were themselves charted on to multiple layers of cosmological significance. Overseeing this was the high god Di. The political world mirrored the world of the heavens, with four spokes meeting at the center of the world, where Di and the ruler engaged, where rituals were performed and power transferred.

The number five worked as a primary metaphor, based in a spatial experience that took on abstract philosophical importance. Five became a constant refrain in the rituals, myths, ideas, and symbols of ancient China on into the contemporary age. As Taoist practices and views began to take hold in the first millennium BCE, the number five was undergirded by the primary dual forces of yin and yang. Supporting these was the Tao itself, the original formless "stuff" at the base of all that exists. As Lao Tzu's *Tao te ching* puts it, the Tao is "eternally nameless." The deepest reality or nature is the Tao, and from this primordial, chaotic realm emerges two forms, yin and yang. These two become associated with male and female, light and dark, hot and cold, and other opposites. They are complementary, equal, and opposing forces. Yin and yang energies then produce a sequence of movements, phases of being numbering five.

In texts from the *Tao te ching* to the *I ching* and later in commentaries on the *I ching*, such as *The Elemental Changes*, the prominence of the number five is reaffirmed as the Five Phases become a religious-cultural-political ordering grid. In this system, the five cardinal points (east, south, center, west, north) match up with the five seasons (spring, summer, transitional period, autumn, winter), the five elements (wood, fire, earth, metal, water), the five primary colors (green, red, yellow, white, black), the five sacred mountains (Taishan, Hengshan [Hunan], Songshan, Huashan, Hengshan [Shanxi]), and the five sense organs (eye, tongue, mouth, nose, ear).* The mythological and cosmological movement—from Tao to yin and yang to the Five Phases—parallels many systems through the history of the world's religions: from primordial chaos to increasing differentiation and categorization. In broad strokes, the Way of the Tao then is not dissimilar to modern art, or mystical visions of Christians, or Kabbalistic conjurings of incense, or drummed rhythms of the Yoruba. All these traditions use technological tools of differentiation to bring practitioners back to a primordial state where all is unified, to the formless and seamless origins of nature. One basic tool is the formation of crossed lines, a spatial accounting of how the cosmos maps onto cardinal directions and mountain peaks, and ultimately the human body and social life.

The Taoist symbol of yin and yang has become a well-known image, often misused in modern consumer culture as a logo. It consists of a circle with a black swirling segment with a white eye, contrasted with a white swirling segment with a black eye. They enfold each other, and are the mirror image of each other. It is the Chinese version of crossed lines, as discussed above—Agnes Martin's comments about her grid paintings being "about formlessness, breaking down form," could be understood in Taoist ways. The perpendicular lines in modern art, among the Egyptians, and eventually for Christians, stand for the basic struc-

---

* Speech was understood as one of the senses, as it was in parts of medieval Europe.

tures of the universe. Within the Taoist symbolism the lines are curved. These are not the same exact ways of seeing the world, and their differences are illuminating, yet it is intriguing to see how each begins with a two-part, interconnected system, each of which is made into primary forms of the universe.*

Centuries and continents away, nestled in the highest mountains of South America, lies the Andean village of Misminay, between the Peruvian city of Cusco and the famed Inca temple ruins of Machu Picchu. In Misminay's symbolic mythology, cruciform imagery stands for the general layout of the cosmos. The universe is structured around dual intersecting axes, one on earth and another in the heavens, astronomically observable in the rotation of the constellations in the clear, high-elevation night sky. The heavens are divided into a four-part (*suyu*) system, and each of these has its own stellar cross overseeing it. Each of these is, in turn, associated with solstices and equinoxes, and thus also with seasons. After contact with Christians, and an appropriation and reuse of the Christian theology of the cross, the Quechua-speaking community adapted the Spanish term "Cruz Calvario" (Cross of Calvary) to refer to the Milky Way at its annual zenith in the sky—the Milky Way forming the chief axis that divides the celestial firmament. Mixed with these Christian concepts are the gods of the mountains, the Wamanis, who are sometimes represented by crosses standing at the apex of mountains, looking not unlike Jesus's cross at the top of Mount Calvary. Irrigation canals then flow downward from that point, supplying divine water to the people and water for food crops.[7]

These cosmic quarterings are taken up in everyday objects

---

* Indeed, if I weren't writing this chapter on the visual object of the cross, I would be writing it on circles. The cross and the circle together are the most widespread, ancient and modern, globally recognizable visual symbols. And of course, the two are often seen together: in the ankh, the Celtic cross, the neolithic circle cross, and even the Buddhist wheel of dharma.

and spatial orderings of the Misminay village. At the village center is a chapel called Crucero ("cross"); within it are three community crosses. The chapel is the center because it draws people to it for communal gatherings and religious events, but also because it is the geographic crux of the community, the point at which two footpaths intersect and the point at which two irrigation canals cross each other. The two footpaths and two irrigation canals run parallel to each other, and they serve to divide the village itself up into four sections, with a social organization and hierarchy based on the four quarters.

As with the Misminay, cruciform imagery is found across indigenous traditions throughout North and South America. The number four, for example, permeates the culture of the Navajo (Diné) of the southwestern United States, indicating everything from the four cardinal directions, four colors, four sacred mountains, four times of the day, and four periods of a human lifespan. As such, a cross with its four points appears on weavings throughout Navajo culture. The Sioux use a sacred hoop (medicine wheel), a cross within a circle, as a representation of the four directions within the world. And the Ojibwe make the shape of a sacred hoop from stones laid out on the ground, with each stone in the cross and circle representing a different spirit, direction, animal, or virtue—the setting can be used for healing purposes. Uses of crosses as icons, cosmic maps, healing objects, talismans, and metaphorical principles within the Americas predate Christian contact. The European colonization of the Americas nonetheless brought new, synthetic ways of seeing both the traditional crosses of the native peoples and the Christianized versions of the image. The crossing of crosses produced ever-new stories and traditions.

Somewhere in the movements from centripetal to centrifugal and back, from intersection to ends, the cross forms a basic grid for mapping the world, a technological orientation device interlinking the mythical world of the heavens and gods with the perceivable physical world of humans. The cross is a bridge transporting us across, through, over, up to meet our stars, our gods, our people.

A collection of crosses hangs on one of my office walls. The crossbars of a Celtic cross I purchased on the Isle of Iona in Scotland bloom into a Tree of Life. The post and crossbar of a brass crucifix from Spain is meticulously ornamented with fine floral lines. A wooden cross from Mexico, given to me as a gift, has brightly colored tile work attached to the standard slats. Another Mexican cross has tiny mirrors inserted behind tin frames at the four points—a fact that I've always associated with Martin Luther's statement about how we all carry the very nails of Christ's crucifixion in our pockets: we look at the points of this cross and see ourselves reflected.

If traditions from Central America to China to Egypt took two crossed lines and made them a fundamental marker for connecting with the contours of the cosmos, Christians took the simplicity of the crossed lines and created elaborate structures. Deriving from the iconoclastic, Protestant reform heritage of the Netherlands, Mondrian was able to pare down the symbolism of crossed lines to the barest minimum, but most of Christendom has seldom believed van der Rohe's assertion that "less is more." Christian crosses have merged perpendicular lines with circles or added extra lines here and there, or morphed the crosses into trees, or appended flowers, colors, and ornaments.

For Christianity, the cross is what anthropologist Sherry Ortner calls a "summarizing symbol."[8] That is, it is a material object that sums up and stands in for a larger system; it represents many ideas, attitudes, and meanings all at the same time. This is not the cross as visual contemplation point, as in several of the above examples, but here it is a symbol that has moved into a conceptual framework. Summarizing symbols are not mere abstractions, however; they instead represent for participants, "in an emotionally powerful and relatively undifferentiated way, what the system means to them." Bringing together multiple ideas and feelings, these key symbols do not "encourage reflection on the logical relations among these ideas, nor on the logical consequences of them as they are played out in social actuality, over time and history." Rather, they are a "crystallization of commitment." People act because of such symbols, even to the point of creating a "love it or leave it," either-or mode of being. Such symbols speak, telling people how to behave, how to lay out their land, where to place their valuables, and with whom all these things should be done. But they don't speak with much nuance.[9]

Of course, to say as Ortner does that the cross is a summarizing symbol for Christianity can only be an abstract, rhetorical point, because the reality is that there is no one cross, as we have already begun to see. If we spend time looking with our eyes, we come to a different perspective than if we simply use words, and we begin to gather in the sensual dimensions of the primary metaphor. To explain this further, I want to hold on to the idea of the summarizing symbol for the cross, but to see how far this can be pushed, and at what point it might no longer summarize, at what point the material object no longer becomes recognizable to others for whom it is supposed to summarize ideas, feelings, and commitments.

One cross on my wall was a gift from my mother after she returned from working in Ethiopia. It doesn't really look like a cross. Maybe more like a big key. Or a metal bookmark for a family Bible, its interlaced lines so complex at the top that it becomes more of a mesh than any easily distinguishable horizontal and vertical axes; a gathering of many crosses appears within the singular large grid of lines. If abstract artists in modern Europe took the complexities of the cosmos and compressed meaning into a few lines and colors, the Ethiopian Christian tradition turned in the opposite direction, layering lines and accreting meanings in intricate and beautiful ways. I can get lost in its designs.

The fourth-century bishop Frumentius (known as Abba Salama, the Father of Peace) established the Ethiopian Church. Legends say he carried a hand cross from Egypt, where he had received it as a gift from the Coptic monastic founder, Saint Pachomius. The style of the original cross is not clear, but the Egyptian ankh had been carried over from ancient religious practices into the later Christian culture and was adopted by the Coptic Christian Church in Egypt, its older meanings replaced with the newer Christ-centered theologies. The benefit of the ankh, with its loop at the top, was that it was portable, and it became a well-used hand cross. Whether or not it was an ankh that Frumentius carried or a Greek cross (all four arms are of equal length) or some other style altogether, aesthetic and theological developments in Ethiopia turned the crossed lines into twisted weaves of patterns and details not seen anywhere else in Christendom.[10]

The chapter on drums already noted the lengthy history of Ethiopian Christianity, a historical reality that has given the artistic and ritualistic traditions there a long time to steep, to soak up various influences and to see what works, what doesn't, what sinks and settles at the bottom, and what evaporates away. Mixing Byzantine, Islamic, and indigenous East African aesthetic traditions, Ethiopia has elevated the cross into a richly diverse art form, two crossed lines evolving into elaborate pendants, processional markers, handheld protective devices, necklaces, and other bodily ornaments. Sometimes the cross consists of a simple mark of two crossed lines, which may be tattooed or even branded onto Christian foreheads. At other times, as with many hand and processional crosses, the form involves patterns of interlaced lines, weavings of metal that look at times like they could have come from the Celtic Book of Kells, at other times like the backdrop to a Southeast Asian Buddhist icon, at others like an obscure baroque parlor utensil, or all of them at once. Some copper, bronze, and silver crosses have central plates with etchings of Christ, though usually the representational aspects are minimal. Further, these crosses are a long way from anything that could be effectively used for an execution. In their grandest form Ethiopian Christian crosses are abstractions, improvisations on a theme of a cross. And through that they sensually evoke devotion, feelings, and behaviors among their adherents.

Lay Christians in Ethiopia wear small neck crosses for protection against sickness and evil spirits, while priests will carry a hand cross (10–25 cm) as an identifying sign, holding it up against their breast while being photographed and passing it down to sons and grandsons. Such crosses are both looked at and touched, engaged through two senses. Another type of cross, the processional cross, is larger. It fits onto a pole and is raised, in part so that it *is not* touched, thus insuring some of its sacrality, or at least channeling the sacred element solely into a visual sensibility.

Within the highly developed liturgy of the Ethiopian Orthodox Church, three types of crosses are used. They are difficult to distinguish simply by looking at them, but they each have different functions. One is kept in a special storage area, often not far from the *kabaro*, and taken out and touched only by officiating priests during the worship services. Another is used as the incense cross, carried by a deacon in one hand as he swings a censer in the other. A third is used by the *debtaras*—the liturgical leaders mentioned in the chapter on drums—who hold them during their sacred swaying and dancing to the beat of the *kabaro*.

Crosses in Ethiopia are used well beyond official worship, as they supply magical and healing powers. As throughout the Christian world, crosses perform miracles, protect people from harm, and are weapons in spiritual battles. In fact, the first known image of a crucifix used in Christianity dates from around 200 CE, from the eastern Mediterranean region. It is a small jasper amulet with a Greek inscription that weaves the names of "Son, Father, and Jesus Christ" into a magical chant, alongside other magical names.[11] Similarly, Christian clergy in many places manually enact the sign of the cross, invisible in midair, to offer blessings to people. Clearly none of this would have continued to have impact without the central event of the crucifixion of Jesus on a cross, but looking at the functions of sensual crosses in Christianity reveals at least two things. First, that the cross's evocative power might derive from deep, cosmic connections not dissimilar to those found in many other traditions around the world. Second, crosses have multiple meanings and functions across Christian traditions, and their symbolic value does not readily stay still.

Crosses are monsters. In more ways than one. They are monstrous, serving as symbols of gruesome forms of capital punishment: the accused, accursed body put on display. The word *monster* itself stems from the Latin *monere*, which is "to warn," and related to the verb *monstrare*, which translates to English as "to show" or "reveal."[12] A cross used for crucifixion shows, warns, and portends, lest you too stray from the way of the Roman Empire and end up on display yourself.* No doubt due to its monstrous nature, Christians did not go about using crosses as symbols until a couple of centuries after the death of Jesus. While they are a quick and easy reminder of the two-millennia-old tradition today, most early Christians were rightfully reticent to use such an object to portray their faith, opting instead for quasi-pagan tropes like Jesus as a "good shepherd" or a "fisher of men." Wearing a cross during the time of Jesus would

---

* Material evidence indicates that the Persians and the Greeks, before the Romans, had similar styles of execution.

be like someone today wearing an electric chair as a pendant around their neck, a representation of an instrument of execution. Except that very few of us today have actually *seen* an electric chair, as we keep our executions hidden, away from any monstrous showing.

In the Christian tradition, crosses also take the form of a *monstrance*. Essentially, monstrances are ornate, heavily gilded display cases, anywhere from a few centimeters high to a meter or more, often in cruciform. Within them is contained a relic of a saint or the bread of communion, the consecrated host become the body of Christ.* A small window is typically built into the work, allowing viewers to look at the remains therein; the term *monstrance* is used because the structure puts an object on show. A monstrance provides a beautiful covering for what might be a rather abject object: fingernail clippings of Saint Clare, the tooth of Saint John the Baptist, an arm bone of Saint George, the breast milk of Mary, the foreskin of Jesus. Elaborate, gold plated, finely crafted pieces of technology form the showing room for the more natural, bodily object. (One monstrance, at the Monastery of the Incarnation in Avila, Spain, contains the drawing of Christ's crucifixion as sketched by Saint John of the Cross—after his mystical vision.)

I can think of few things that more ably show the subtle, strange power of sacred objects than a monstrance now in the collection of the Art Institute of Chicago. It is from fifteenth-century Germany and represents the silversmithing techniques of that provenance. Shaped in the form of a cross, about twenty-two centimeters high, it contains a relic of the third century martyr Saint Christina. The relic in this case is a bone, possibly

---

* The term *monstrance* has been used in the past for the cases that display either relics or Eucharist, though *reliquary* has become more common for those containing relics and *monstrance* for those with the host. The two are often used interchangeably.

a finger bone, but none of that can be readily verified.* In finely crafted, perfectly symmetrical silverwork is a small window at the crux of the cross, allowing us to peer at the specially situated bone fragment of an eighteen-hundred-year-old human. Some devout people would call this disgusting. Many secular-minded would see it as evidence of backward beliefs. Others have traveled many miles, spending and risking much, to see such a sight, now placed in the clean, well-lit galleries of a major museum. The material body, decaying and imperfect though it may be, stands at the heart of the seemingly smooth operations of religious worship.

A number of other religious traditions also enshrine relics. They are especially prominent in Shia Islamic traditions (clippings of Muhammad's beard are key), Mahayana Buddhism (the Buddha's teeth), and Greek religions (Agamemnon's scepter).[13] In this vein, we might also consider Vladimir Lenin's body, embalmed and behind glass in his mausoleum near the Kremlin, or Britney Spears's chewing gum (auctioned at up to $14,000), or William Shatner's kidney stone (sold for $25,000) as modern secular versions. While a fuller description is beyond the scope of this book, relics do portray the power of objects to shape religious devotion and the prominent function of the body within devotion. Bodies devoted to other bodies.

The most monstrous cross in the modern world is the Nazi swastika. Its sign has sanctioned violence, greed, deception, the rampant yet restrained lust for power, and ultimately genocide. Writing in *Mein Kampf* in the 1920s, Adolf Hitler claimed, "In

---

* The Cathedral of Saint John the Evangelist in Cleveland, the mother church for nearly one million Roman Catholics in Northern Ohio, has a reliquary of Saint Christina's "entire skeleton and small vial of her blood." Pope Pius XI gave it to the Cathedral in 1928 (three years before the monstrance was given to Chicago's Art Institute), and it was only the second time the Vatican had given the complete relics of a saint to a place in the United States.

the swastika [the National Socialists see] the mission of the fight for the victory of Aryan man, and at the same time also the victory of the idea of creative work which in itself is and will always be anti-Semitic."[14] That is a lot to claim for a few perpendicular lines. The first half of the swastika's mission failed (the Aryans were not victorious) but the second half arguably did. Today, across the Western world the swastika is an instant visual trigger of anti-Semitism.

Swastika is an ancient Sanskrit term meaning "good luck" or "good being"; in other words, for a few millennia, the image has signified happiness and pleasure, appearing across devotional images of the *devas* and *devis* (gods and goddesses) of South Asia and beyond. Max Müller, one of the earliest champions of comparative religions, argued in the late nineteenth century that the right-turned swastika was the true one and the left-turned one false—a notion occasionally and optimistically reiterated still today in an attempt to sever the connection between Hindus and Nazis.* There is no real evidence for this assertion in general, and indeed left- and right-turned swastikas appear side by side on temple walls, pottery, and palms of hands. In its more profane sense, the swastika has traditionally been a charm or amulet that is worn, adorns walls, or is carried. Historically, its sacred uses have taken these well-meaning purposes and amplified them. It is one thing to receive a blessing as you enter your neighbor's house. It is another to have the Buddha or Ganesha give you a sign of blessing, palm facing out, swastika in hand.[15]

Müller himself said that the term *swastika* should not be used outside its South Asian context, calling its many misuses "promiscuous." And there is something to his point, because he attempts to keep meanings strictly separated. But symbols seldom obey the limits of nations, cultures, religions, or languages (or

---

* We see something similar when we cross our fingers for good luck, but if we cross our fingers behind our back while making a promise, the promise is undone.

an academic philologist), and so the term has spilled over into many contexts to name the same visual figure. I use it here as shorthand for a specific style of cross (thus akin to speaking of a Greek cross, or an ankh), just as I use the term because it affects response, and it is the ongoing visual-verbal repercussions and reverberations that are of interest. It is the endless morphing of meaning of this cross that makes it a curious object for a history of religions.

Perhaps the original visual symbol was, if we dig back far enough, a sun in motion or some version of a sun god, a spinning wheel of life with spokes, whirling logs, stages of human spiritual evolution, or a calendar. A millennium-old monument of runes in Denmark has the mark, as does a burial ground in Ohio from two millennia ago. Buddhist temples have long been marked by swastikas, and one old written source says that the Buddha himself had a swastika mark on his chest. A nineteenth-century archaeologist, Heinrich Schliemann, excavated the archaic city of Troy and found similar images of the crossed lines throughout its architecture and objects. Jains will spread a handful of flour or rice on a flat circular space and draw four lines into it with their fingers, swiping away portions of the substance and leaving the imprint of a swastika as a blessing.

The history of the imagery is diverse, while the quest for the swastika's origins became especially fanatical, starting in the late nineteenth century. Edward Butts, a civil engineer from St. Louis, made finding its genesis his life's avocation. Writing in 1908, he fell under the swastika's sway, rhapsodizing in ways almost unthinkable today: "To our minds it appears much like a beautiful cloud that once floated above a setting sun, tinted with brilliant colors."[16] Between 1870 and 1933 around a dozen books and numerous articles were published in English on the subject of the swastika—some by eccentric hobbyists, others by earnest anthropologists. During that time the symbol was used by individuals as diverse as a Philadelphia gathering of the Girls

Club of America, the US 15th Infantry, and the personal logo that accompanied Rudyard Kipling's signature.

During this time too, those constructing the history of the "Aryan race" were consistently using the symbol—Hitler's quote above summarizes this connection. The quest for origins (of art, religion, symbols, language) that so dominated Western cultures, arts, and scientific endeavors in the nineteenth century took hold in the quest for racial origins as well. The European push to establish the legacy of the Indo-European peoples resulted in a new set of distinctions, including terms like *Caucasian* and *Aryan* (Aryan being a subset of the larger category Caucasian, which also included Semitic people). Max Müller used the term Aryan to think historically about the roots of language, but others took the distinctions engendered by the term and used these differences to construct physical anthropological histories that, not unsurprisingly, wound up portraying the Aryans as a superior race.

Through these creations of history, the swastika was part and parcel of the search for (or construction of) the Aryan race. At the Paris Exposition of 1889 a Polish archaeologist named Michael Zmigrodski exhibited more than three hundred of his drawings of the swastika found around the world—many of these inspired by Schliemann's Troy excavations. Zmigrodski was but one of many of his time engaging the simultaneous search for the pure race alongside the search for the pure image. A hundred years later, Malcolm Quinn observed the visual outcomes of this connection coalescing in Nazi Germany, suggesting that "the swastika was the sign in which a modern mass was encouraged to see itself as an ancient community."[17] Quinn draws attention to the ways people at pageants and party rallies in Nazi Germany would arrange themselves in a giant, human-made swastika—thus reinforcing the summarizing symbolism. Hitler, Joseph Goebbels, and the rest of the Nazi propaganda team turned out to be shrewd designers, blending religious myths, rituals, and symbols to create identity to their liking. To be pro-Aryan was the correlative of anti-Semitism. Identity consistently formed out of difference, and the swastika was the identifying mark.

Contemporary graphic designer Steven Heller gets at much of the symbol's appeal, not because of grand mythologies but through its modest design: "Like most effective symbols, the swastika's geometric purity allows for legibility at any size and distance."[18] "Purity" was a virtue, the geometries of the world stripped down to a few lines, like the modern art of the time. Even so, the Nazi's sense of purity was not that of the artists: Hitler, Goebbels, and others were adamant in their denunciation of abstract art. Their much-publicized *Degenerate Art* exhibition of 1937 included works by Kandinsky and Mondrian, as well as other abstract painters who were also seeking a newer, more primal mode of expression, but in strikingly different ways and for different purposes. Though its intent was to showcase the negative dimensions of modern art, those in opposition to the Nazi ideals, the exhibition was the largest viewing of modern art the world had ever seen, and was bigger than almost any other modern art exhibition to this day. More than six hundred works were displayed over three months in Munich, attracting more than three million visitors. Symbolic battles are not merely ideological, but they are often battles over symbols themselves—an understanding of political, social, and religious warfare cannot afford to disregard the material basis of symbolic and metaphoric communications.

Having been resymbolized, reappropriated, and renamed as the sign of the Nazis and the sign of mass genocide, the swastika can never be renamed again, some assert, can never be rendered benign. Quinn convincingly argues that the contemporary use of examples of pre-Nazi swastikas (such as those given above) can be seen in the present day for their seeming innocence only because of their Nazi usage (in other words, "Isn't it quaint that before the Nazis a Girl's Club in Philadelphia used the swastika for its group?"). And just as the Ethiopian processional cross retains a sense of sacrality because it is lifted up beyond tangible access, banning the display of the swastika in Germany may actually reinforce its ongoing cultist power.

While copious books have been written on the swastika, and my sketches here just scratch the surface of the multitude of meanings, it is essential to include it among a historical view of crosses. To conclude this section I relate two brief stories that bespeak the power of images, the power of crossed lines as a visual image, and the ways that cross-cultural understandings overlap, conflict, and are remade.

A picture in the February 29, 1940, *New York Times* shows a half-dozen Native Americans lined up in front of a poster with a large swastika on it. Looking closer, one realizes they are signing the poster. Barely visible on the poster are two lines crossing out the swastika. The caption tells the story: "Arizona Indians ban their swastika to show disapproval of the Nazis." I could not find any deeper information about this story, who the people were or what tribes were pictured (four tribes were supposedly represented), but I was moved by the gesture, by the crossing out of the already crossed lines, lines quite truly stolen from them,* and the fact that a group of people who had suffered near genocide themselves saw the dangerous and powerful use to which symbols can be put.

The other story involves the modern artist Joseph Beuys, one of the most influential artists of the modern age, who began incorporating crosses early in his artistic career. Beuys was a pilot for the Nazi Luftwaffe, and he would have displayed the swastika in some form or other during his flying time. He later turned

---

* I don't mean the Nazis took the symbol from Native Americans, but that the long-used native sacred symbol would no longer be used because of the Nazis' colonizing the symbol's meaning.

to art, famously incorporating materials not before found in museums (felt and fats were the two most prominent media) and continuing to challenge social perceptions of art. Situated in a divided Germany after the war, Beuys's work aimed for social change. The figure of the cross—though not a swastika—hung over his works as he sought mendings: of the past and present, of West and East. His first image of a cross was a 1943 sketch of a nurse with the medical cross on her hat, and thus for him an initial sign of healing. His friend Heiner Bastian succinctly tells of the artist's attachment to the simple form: "The cross stands for a possible society, for an infinite guilt indefinitely in need of absolution; for silence, but not the silence of death; for morality, but not that felt in the face of death."[19] Beyond—though not without—Christianity, the cross divides while it might also unite.

"In this sign, you will find victory." These are the words Jesus is said to have spoken to Constantine, accompanied by a vision of a cross of light.[20] The words and image together did lead to victory for the emperor, marking the moment of his conversion to Christianity and altering human civilization forever after. Crosses and civilizations are bound up with each other, meaning also that crosses and war frequently meet.

Since Constantine's time, Europe has fairly consistently been governed and gone to war under the sign of the Christian cross, and even today many European nations carry a cross as a primary symbol in their flags. As Christianity became dominant and politics, social life, and theology intertwined, the cross shifted from a sign of crucifixion to a sign of victory. The cross may be a focal point for meditation and prayer, and devout Christians will pray before a cross at the front of a church or on a household wall, but the cross has also often been used as a symbol of courage and group loyalty, leading the holy into war. As the old hymn puts it, "Onward, Christian Soldiers, marching

as to war / With the cross of Jesus, going on before."²¹ Flags with
crosses led the way across the continent to the Crusades, they
were carried in the midst of the Thirty Years' War, and they
were present on various sides in the Crimean, Franco-Dutch,
and Napoleonic Wars, to name but a few. Crosses and swords
crossing each other.

And it's not just Nazis and Christians who go to war with
crosses. In the Yucatan Peninsula in 1850 a cross appeared near
a well and began to speak of God's love and power, and the
Mayans who heard it were summoned to battle against their
oppressors, the European-descended Yucatecos. The story of
the Talking Cross of the Caste Wars of the Yucatan has been
told and retold through Christian and indigenous perspectives
many times. The Talking Cross was not so much an *apparition*
in the Roman Catholic sense as it was an indigenous Mayan
cosmological event. The cross was not an unsurprising image for
the Mayans, who had long communicated with ancestors and
deities through cruciform icons. Even after the Mayan rebels
were defeated in war, the Talking Cross continued on, forming
its own religious following. The cross continued to speak to the
people and to provide holy water for them in the well, and it
motivated the rebels to continue their struggle for independence
for many decades. Shrines were built to the Talking Cross, and
these have remained active into the present day. At times, Mayans have even used Roman Catholic crosses, and repurposed
them for their own significantly non-Christian means.²²

In a wholly different yet parallel context, crosses have created
conflict in contemporary high schools in the United States. In
numerous separate events in recent years, students have been
asked to stop wearing cross necklaces at school. A student in
Minnesota was told to take off his cross and rosary beads even
though he said he was wearing it in honor of his cancer-stricken
grandmother. Two boys in Albany, Oregon, were suspended
for wearing cross necklaces after they had been warned to take

them off. And a student in Central New York was suspended for wearing rosary beads with a cross attached. There are a number of similar cases, and in many of them the ACLU has been outspoken about the students' right to wear the crosses, as this should be protected under First Amendment rights. Looking again at the stories, it becomes clear that the schools did not ban the crosses because of a seeming conflict of church and state. Instead, school officials believed the crosses and rosaries were gang symbols. Indeed, many gangs have used crosses as symbols of identity, from Celtic crosses to swastikas to the Pachuco cross tattooed on the hands of many Latino gang members (though not only gang members). Adornments, whether flags for a battalion of soldiers or necklaces for an individual body, are signs of power and belonging.

Double crossing. Crossing out. Crosses stand at the heart of conflict, and even cause conflict. In and through their capabilities to identify groups of people collectively they become powerful sources of cohesion. And they simultaneously become forces to show how one group stands over and against another.

Mark Twain once quipped, "Clothes make the man. Naked people have little or no influence on society." We are what we wear, dressing for success, dressing up or down, ornamenting our bodies in order to have influence, to be noticed (or not), and to provide a sense of self and inclusion in a larger circle. In *The Language of Clothes*, cultural observer Alison Lurie writes about the ways clothing and identity are bound to each other:

> For thousands of years human beings have communicated with one another first in the language of dress. Long before I am near enough to talk to you on the street, in a meeting, or at a party, you announce your sex, age and class to me through what you are wearing—and very possibly give me important information (or misinformation) as to your

occupation, origin, personality, opinions, tastes, sexual desires, and current mood. I may not be able to put what I observe into words, but I register the information unconsciously; and you simultaneously do the same for me. By the time we meet and converse we have already spoken to each other in an older and more universal tongue.[23]

Dress is visual, tangible, political, and personal; visible clues speaking silently about who we are and to whom we belong. Our clothing and bodily adornments signal to others our social status, including our religious status.

Religious people wear things. That's a strange and direct statement, but the basic truth of it leads quickly to the question, what do religious people wear? And when and where and why do they wear these things? A shaved head of a man peers out from long, saffron-colored robes, and we might realize he is a Buddhist monk, probably from Tibet. A woman at the farmers market wears a simple, blue billowy dress with a small, laced head-covering and her status among the Amish is noted. A young man's tattoos up and down his arms and neck and across his face will denote his identity within a particular gang, the group with which he most identifies and that provides him with a sense of purpose (leaving aside ethical questions about that purpose). A man with long, curling sideburns, beard, and a black cap indicates his Orthodox Jewish attachments. The clothing of a young woman walking down a city street in contemporary business attire may simply indicate she has a decent job or is hoping to find one; looking closer, a small gold cross is noticed dangling from a thin gold chain around her neck, subtly announcing her Christian convictions.

Crosses have become dress, indicating identity. Crosses are emblazoned on T-shirts, attached to charm bracelets, and especially worn around the neck. They are also imprinted directly on the body. This was true long before fashion became an industry.

(Arguing against such fashion decisions, I recall a fundamentalist preacher from my childhood once pronounced, "People are not meant to wear crosses, crosses are meant to wear people!")

Take away the oval at the top of the ankh and you are left with the T symbol: a tau cross, so called after the Greek letter it resembles, which was itself taken from the ancient Hebrew character *tav*, which used to be drawn in the form of a cross. This is another ancient image of eternal life and one used often as adornment. In the apocalyptic Hebrew scriptures of the prophet Ezekiel a sign is given to those who will be spared the mass slaughter at the end of the world, a "mark [*tau*] on the forehead" that exempts them from judgment.[24] In the book of Job, as he concludes his plea to God, Job defends his faithfulness in the face of tribulation, even offering his signature, his *tau*, to show his steadfast devotion and to keep from being indicted.[25] Christians such as the Franciscans have continued to use the tau-shaped cross as an identifying mark of their order, referring to the Ezekiel passage. Saint Francis himself used this style of cross, signing his letters with it, tracing its mark on his body, drawing it on the wall of his residence, and using it, as Saint Anthony had before him, in his work with lepers. The Franciscan habit (tunic) is also meant to mimic the tau cross when the friar stands with arms outspread.

Jump ahead many years to the Ecclesia Church in Houston, part of a recent wave of Christian groups often referred to as the "emerging church" movement. During Lent in 2012, pastor Chris Seay and the artist in residence at the time, Scott Erickson, encouraged congregants to get tattoos, designed by Erickson, as part of their Lenten practices. About fifty people got their skin inked and set up a special art exhibition called "Stations on Skin" to display them. Crosses were not blatantly evident in the epidermal imagery but set within larger pictorial designs. "I totally think the cross is important," Erickson said, "but as a symbol, it doesn't inspire thought anymore. It's become decorative."²⁶ Perhaps too much of a summarizing symbol—too many uses theologically, politically, culturally, artistically—makes the thing lose its strength.

If tattoos are considered a new trend in the faith, a longer history of Christianity shows otherwise. Tattoos (a Polynesian term) were otherwise known by the Greek term *stigma* in the ancient world (plural, *stigmata*), a term that carries over into contemporary times, bringing with it the negative connotations of the original.²⁷ A stigma was an indelible bodily mark, painfully applied with needles or brands, which showed the downgraded social status of the person—slaves and criminals were thus distinguished this way. Certain Christians adopted the stigma as a way to show their commitments, sometimes in the face of adversity, sometimes to the face in the mirror, indicating their status as a slave to God. Later deemed heretical, the fourth century Montanists used crosses as a stigma on their bodies. Persecuted Coptic Christians tattooed crosses on their own inner arms to keep them on the straight and narrow path as their faith was tried. And as mentioned above, Ethiopian Christians sometimes have a cross tattooed on their forehead to display their faith.

Most of the previous examples are voluntary donnings of the cross, but there are many involuntary uses as well. Early in the fourteenth century, Béatrice of Planisoles was accused of Catharism. Among other heretical ideas, the Cathars conceived of a dualistic world in which the devil, the god of darkness, was "in the beginning" with the god of light, overseeing the earthly, physical realm. The Cathars also adhered to nonviolence (taking it as far as keeping a vegetarian diet), believed in a universal redemption, and were progressive regarding the role of women in religious environments. Like many groups opposed to the official teachings and practices of the Rome-based Church, the Cathars thought the official rituals to be a bit excessive. They did not make the sign of the cross upon entering a church, partly because it was linked to the violence of the crucifixion. Instead they would touch head, nose, beards, and ears and say, "This is my forehead and this my beard, and this is one ear and this the other." They mimicked the outward sign while reconceiving the inward aspect.[28]

The Cathars were persecuted by the Inquisition and their followers were labeled heretics. Béatrice was accused of this heresy, largely because of her father's associations, and received a prison sentence. She was released from prison only if she would continue her penance with a common chastisement of the day: she had to wear a double yellow cross. Yellow was the color of shame (a symbolic value taken up centuries later when Jews were forced to wear yellow Stars of David), and wearing the double cross meant that every piece of their clothing except the shirt had to have two crosses stitched on them. Especially crucial was that the crosses had to be openly displayed anytime the guilty were in public.

Likewise, if you walk through the old Jewish quarter (Barrio Santa Cruz) in Seville, Spain, today, you might stumble through the labyrinthine streets to find the Calle de las Cruces, and see a couple of wooden crosses embedded in the siding of a house. These date back hundreds of years and were meant to signal the homes of Jewish people who were forced to convert to Christianity. Seville was under Muslim rule from the eighth through thirteenth centuries, and Muslims, Christians, and Jews lived together during this time—not always peaceably, though they did share many theological ideas, sacred texts, foods, symbols, and architectural styles. But when King Ferdinand III of Castile conquered the city and made it a Catholic space, he didn't extend much tolerance to the others, and Muslims and Jews were forced to convert. All synagogues in the city were disbanded by 1391. In 1492, while Columbus was sailing the ocean blue, starting his journey from Seville, the newly formed nation of Spain made clear they were the Catholic nation of Spain and expelled all Jews under that year's Alhambra Decree, as the last of the Muslim strongholds in Granada was taken by the Catholic monarchs Ferdinand and Isabella. Hundreds of thousands of Jews were forcibly sent away (the Muslims would be expelled sometime later), while a significant minority stayed and converted. These conversos had crosses affixed to their walls, showing their conversion status as well as supplying a medieval surveillance system so that others could keep watch on them and be sure no backsliding was taking place. As has become evident in later years, the conversos often kept up appearances but continued their Jewish practices in secret, often in the basements of these very houses marked by a cross.

In the generation after Columbus, Hernán Cortés left Spain to conquer the peoples of Mesoamerica. The cross was already so prominent in the New World that Cortés saw the indigenous symbol and became convinced Christians had been there before. No evidence has ever emerged to confirm this, and clearly the native use of the cross had little relation to the Christian understanding of it: the Aztecs had used it as an emblem associated with the god Quetzalcoatl, while the Maya had used it for the god of maize, and others used it as a four directions symbol. The fact that Cortés and his men would have prominently displayed crosses on flags and staffs, and possibly around their necks, has led historians to suggest this contributed to the native Mayan and Aztec people's initial acceptance of the Spanish: they believed, as did Cortés, that they each had the same symbol and thus the same mythologies and understandings of the world.

In Chiapas, Mexico, we can see the mixing and merging of traditions, with crosses in particular standing at the heart of the symbolism. Families in towns such as San Cristóbal de las Casas adorned their rooftops with crosses, a practice that reached its zenith in the late-nineteenth and early-twentieth century. These were usually made of iron, fashioned in elaborate designs that improvised on the basic cross, twisting and turning the iron lines in new ways, adding suns and moons and flowers and stars and the occasional occupational symbol. On first glance Roman Catholicism is dominant in the contemporary religious life of the communities, with churches dotting the landscape. Yet, roof crosses meld various meanings. They are often used in strikingly unorthodox ways: as protective devices against floods, earthquakes, lightning storms, and volcanoes, all of which have occurred in the area. Virginia Ann Guess has studied this tradition more than any other native English speaker, noting that, in spite of the variety of symbolic values that may be attributed to the roof crosses, they "share a common goal: to manipulate or live in harmony with supernatural or natural elements they can neither explain nor control."[29]

As Mesoamericans took on the cross symbol of the Spanish, they morphed and mixed it, and it became a hybrid entity, its meaning lying somewhere between European and indigenous traditions. Devotion to the cross reaches such a fervent pitch today that in Latin American practices surrounding the Festival of the Cross (Fiesta de las Cruces, or Cruz de Mayo) on the third of May, the cross is treated as a living being, not unlike some drums and stones we have seen. In Chiapas, crosses are dressed in new clothes, ribbons, and flowers. Devotees gather to pray, burn incense, and light candles. It is a Catholic festival, though not mandatory, even as the meaning of this cross often moves away from strict, orthodox conceptions.

Jewelry, clothing, and house markings may be "accessories" or "adornment," yet there is no such thing as mere ornament. A fresh coat of colored paint on a wall does not physically change the structure of a room, but the room will be experienced in a different way. (One study shows that couples argue more in yellow kitchens.) Likewise, the external bodily adornment changes the person who wears it, mainly because she or he is treated and experienced differently by those around them. It's like the parable of the man who wanted to hide his real identity and so he wore a mask for such a period that his face eventually morphed to match the mask. The cross is one bodily mark of identity for those who wear it and those who see it, an identity connected to salvation and preservation, of life in the face of death.

Sometimes, as Freud once quipped, a cigar is just a cigar. The same may be said for crosses: sometimes two crossed lines are just two crossed lines. Sometimes the crossed lines are nothing more than profane—though crucial—black lines on a yellow road sign warning drivers of an upcoming intersection. Sometimes they help us add up our bills and debts. Or I can look to the top right corner of the keyboard I am using now and punch in this character: **+** . Sometimes, perhaps with nowhere else to go, two lines just cross.

But symbols are sticky, attaching themselves to our collective conscious and unconscious bodies and minds. We've been trained to think about an image in one way, and no amount of rewiring seems capable of changing it, short of desires for world domination. In some ways the simpler the symbol the stickier it is, which is a large part of the reason crosses are such powerful sacred objects.

In the middle of the National September 11 Memorial and Museum in lower Manhattan stand two steel I beams crossed at a right angle. You might be able to picture this in your mind, since images of it flooded the news after the terrorist attacks on the World Trade Center and the ensuing cleanup. This one, framed infrastructural remnant seemed to be the only thing left standing, and it became symbolic for many doing the rescue work. The memorial's website itself calls it an "icon of hope." The American Atheists sued to have it removed, so concerned were they that religion should not be part of the memorializing process, but most people were willing to forgo what might be deeply held beliefs about the separation of church and state in order to significantly memorialize a traumatic event.* The crossed beams in the setting of the World Trade Center ruins have no actual connection with the Christian mythology of the crucifixion of Jesus, except as some believers (and nonbelievers) might make the connection. Jon Stewart, comic host of television's late-night spoof on news *The Daily Show*, poked fun at the atheists and suggested they didn't really need to see it as a Christian symbol. Instead, Stewart offered in ways that would make Freud proud, "Why not just think of it as a metal T-shaped thingy?"[30]

Two other metal posts meet at right angles and cross purposes in contentious space, in this case in the middle of the Mojave National Preserve in California. The T-shaped thingy was put there by the Veterans of Foreign Wars in 1934 to honor the dead from World War I. Originally made of wood, the cross was rebuilt several times until four-inch steel pipes were welded together and drilled into Sunrise Rock in the Mojave in 1998 by Henry Sandoz. At this point controversy ensued—religious symbols on public land being the problem—eventually sparking a court case (*Salazar v. Buono*) that went to the US Supreme Court, which handed the case back down. Initial court cases told the VFW to board up the cross (which they did, leaving a big wooden box on a pole on a rock in the desert), but after the Supreme Court case the cross could be displayed again. To complicate things further, the metal-pipe cross was stolen in 2010 as an act of protest, only to turn up in Half Moon Bay, California, a couple of years later. In November 2012 a hundred people gathered for a ceremony to rededicate a new cross on the site, which through the decade-long legal battles, had been turned over to private ownership. Countless hours of work, millions of

---

* The National September 11 Memorial and Museum is a public charity [501(c)(3)].

dollars in private and public funding, hostility, theft, deception, and anger, and now it looks little different than it did twenty years ago: two metal poles in the desert.

Even Christian uses of the cross have been employed to the point that they carry little theological gravitas. Recall Christian artist Scott Erickson quoted above, saying the cross "doesn't inspire thought anymore." Or one might think of the use of the cross as a grave marker: picture a cemetery here with rows and rows of white crosses, especially those for the war dead, their replicated forms stretching for acres. The cross that initially indicated the religious identity of the person who passed on simply became a marker of death itself. The crossed beams might offer hope to those left behind, but the threat remains that repetitious use relinquishes some of its sacred capital.

I must admit, as someone who has spent a large part of my professional life researching the power of visual symbols and icons in the lives of people, the pragmatist in me wants to say, "Those are just two steel beams! A T-shaped thingy!" But then again, they cannot be just that. Two crossed lines become a Rorschach test, evaluating a society's collective fears and desires, needs and entreaties. The simplest of marks debated in the highest of courts of law, the most respected of newspapers, the most serious of religious institutions.

How can we explain the worldwide appeal of a cross as a primary visual symbol? How is it that two crossed lines might represent fundamental structures of the world (four directions, meetings of heavens and earth) from ancient China to Egypt, India, the Andes, and the United States? The traditional scholarly answer would be to take a historical approach, to trace influences and immigrations across seas, rivers, and continents, and to show linguistic developments merging and emerging in new times and places. If we just keep digging up enough old bones and uncovering sacred scriptures, we might get to the heart of it all, or so the promise goes. To be sure, this chapter could not have been written without my reliance on important historical, anthropological, philosophical, linguistic, and archaeological work, undertaken by people who believe there are such singular beginnings. But I remain skeptical, as do many contemporary scholars, that a final origin can ever be found. I do not believe there is a singular, original cross from which all these traditions derive their cultural meaning. Besides, what such quests are seldom able to answer is *why* certain objects and ideas stick and others don't. Some words and things find their way translated into other vocabularies and cultures. Others don't.

There is another approach, and that is to look not just to the past but also to the present, to the varieties of human bodies and their sensual quests to find meaning, order, and purpose in the things of the world. We seem to be wired this way. Our bodies, one-half and incomplete, desire connection as we fill our visual perceptions with visible objects. Art historian David Freedberg begins his grand study *The Power of Images* this way: "People are sexually aroused by pictures and sculptures; they break pictures and sculptures; they mutilate them, kiss them, cry before them, and go on journeys to them; they are calmed by them, stirred by them, and incited to revolt."[31] It's a great summary of the myriad ways images have provoked people to act, to respond, stirring joy and anger, lust and fear. And, as we've seen in this chapter, the imagery does not even need to be complex.

In this light, one might believe that the cognitive neurosciences could tell us why crosses have kept emerging in various times and places. Cognitive and developmental psychology might point out the ways crosses relate to rudimentary forms of our first childhood drawings, and thus become a primary metaphor for our later years. Neurobiologists might use visual technologies to allow us to see deeper and deeper into the neurochemical processes of the body, observing our impulses at a base level and marking our responses to sensual stimuli. From CT and PET scans to fMRIs and MPIs, new imaging technologies are representing the body in sophisticated ways and providing newer answers to our perceptual ponderings. These hold a lot of promise, though I suspect the field is currently looking through the equivalent of Galileo's lenses when what is needed are telescopes like Hubble's or Webb's.

Ultimately, I wonder if it's not the artists and poets who have already been there, who have deciphered the meanings of the sensual signs, observed the origins of the cross, and sculpted, painted, photographed, and rhymed the creation, purifying and condensing, improvising and elaborating.

BREAD

When I hear bread breaking,
I see something else; it seems to me
as though God never meant us to do anything else.
So beautiful a sound; the crust breaks up like manna
and falls all over everything and then we eat;
bread gets inside humans.

—Daniel Berrigan, Jesuit priest and peace activist[1]

Around the same time modern artists were taking sacred symbols such as crosses and turning them in profane ways, another artist, Sister Mary Corita Kent, was working in reverse. She joined the Order of the Immaculate Heart of Mary in 1936, studied and then taught art, and eventually chaired Immaculate Heart College's art program in Los Angeles. From the 1950s onward Kent created screen prints that expressed her devotion to her Christian faith and related interests in social justice. Buckminster Fuller and Charles and Ray Eames championed her work, and her college department hosted lectures by John Cage, Alfred Hitchcock, and Jean Renoir.

While Vatican II meetings were taking place (1962–65) and the church expressing an interest in situating Roman Catholic traditions more firmly within the modern world, Kent's work stood as an ideal example of how this could be achieved. In the era of Andy Warhol's soup cans, Madison Avenue's "mad men," and growing critiques of the excesses of high capitalism, Kent simply suggested, "We lift the common stuff out of the everyday and give it a place in our celebration."[2] Her 1964 work *The Juiciest Tomato of Them All* repurposed a slogan from Del Monte canned tomatoes into praise for the Virgin Mary—Mary being "the juiciest tomato." The piece pays homage to Warhol, while squeezing devotional purposes out of consumer goods and pop art. Slogans, under Kent's gaze, became parables.

At the time of Kent's death from cancer in 1986, prominent Harvard theologian Harvey Cox opined, "The world of signs and sales slogans and plastic containers was not, for her, an empty wasteland. It was the dough out of which she baked the bread of life. Like a priest, a shaman, a magician, she could pass her hands over the commonest of the everyday, the superficial, the oh-so-ordinary, and make it a vehicle of the luminous, the only, and the hope-filled."[3] In his eulogy, Cox conjures Kent's 1965 silkscreen print *Enriched Bread*, a work that borrowed its vibrant color scheme and symbols from a package of Wonder Bread and is overlaid with a quote from Albert Camus's essay "Create Dangerously." In so doing, Kent draws on Christianity's central ritual of Holy Communion, a rite of wonder, of enrichment. *Enriched Bread* merges and mixes sacred and profane, high art and low, recreating commercial products for new contexts, for spiritual ends. All of which offers an enlivening way to approach the place of bread in religious traditions.

Simple and standard as it is, bread is deeply complex and full of wonder. If you haven't tried making it at home, please do so. Now, in fact. For it is in the tactility of the ingredients, the robust, scented space of the kitchen, the natural-yet-contained fermentation processes that one begins to appreciate the intricacy of this daily meal. Meat can be taken straight from the animal source and eaten with nothing more than a fire to roast it over. Apples and pineapples, grapes and carrots, almonds and pecans are eaten directly from their plant sources with little pro-cessed intervention. But the most basic bread derives from care-fully cultivated species of particular grasses that are harvested, ground, mixed with other ingredients, formed, and baked in ovens that have some consistency in temperature. Go to your refrigerator and pantry and you will find there no staple foods that are more elaborately made.

Vary any of the ingredients of bread, even to a slight degree, and the end product will be different at each and every baking. One type of grain varies significantly in taste from another, just as the shape of the dough, the fineness of the flour, and the ad-dition of eggs or fruits or nuts all transform the end product. The ingredients are under human control, but only to a degree. Climatic changes from season to season can affect the protein structures of the grain crops, as can humidity and heat levels while making the dough. And that's to say nothing about the cultural and religious divergences that go into making bread.

Apollonia Poilâne understands all these details better than almost any living person. She is the young CEO of what is prob-ably the best-known, most respected bakery in Paris, possibly the world. Begun by her grandfather in 1932, Poilâne Bakery now employs 160 people and grosses more than $18 million a year. Those around the globe who have fallen for the spells and smells of Poilâne Bakery bread have it shipped to their homes by Federal Express. Poilâne is a business in the middle of one of the most modern, fiercely secular cities the world has ever known. And yet, to hear Apollonia discuss the making and par-taking of bread, one begins to find something like a sensual, mystical encounter. "You must listen to the breads," she says. In the bakery's training programs, bakers learn family secrets (in ways perhaps akin to the ancient Abtinas family's secret incense recipes for the Jerusalem temple), and apprentices are taught to use eyes and ears as much as scales and clocks. She finds bread to be "the perfect vehicle to talk about really essential things—a revolution, a religion, a theory."[4] Bread's intimate sensuality leads quite naturally into the body politic.

Like other sensual objects, bread turns the stuff of religion upside down, as Sister Corita Kent has provocatively suggested. Its ubiquity in space, its characteristically quotidian existence in time would at first appear to be the opposite of the sacred. We are given our daily bread (when we ask), people who work are "breadwinners," and what could be more profane than Wonder Bread? But bread stirs wonder, works its magic as its glutinous mass binds people together. It has done so for many eons and will likely continue to do so for years to come.

Yet, bread's omnipresent dimensions can be overrated, and we find that not all people have put the natural lands on which they live to the same agricultural uses. I will point to several traditions' use of bread, though we will also come to realize that crosscultural and interreligious studies have limits. While it is not as widespread as the other objects in this book, I felt it important to include bread in part because it serves as a warning of sorts, that actually none of these five objects should be discussed as being a universal aspect to religions and cultures. At the same time, we will see, when sensual objects are introduced into new places they remake practices and customs. Tradition is a story of changes, as edible objects meet hungry bodies in novel circumstances, and there is little question that bread has changed the world. A history of religions is incomplete without it.

Our oldest literature in the Western world offers proof of the more than five-millennia-old existence of bread as a food for humans. Unearthed inscriptions indicate more than forty varieties of bread were in use in ancient Egypt and more than two hundred in Mesopotamia. Yet it is also clear in the beginning that bread is bound up with human identity, marking types of people as distinct from others—we eat this bread, not that—and ultimately as a sign of civilization. The great ancient Mesopotamian myth of *Gilgamesh* tells the story of the wild man Enkidu, who is transformed as he learns of the existence of bread and eats thereof, just as he learns about lovemaking. Significantly, bread is introduced to the man by a woman, Shamhat, who has knowledge about such things. And in both *The Iliad* and *The Odyssey*, the term *bread eaters* is used to refer to humans in general. It is the sign of culture and juxtaposed with the *lotus eaters* and others who do not cultivate the land or work, who lose sight of the journey of life. Bread is a human invention, bound up with hard work and the establishment of civilized life.

The Stone Age saw the emergence of *Homo sapiens* and the coextensive rise of religion, art, settled social communities and their related social codes, and the cultivation of plants. Historians have called this the great Neolithic revolution, and it enabled humans to get on with the business of culture and civilization. Which invention lifted the human to abilities beyond other animals is disputed. The use of tools is clearly a vital one, but other scholars have recently argued that the ability to cook and bake (which presuppose tool use) are what prompted the evolutionary leap.[5] Shifting from hunting and gathering to planting and harvesting specific crops, then turning these natural substances into something edible, allowed for a greater diversity of energy sources and allowed humans to eat lower on the food chain. Bread can be stored and transported and became an important source of carbohydrates and nutrients. In return, the grains that we grew influenced us. Grain growing and bread making allowed us, and forced us, to settle in particular places for long periods. All of which led to larger brain development. It is how and what we eat that makes our brains big, not so much how and what we think.

Mythologically and historically, bread signifies the transition of cultures from hunter-gathers who use meat and fats and beer to civilizations that cultivate the ingredients and processes needed for bread and oil and wine. Adam and Eve were hunter-gatherers. After the Fall, Adam and Eve themselves became farmers, and Adam's curse was to have difficulty in raising crops and making bread: "In the sweat of your face you shall eat bread till you return to the ground, for out of it you were taken; you are dust, and to dust you shall return."[6] Their sons, Cain and Abel, were farmers. Cain raised crops and Abel raised animals. After the first murder, occurring "in the field," Cain went on to build a city. The move is from garden to field to city. Culture relies on agriculture. As an old Albanian proverb puts it, "Bread is older than man."

Even the Middle Eastern cultures that were exceptional for not eating bread understood its significance. Due in part to arid land, amber waves of grain on a mass scale were not an option in ancient Arabia, though Arabians did eat grains mashed into a pancake and cooked on a heated stone, while others crumbled them into a broth. Bread (Arabic, *khubz*), in the fuller, leavened sense of the term, was not widely available, and the expression "bread eater" was here used for people of some socioeconomic status. This is partly why, in the hadith, Muhammad speaks highly of bread. The sayings compiled by Muhammad al-Bukhari quote the prophet Muhammad: "The planet earth will be a bread on the Day of Resurrection." Bread will be one pleasure of Paradise. Al-Bukhari continues his quotations of the Prophet, saying that Allah "will topple turn [the earth] with His Hand like anyone of you topple turns a bread with his hands while (preparing the bread) for a journey, and that bread will be the entertainment for the people of Paradise."[7]

The existence of daily bread, especially because so many activities are needed to bring it from field to mouth, can be precarious. Droughts and floods, hail and fire can devastate an entire season's worth of food. So, empires that support massive distribution systems become crucial. Empires have risen and fallen on the basis of bread, on how well their people can be fed with the most basic of substances.

Jump ahead a few millennia, and we find evidence of bread and civilization again pitted against the wilderness, only by this time the progress is not so welcome. Writing in the *Atlantic* in 1897, naturalist John Muir argued against the wholesale deforestation that was occurring across the North American continent at the time, turning nature into empire. In the midst of his objections, he lays it clear: "In the settlement and civilization of the country, bread more than timber or beauty was wanted; and in the blindness of hunger, the early settlers, claiming Heaven as their guide, regarded God's trees as only a larger kind of pernicious weed, extremely hard to get rid of."[8] In Muir's account, bread stands for blind hunger—greed and gluttony—and operates as a synecdoche for civilization as a whole. Civilization is human, but the trees are "God's." Progress isn't all it's cracked up to be.

Muir is responding to a time when European Christians colonized North America, and their diets shifted. The richness of the continent's natural resources, abundant in fish, fowl, and fertile soil, enabled indulgence. The excesses of eating reached such a degree that by the early nineteenth century a number of evangelical reformers and revivalists began to talk about the morality of diets, seeking more austere approaches to food consumption. Among them was Sylvester Graham, a Presbyterian minister who lectured on healthy lifestyles, advocating fresh air, cold baths, and hard mattresses, as well as abstaining from alcohol and tobacco use. Ultimately he called for a move away from the meat-and-grease-heavy cuisine that had become the daily bread of Americans. Observing the diets of Native Americans and Pacific Islanders and biblical references to food, Graham became convinced that the best diets were based on bread, with fruit, vegetables, and nuts supplementing the carb-rich staple. (Not only would these foods be healthy, the eating of them also would curb enthusiasm for masturbation, which Graham believed was not only impure but also would lead to blindness.)[9]

Graham's arguments, especially laid out in his 1837 "Treatise on Bread and Bread-making," saw natural ingredients as closer to God's own intentions, and coarse, dark bread was the closest to nature. At the time, across the Americas and Europe, dark breads were considered the stuff of peasants and the poor, while refined, heavily sifted flour was for refined people; it took alum and chlorine to peel away husks and germ, leaving a white but nutritionless, chemical-laden loaf.* Against the established bread-making practices of his day, he used unsifted whole-wheat flour without chemical additives. Championing the dark, coarse breads, Graham's flour was eventually solidified into little flat squares we now know as graham crackers.

Graham was the Doctor Atkins of his day, only with a reverse strategy of making carbohydrate- and mineral-rich foods the base, and his influence was felt on many prominent people and institutions.† The revivalist Charles Finney—a notable figure in the Second Great Awakening—became president of Oberlin College in his later years and incorporated Graham's vegetarian diet as the standard fare for students at Oberlin. Students and businesspeople had their own preferences, however, and private boarding houses in town began offering hot meat-based meals that became popular with students, leading to Oberlin's eventual abandonment of the diet.

Around the same time and place, and as a direct result of the Second Great Awakening, a wheat farmer turned Baptist minister named William Miller predicted the second coming of

---

* At the same time as Graham's movement began, a roller mill was invented in Switzerland that made an easy separation of the wheat germ and bran, and thus simplified the process of making "white bread." By the end of the nineteenth century, white bread became a global staple, no longer the stuff of the upper classes. Today's white breads still remove the nutrient-rich bran and germ, so commercial brands are required by law to "enrich" their flour with iron and other vitamins.

† The term *carbohydrate* does not appear until 1844; *protein* a few years earlier, in 1838.

Jesus would occur on March 21, 1843. This was based on his extensive study of the numerology of the Bible. When the end did not come, he revised his calculations for October 22, 1844. Time passed and the end of the world did not come on this date either, leading to what would become known as the "Great Disappointment." Many of Miller's numerous followers lost faith, at least in his cause, and turned to the Shakers and other Christian groups for connection.

However, one follower named Ellen G. White took up where Miller left off. Beginning at age seventeen she had a series of visions that led her to believe worship services should be held on Saturday, not Sunday, and that God cared deeply for the human body, especially for what goes into it. White's visionary leadership earned widespread respect, and out of her work, along with that of several others, the Seventh-day Adventist tradition was born. Initially influenced by Graham's diet, the Adventists to this day are vegetarian and place high value on exercise and general health. Holistic health is emphasized. White advocated good eating, and many of her writings deal with cooking and preparing foods in ways that are wholesome for both body and soul. For her, good food such as whole wheat bread (she often mentions the importance of graham flour) was essential as the basis for a healthy body. At the same time bread remained a key metaphor of Jesus Christ himself, and the spiritual and physical dimensions coalesce through her teachings.

One of White's later visions included a plan for a health center, and soon the Adventists opened the Western Health Reform Institute in 1866 in Battle Creek, Michigan. In the generation following White, one Adventist named John Harvey Kellogg took White's ideas and practices further, becoming superintendent of the institute in 1876. When the building burned down in 1902, Kellogg and his brother had it rebuilt on a grander scale, renaming it the Battle Creek Sanitarium, a place that would be host to many famous people, including Henry Ford, Amelia

Earhart, Mary Todd Lincoln, and Sojourner Truth (and play-fully recounted in T. C. Boyle's novel *The Road to Wellville*). Around this time, Kellogg invented corn flakes, revolutionizing the concept of breakfast as cereal grains were harvested and pounded into flakes that could be kept for longer periods. Kellogg and his brother ultimately founded the company that would become the world's second largest snack-food seller, producing foods that are miles away from nineteenth-century Adventist diets.*

At the end of a summer in the middle of my college years, I returned to my family home after spending two months in rural Kenya doing quasi-missionary work. I walked through our local grocery store in San Diego and gazed upon the rows and rows of cereal—produced by Kellogg's, General Mills, and Post—in their rainbow-colored, enticing boxes, full of sticky processed ingredients. In aisle five I had a slight meltdown, weeping at the choices, wondering why it is that I should have access to so much when others have so little. Danish philosopher Søren Kierkegaard once called anxiety the "dizziness of freedom," and while he certainly was not talking about breakfast meals, it is not far removed from the emotional state many of us are left with in a land of too many choices. The cereal aisle is but one indicator of the ways we have moved from a mode of eating that is cultivated yet still reliant upon nature to one that relies on the massively produced, multilayered packaging of food inside well-lit box stores, which leaves us with some real, some imagined-but-possible, and some imagined-but-impossible choices.

The name *cereal* itself comes from the goddess Ceres, Roman pagan deity of agriculture. (The first uses of the term *cereal* in English are found in the early nineteenth century, predat-

---

* Among other products, Kellogg's owns and distributes Cheez-It, Pringles, Gardenburger, Famous Amos cookies, Pop-Tarts, and MorningStar.

ing Kellogg's invention, but at the same time as dietary reforms were emerging.) In her connection with growing grains, Ceres was also associated with fertility—not only of crops but also of people, and Ceres thus became linked with marriage ceremonies. Preceding Ceres was Demeter, the Greek grain goddess of Eleusis, also linked with fertility, agriculture, and marriage. The Greeks believed she discovered grain, and she is typically depicted carrying stalks of wheat. The underground cult that grew up around Demeter became a key religious movement in Athens. The root of her name, *meter*, means "mother." Like many of the goddesses of the ancient world, she is the earth mother. In Norse mythology, we find the goddess Sif, the wife of Thor, playing the role of the earth goddess. Loki the trickster cuts her hair off; dwarfs are called upon to form a new headpiece, its golden waves becoming associated with fields of wheat.

As agriculture splits the difference between nature and culture, the growing of cereal grains creates a link between the heavens and the earth. Rains come down from heavens, falling to the waiting earth out of which the crops grow up. Throughout these myths we find the convergence of opposing forces, of male and female paralleling the relations between the heavens above (Thor and his thundering hammer) and earth below (Sif and her flowing fields of grain). Erotic relations of the cosmos are evoked in the growing of wheat.

Through such erotic-cosmic connections, the making, baking, and partaking of bread become activities that offer a binding force for religious life. Religion has traditionally functioned as a medium between nature and culture, joining us to, as it simultaneously distances us from, "God's trees." Myths, rituals, and symbols are all predicated on natural substances and rhythms, and as humans participate in them, we are also put in synch with the cosmic order. Worship of the ancient goddesses was no different: breads and cakes were the normal offering, with a special divine bread offered upon a table before the deities. This offering was charged with spiritual energies, and as the worshipers ate the now-consecrated meal, they would gain some element of its healing powers. The goddess tradition was strong in the ancient world; goddesses were deeply engaged with creating and nurturing the cosmic realm, and thus sustained our human relations to the heavens and to each other.

Glance at many old images of Ceres and you would not be amiss to think it was an image of Mother Mary: long, flowing robes, gently seated, and benevolent gaze, though Ceres generally carried a staff while Mary did not. Indeed, many early Christian images were taken from pagan imagery (Jesus as the good shepherd was a rendition of ritualistic images of sheep being brought to a sacrifice; the golden halo of Jesus taken from depictions of the Sun God) and syncretized into a new form of worship that became seemingly unique and yet familiar to the people of Europe and beyond, where Christianity was quickly spreading.

Mary takes her place along a continuity of mother earth goddesses. As she absorbed many of these earlier traditions, she also supplanted them, effectively and over time erasing them from the emerging histories, appearing fresh and unique. While we might be tempted to think the sacrifice of grain and bread that had been given to the earlier goddesses transferred to the Christian Eucharist, to the glory of Jesus Christ, it was not always that subtle. In fact, a curious sect of Christianity—eventually labeled a heresy—emerged in the first centuries of the new religion. They were the Kollyridians, mostly seen in Arabia and Thrace, which was a group of Christian women devoted to Mary and who regularly offered her sacrifices of bread (the name *Kollyridian* refers to the type of bread they offered). They brought bread to an altar "in the sacrifice and name of Mary." As one scholar writes about the importance of this tradition, "In the sacred mystery of bread, every woman could view herself as possessing a portion of the creative power of the gods, for in every act of intercourse, conception and birth, the sowing of the seed, the miracle of death and life, is repeated."[10] While the Kollyridians would disappear from history, a more orthodox cult of Mary would grow strong within Christianity. Mary offered opportunities to identify with femininity, motherhood, and nurturing in powerful ways between nature and culture, heavens and earth.

If frankincense is the gold standard among incense varieties, wheat is it for bread flours. Historians of food tell of wheat as the king of grains, the imperial grass. Many cereal grains have been grown, milled, and baked, but none other supplies everything that wheat can. Wheat is adaptable to diverse growing environments; it invades new habitats and has evolved faster and more successfully than almost any other living organism, save humans. Wheat is high in nutrient content, and ultimately has great gastronomic appeal.* This is especially so because of the gluten levels, which allow a coherent dough to stay together, to be shaped and baked, and ultimately to be savored.

According to some estimates, 20 percent of all human calories consumed around the world come from wheat flour, though in many times and places that number has been 50 percent and higher. Around fifty million acres of US land are used each year to produce more than two billion bushels of wheat. (The European Union collectively and China, India, and Russia all produce even more than the United States.) Not all the wheat grown goes to making bread, but a vast majority of it is milled for flour, and a majority of that does end up in loaves, rolls, biscuits, pancakes, and bagels.

The precise origins of leavened bread are unknown. Evidence

---

* The earliest breads were flat breads, made from grasses such as barley, emmer, and einkorn. Rice and corn are grains that globally are grown more than wheat, though they don't count for as much of the world's actual nutrients and, of course, they aren't used often for bread.

points to its beginnings in Egypt, around six thousand years ago. Due to some ancient accident, some flour and water had probably been left out too long, some free floating yeast found its way to the sugars, someone eventually noticed, perhaps befuddled by the expansion of the dough and the fermenting bubbles, and decided to cook it anyway. It's hard to imagine what that old loaf tasted like. Certainly a long way from the loaves of now, but also a marked contrast to the gruel and cakes of then.

As I was looking into the origins of bread and reading books from anthropological, culinary, historical, sociological, and philosophical perspectives, I noticed an interesting element in many of the studies. Curious is the way that most everyone who writes about a history of bread feels compelled (as I do here) to tell its creation story. We have no idea what actually happened in the beginning, but because we know something about the ways yeasts can interact with the starches-become-sugars of ground grain mixed with water, we can take a guess. That's the gist of what we know, and so we all tell various versions of the same fictional story, a tale that begins "Once upon a time in ancient Egypt . . ." and carries through to the astounded observations of those who might have been around to witness that accident. There is a deep-seated human need to know origins, to pin down a time and place and, ideally, a person that we can point to as the generating force of things. If we don't know, we deduce, theorize, and mythologize. At the same time, we like the mystery of being unsure of its first time and place, as it adds to the appeal of the substance, as if the unknowing is evidence itself of the long-lasting power of bread and its role in human life.

So, bread's history is written from secular standpoints, but we writers are overtaken by the bread, by the story of bread, and draw on the supernatural to explain. British historian Felipe Fernandez-Armesto's history of food puts it this way: "No convincing theory of how or why bread making began has ever been proposed. Perhaps that is the key to bread's success: it is one of those 'magical' foods, in which human mastery effects an unrecognizable change on the ingredients of the recipe."[11] Journalist and author Michael Pollan, in a chapter on bread in his book *Cooked*, suggests how seeing dough rise must have seemed "miraculous" to those who first observed it, as if "the spark of life had been breathed into it."[12] H. E. Jacob in *Six Thousand Years of Bread* ponders the wonders of baking the risen dough, imagining ancient Egyptians around the oven: "In awed admiration family and friends stood around to watch. In this chamber grew something which so far was the product of their familiar labors but which they had now entrusted to supernatural forces over which they had no control."[13]

What Fernandez-Armesto, Pollan, and Jacob are getting at is the ongoing quasi-miraculous nature of bread itself. An object that draws us to it: for smelling, for eating, for sustenance, for sharing with others. Triggering our creative capacities, bread connects us with creation itself. Pollan, as he so engagingly does with most of his studies, learns about bread by making it himself. He gains know-how with his knowledge. It's not an academic study for him, and this is part of what has made him a successful writer: he gets his hands into it. Pollan has felt, and many others of us have felt, the creative activity of making bread: "the fresh-baked loaf still feels like a creation ex nihilo, its from-mud-wrested form a refutation of cosmic entropy."[14] This run-of-the-mill provision engenders epic and mythic response.

Bread is there in the beginning. As communities share stories of their most formative events, we often find bread in the midst of them. This is especially true for the history of the Jewish people. Every spring, Jews around the world sit down to share an evening in the presence of family, friends, and God. We know this ritual as the Passover seder, a gathering that signifies the mythological makeup of the ancient Israelites and their release from captivity in the land of Egypt. This too is what Jesus and the disciples were celebrating at the Last Supper, and out of this sprang the Christian ritual of communion. Even so, textual and archaeological evidence suggest that Passover itself initially came from older rites that celebrated the grain harvest. Rituals, like bread, rarely have simple origins.

Among the various foods and drinks, all with their own symbolic dimensions, matzoh is perhaps the quickest trigger of Passover, the substance most connected with the annual gathering as well as the substance most connected with the ancient stories from which it rises. Indeed, it is sometimes known as the Festival of Unleavened Bread. Matzoh meets the minimal requirements of what might be called bread: some water and flour. No eggs, sugar, or other additions, and certainly no yeast.

Flour and water made into dough will of course rise in the presence of yeast. Yeast is a living, single-celled fungus, and there are around fifteen hundred known species of it. One gram of yeast contains twenty-five billion cells, tiny little fungi that eat sugars found in grains like wheat. As the fungus eats the sugar, the by-product is carbon dioxide gas; the microscopic carbon dioxide gas bubbles make dough expand, resulting in bread's porous texture, the little craters that deliciously hold melted butter and jam. The process of consuming sugars and producing gas is the process of fermentation, the same activity that makes alcoholic beverages like beer and wine, food products like sauerkraut, miso, yogurt, and kimchi, as well as fuel for rockets and cars. So, besides being quick to make, matzoh fulfills another function by being pure, unfermented, not in a state of decomposition.

Without yeast, the bread is flat and typically crispy, though in several food cultures (such as Iraq's) there is soft matzoh. Its unleavened flatness is significant: when the Israelites were freed from slavery under Moses's leadership, they had to bring food with them but didn't have time to let the bread rise (leavened bread would certainly have been known to them after the years of captivity in Egypt). They quickly baked the simple dough and took it with them into the wilderness. Deuteronomy puts God's Passover command this way: "You are not to eat any *hametz* [leavened food] with it; for seven days you are to eat with it matzoh, the bread of affliction; for you came out of the land of Egypt in haste. Thus you will remember the day you left the land of Egypt as long as you live."[15] Matzoh thus helps signal the liberation from slavery, the start of a new life, and the movement toward the Promised Land.

Matzoh is called poor man's bread and bread of affliction. Its simplicity evokes humility. As it is eaten, participants in the seder read from the Haggadah, the ritual manual that provides prayers and stories to help guide and remind the observant. Describing the place of the ritual observance of this ancient story, the Jewish historian Yosef Hayim Yerushalmi looks at the role of remembrance (*zakhor*) through the Hebrew Bible, and says that the memory enacted in the seder is not "recollection, which still preserves a sense of distance, but reactualization."[16] The Talmud puts it directly and forcefully: "In each and every generation let each person regard himself as though he had emerged from Egypt."[17] In the eating, the praying, the drinking, and the communing, the present-day community begins the evening in bondage; then they are liberated, and finally redeemed. Eating is remembering; the past made real to us through the palate.

Bread stuck with the Israelites. Perhaps during their time in Egypt, the growing and baking of cereal grains becoming deeply engrained in their cultural life and prompted them to make bread an integral aspect of several rituals. Sometime after the exodus, the grain product became associated with the Torah through the ritual of Shavuot. This Festival of Weeks began as a grain harvest (Exodus 34:22) that ultimately overlaid the agricultural ceremony with God's giving of the Torah to Moses. The founding story in this case tells of the Israelites wandering in the Sinai desert on the way to the Promised Land. They stopped for some time at the base of Mount Sinai while Moses climbed the mountain to commune with God. God spoke and gave Moses and the people the Torah, the teachings and law that sustained Jews for the next several millennia. To celebrate this monumental event, in the ancient ritual of Shavuot the Israelites used two loaves of wheat bread, as well as other first fruits, as an offering to God. (In contemporary versions of the ritual, all-night Torah study might occur and the book of Ruth is read, though curiously, there is not a lot of agreement on why Ruth.)

As the Torah became embedded in the social life of the people and rituals were structured for offering and worship to the one, true God, bread continued to be present. The laws surrounding the tabernacle, the main place of worship through the wilderness, and ultimately the temple in Jerusalem included space for bread. Alongside the Altar of Burnt Offering and Altar of Incense, God also instructed that they are to keep a "showbread" upon a table near the altar. This bread, *lechem HaPanim,* is the "bread of the presence," for it is to always be in the presence of God. Twelve loaves were laid out during the week and changed every Sabbath—the leftovers were to be eaten by the priests. One set of instructions in Leviticus states that the bread was to be accompanied by cups of frankincense. It is not clear that the bread was unleavened (the initial biblical accounts do not mention this) but one can't help wondering about the priestly task of eating week-old bread. Then again, according to Talmudic sources, the matriarch Sarah was able to make bread that stayed fresh from Friday to Friday, and the manna that fell from the heavens on Fridays during the wilderness wanderings would keep through the Sabbath, so perhaps here too a small weekly miracle occurred to preserve the perishable matter.

Ancient customs often carry ancient secrets. According to 1 Chronicles, the Kohathites were the clan charged with taking care of the showbread. As with the frankincense recipes kept by the Abtinas family or the bread-making skills of the Poilâne family, it seems the Kohathites also kept secret instructions for the bread recipes and preparations. Years later, the great Kabbalistic mystic Rabbi Isaac Luria encouraged the use of twelve breads on the household Sabbath table as a replica of the temple and as a symbolic reference to the unspoken name of God—the name can be seen or invoked but not uttered. (On Luria's table, by the way, would have been twelve loaves of pita.) And a Moroccan explanation of the challah says, "The bread contains within it divine secrets."

While the showbread was linked to the ancient temple, and thus specific rituals surrounding it disappeared with the destruction of the temple in 70 CE, bread sacrifices continue. At 4:30 every morning on the Lower East Side of Manhattan, a rabbi arrives at Kossar's Bialy to bless the day's dough and to make a burnt offering of the challah.* Contrary to popular understandings, challah is not necessarily the eggy, sweet, braided loaf you find at your local grocers, but has its roots in the Hebrew scriptures and refers to an offering of the first part of kneaded dough that is given to a priest. It is a mitzvah, a command. There are several layers to this command, many parsed through rabbinical literature, and one of them is meant for the challah sacrifice to trigger the bread of presence and the offerings involved there. Another is to always remember our reliance on God, from whom the food comes in the first place.

Today, *challah* still refers to the sacrificed portion, but it also names a diverse range of bread types, standing for a diverse Jewry. It is probably only since the fifteenth century that the braided bread has been used specifically on the Sabbath, and this began among the Ashkenazi in Germany, most likely adapted from the baking practices of non-Jewish neighbors. Sephardic

---

* Rabbi Fishelis also oversees the kashrut operations of the Pickle Guys on Essex Street and Murray's Falafel on First Avenue, also on Manhattan's Lower East Side.

Jews have continued to use flat bread for their Sabbath challah. Challah loaves may be flavored with poppy seeds, figs, raisins, caraway, or apples and sweetened with honey or sugar. During Purim some Ashkenazi will shape it into a rose (after a traditional medieval liturgical song "The Rose of Jacob"), while the Moroccan Jewish community at Purim bakes hard-boiled eggs into the loaf to resemble Haman's eyes. With their symbolic dimensions of liberation, purity, memory, and offering to God, specially flavored and shaped breads create a wide range of meanings for Jewish people.[18] Bread preserves history.

A companion is someone we share bread with. That's what the word *companion* literally means: from *com* meaning "together," and *panis* meaning "bread." When company comes over, we break out the bread. Bread is a pervasive symbol of being together, of gathering, of community, a symbol that we engage, chew, taste, swallow, and digest in the presence of others. Historians of social life are clear that commensality, eating together, has been vital to ongoing political power, and peaceful coexistences. A Moroccan proverb tells us, "By bread and salt we are united."

In the first few centuries of the Christian church BYOB was the norm. Worshipers brought their own bread and wine, contributing to the community life at large, sharing with their companions. The elements were blessed through prayers, and the faithful ate and drank. Whatever was left would be distributed to the catechumens (those undergoing a preparation course for admittance to the church, but not yet full members) and members who were absent. These leftovers were initially called the *eulogia*. A eulogy is a blessing, but in this initial usage it is about the object blessed, which in many early uses was specifically communion bread. Before there were words of blessing, there was bread of blessing. By the fourth century, Christians were sending *eulogia* to each other as symbols of their union, their life as the body of Christ. In ordination and canonization ceremonies within the Roman Catholic tradition today, loaves of bread are often passed from one party to another as symbols of power and blessing. The Eucharist eventually became so central and centralized that not just any bread would do. It needed to be authorized and maintained by the clergy, and thus grew the altar bread tradition that protected the quality of the breads, ensuring they were made with pure, natural water, of wheat flour only, and baked.

Christianity would not exist without bread. Or if it did, the tradition would be in a form unrecognizable to Christians then and now. Jesus was born in Bethlehem, the town's name literally meaning the "House of Bread." In Hebrew, the term *lechem* is generally translated as "bread," but also is used to refer to food in general throughout the Bible. (Similar parallels are found in several languages.) The translators of Proverbs 28:19 put it, "He who tills his land will have plenty of food [*lechem*], but he who follows empty pursuits will have poverty in plenty." Bread becomes a synecdoche of food and connected to good life. This relation of the part to the whole unfolds to encompass an even larger idea, as bread becomes the symbol that stands for life itself.

Into the House of Bread is born the Bread of Life. The Jesus of John's Gospel says, "I am the living bread which came down out of heaven: if any man eat of this bread, he shall live forever: yea and the bread which I will give is my flesh, for the life of the world."[19] Throughout the Gospels, Jesus refers to himself in the language of bread, perhaps calling to mind the cult of Ceres as well as the showbread and challah. Ultimately, at the Last Supper, Jesus identifies himself with the bread and wine. With his disciples he observes the Passover seder, taking the bread and wine, telling them to eat of it, and saying, "*Do* this in remembrance of me." As with the Jewish tradition, Christian memory is not some type of thinking we do with our brains; it is something we enact through our bodies. Memory is ingested, chewed, and swallowed.

Early Christians drew many of their myths, rituals, and symbols from their Jewish and pagan precursors, and what came to be known as the Christian Eucharist or Holy Communion was no exception. From the ancient mother goddess traditions of Demeter, Ceres, and Isis and the showbread of the temple came a practice of offering bread upon an altar table. Several prominent early Christian theologians, such as Ignatius of Antioch, Irenaeus, Ambrose of Milan, and Saint Augustine, discussed the power of the eucharistic bread to effect healing and even ward off death and lead toward immortality. We might easily read this as metaphorical language today, but in the time and place in which they were writing, the distance between the magical and metaphorical was not so easily discerned (whether it is today is another question). Early Christianity itself is full of accounts of miraculous effects of the Eucharist: warding off evil, blessing, and curing.[20]

In many ways the notion of the bread and wine functioning like an amulet dissipated over time, but many miraculous events were linked to the substance. Throughout history, Christians have used the activity of eating bread and drinking wine to remember, to signal their devotion, and to join together as the body of Christ. There is a "presence" in the bread, and as the community takes communion, we are bound to the past, bound to Jesus Christ, and bound to each other in the present moment. The first explicit theological statement by the Christian church on the presence of the divine within the food substances was given at the Fourth Lateran Council in 1215:

> In this church, Jesus Christ himself is both priest and sacrifice, and his body and blood are really contained in the sacrament of the altar under the species of bread and wine, the bread being transubstantiated into the body and the

wine into the blood by the power of God, so that to carry out the mystery of unity we ourselves receive from him the body.[21]

This statement (eventually known as the doctrine of transubstantiation) merely reaffirmed what laypeople had been assuming in their practices for centuries. What is stated here is that this most basic of foods, ubiquitous in its form across the known cultures of the day, became divine within the specificities of the Mass. And by eating this bread, believers take divinity into themselves.* Thirteenth-century mystic Mechthild of Magdeburg had eucharistically ecstatic visions of God recorded in her work "The Flowing Light of Divinity." She says, "Yet I, least of all souls, Take Him in my hand, Eat Him and drink Him, And do with Him what I will."[22]

Living on bread alone became a mark of piety through much of Christian history. The Carthusians, for example, fasted three times a week, during which they would take only bread, water, and salt. This is not to say that very many Christians ate only bread and water, but the sustenance of bread alone is a key element in the hagiographies of many saints. Saint Jerome, the fourth-century historian who gave us many accounts of early church events, tells of the life of a third-century Desert Father called Saint Paul the Hermit. According to Jerome's account, a raven would come every day to bring the aging ascetic a half loaf of bread, and thus he was sustained for many years. This component of his life was so key that the image of the raven and bread has become the standard depiction in Saint Paul the Hermit's iconography. Once, when Saint Antony paid a visit, the raven

---

* There are a number of religious traditions that have rituals surrounding the eating of deities. The Aztec deity Huitzilopochtli, for one, was communed with by people who would take crushed seeds of a prickly poppy and form the dough into a figure of the god, which was then consumed.

brought a whole loaf, and a humorous tale follows. Antony and Paul give thanks for the Lord's loaf; then, rising to partake of the meager food, they dispute who should be the one to break the bread, each wishing to show the other humility and hospitality. Their argument lasts the whole day, with Paul saying Antony should break it because he is the host in this circumstance, while Antony defers to Paul's age, wanting to offer the bread to his senior brother. As evening rolls around, they decide that they should each grasp one end of the loaf and pull. And so they do, with each one feasting on their morsels and then keeping vigil through the night. That evening proved to be the final one of Saint Paul the Hermit's time on earth.

Into the Middle Ages, pious Christians, many of them women, went for long periods subsisting on the Eucharist alone: a diet of bread and wine. Mystical visions occurred as the bread and wine would transform into the human body of Christ before their eyes—transubstantiation taken to its extreme—as their physical bodies became emaciated. The obsessions of these mystics could become so engrained in their minds and bodies that modern historians have considered some of these to be cases of anorexia nervosa. Caroline Bynum, one of the most knowledgeable medieval European historians of our day, puts it this way: "Eating God in the host was both a sweet tasting that focused and transcended all hunger and an occasion for paramystical phenomena of the most bizarre and exuberant sort."[23]

Catherine of Genoa, for one, was so desirous of God's love that she went through long periods of fasting, ingesting only bread and wine. As a result, bread became a constant refrain in her language. Hunger was a metaphor for desire in general, satisfied only by the bread of God. "Let us imagine," she says, "that in the whole world there was but one bread and that it could satisfy the hunger of all."[24] She acknowledges the metaphorical quality of her writing, while at the same time she was physically partaking of the communion, but very little else, leaving her with constant bodily afflictions: convulsions, feelings of extreme heat and cold, and trance experiences. It should be made clear that for Catherine, as for much of medieval spirituality, such diets were never undertaken simply for the individual him- or herself. Instead, they are set within the physical-spiritual action of service to others, as mystics like Catherine often worked with the sick in hospitals and helped feed those with few resources. Fasting was social, spiritual, and physical all at once.

Questions about the material substance of bread and the presence of God within it have been evolving over the centuries. At times, the metaphorical language *about* bread gets ignored, leaving only literalism. In a 1995 letter, writing from the Vatican as Prefect of the Sacred Congregation for the Doctrine of the Faith, Cardinal Joseph Ratzinger stated, "Given the centrality of the celebration of the Eucharist in the life of the priest, candidates for the priesthood who are affected by celiac disease or suffer from alcoholism or similar conditions may not be admitted to holy orders." Wheat bread and alcoholic wine are the Roman Catholic–approved ingredients of the Eucharist, and there is to be no substitute for them: no gluten-free bread, no alcohol-free wine. Thus, people who have bad reactions to these substances need not apply. In his letter, Ratzinger reiterated Canon Law 924.2, which states: "Special hosts *'quibus glutinum ablatum est'* [that are gluten free] are invalid matter for the celebration of the Eucharist."[25] As gluten intolerance has become a widely known medical condition, the symbolic tradition has had to be revisited, but the Vatican has reaffirmed its longstanding doctrinal position.

Nonetheless, in broad, creative, Catholic fashion, many parishes have found their ways around the rigid canon law. Practice always proves more pliable, and more interesting, than doctrine, and so some parishes have allowed communicants to receive communion under the form of wine only. Others have turned to low-gluten wafers. In fact, the Benedictine Sisters of Perpetual Adoration, in Clyde, Missouri, have become the go-to suppliers for practicing Catholics with gluten intolerance. The sisters began in 1874 when a small group of women left Switzerland and came to the United States, founding a monastery in Clyde that ministered to a German immigrant population. There the sisters taught, ran an orphanage, and eventually started a farm that provided food for the community at large. In 1910 they began to make altar breads, initially using a single gas stove, turning to electric stoves by 1920, and increasing production with new technologies up until the present day. In the past century, an estimated five billion wafers have been distributed across the world for use in Catholic Mass, and they are now the world's largest religious producer of altar breads.

In 2003 the sisters began making low-gluten wafers, and these have proven to be highly popular. I contacted them to learn more about this product, and they told me that they have been overwhelmed by demand for them, and their customer list is over six thousand, primarily in North America but in other parts of the world as well. In conjunction with the US Conference of Catholic Bishops they came up with a recipe that uses a wheat starch with most of the gluten removed. It is still "wheat only," and thus fulfills the Roman Catholic dogma, but the gluten content is less than .01 percent, making it safe for most people who suffer from gluten intolerance.

On the other end of the spectrum, Protestants have in general been a good deal looser with interpretations and practices than the Vatican. As part of the Protestant Reformation, Martin Luther, John Calvin, and others pruned the official sacraments of the church from seven down to two: baptism and communion.* These reformers, like most reformers of religious his-

---

* Some elements of the Anabaptist tradition, initially spearheaded by Ulrich Zwingli, also include foot washing as a sacrament.

tory, have believed that too much ritual creates hierarchy and fosters a spiritual focus that is external instead of internal. As a result, the doctrine of transubstantiation also became watered down. Luther still understood the presence of Christ to be in the bread and wine, but they did not *become* the actual body (later theologians would call Luther's view *consubstantiation*). Calvin, Ulrich Zwingli, and other theologians at the time offered their own versions of what happens to the bread and wine during communion, moving further and further from earlier church doctrine as they intended to show their own uniqueness in relation to the others and in ways that distanced themselves from anything that might seem superstitious or overly reliant on magic. The mystery made safe.

Today's Protestant denominations, stemming from the various offshoots that rapidly multiplied after Luther and Calvin, have trimmed the sacraments to such a degree that even communion, that most central rite throughout most of Christianity, is not often celebrated. When it is, adherence to wheat bread and wine are not necessary. Due to a broad temperance movement in the nineteenth century—and the preservation and pasteurization advances invented by people like the Methodist Thomas Bramwell Welch—grape juice became standard as a replacement for wine at some Protestant communion tables in the United States and United Kingdom. Online businesses like CelebrateCommunion.com offer boxed sets of communion wafers and prefilled, disposable communion cups with grape juice, while Amazon's grocery section sells a number of boxed wafers from different companies. Gluten-free wafers are also available (made of rice and potato flour; 0 percent wheat). The distance we have come from the medieval view of communion can be seen in the reviewers' tongue-in-cheek comments on the Amazon site. A reviewer with the screen name of Cypress Green says of a communion wafer box: "Order several boxes of Jesus, and He'll help you out with that unsightly double chin, just as you prayed!" And "Angela" says simply, "I eat them because they are a good snack."[26]

Yet, even if the miracles are rendered benign and the wonder proven to be nothing more than a stark-white sponge, bread's creative facilities have morphed and spread, adapting to multiple contexts. Bread has become so widespread throughout the Christian tradition that there is a profusion of breads for various seasonal rituals. There is the *bobalky* in Slovakia at Christmas; a *rosca de reyes* for Three King's Day (Epiphany) in Mexico; *lagana* for Greek Orthodox Lent; hot cross buns for Good Friday in the United Kingdom; *kulich* for Russian Easter; and the United Church of Christ, First Churches of Northampton, Massachusetts, have recently introduced the local recipe of fig bread for their congregation during Advent.

The process of making leavened bread includes a step known as the *proof* stage in which the dough ferments and rises to what will be its final form before baking. There are minted proofs for coins; liquor proofs, which tell of alcohol content; printing proofs for book pages (after *their* final fermentation); proof texts, which argue theological points; and legal proofs for solving crimes. A proof relies on the activity of proving something, probing, putting it to the test, creating a measurement by which something might be judged, a body of evidence deemed worthy and ready. Which all presupposes some crime, some doubt, some lingering questions. So with bread, the proofing allows the baker to test the results of the many processes leading up to the ultimate time in the oven: looking at, touching, and smelling the loaf. Proofs for bread, like proofs for God, require some substantiation.

The English word *proof* finds its cognate noun in Spanish as *prueba* and the related verb *probar*. (In French, it is *preuve*; in Italian, *provare*.) In Spanish class, a student might take a *prueba*, and *probar* is generally translated as "to test" or "to try." At the same time, if you want to taste some food or drink, you will *sabor* or *gustar*, but in its transitive form you might *probar*. As with this Spanish connection, in English the words *testing* and *tasting* share origins. "Taste test" is a redundant phrase. Though mostly obsolete now, to taste something used to mean not only testing and trying but also experiencing and feeling.* The proof is in the pudding. We even attach ethical and aesthetical value to our tongues: to say something is in bad taste means that a social code has been violated; someone who has refined his or her sense of décor has good taste. It's not just that a thing tasted can be good or bad but that taste *belongs* to the possessor of the tongue; the collection of objects in her house becomes proof that she has good taste.

Bread is proofed. It is probed, tried, tested, and tasted as it is created. In so doing, the bread tries us, tests our patience, our attention to detail, our ability to work well with others. The activity of making bread—of mixing, blending, kneading, forming, rising, shaping, proofing, and baking, which is to say nothing of the tilling, sowing, tending, fertilizing, reaping, and grinding—is fraught with struggle. The Islamic Sufi poet Jalaluddin Rumi has a wonderful poem called "Breadmaking" that intertwines the activity of lovemaking with warriors in battle: warring and loving are metaphorically applicable to the bread-making process, "a great mutual embrace" taking place between God and humans. And just as the bread of the Bible is the stuff and staff of life, we also find the "bread of wickedness," the "bread of deceit," and the "bread of adversity."[27] Bread is a battle.

One person who knows the double-sided dimensions of bread is the Jesuit priest Greg Boyle. Father Boyle became pastor of Delores Mission Church in 1986, one of the poorest parishes in Los Angeles, situated among the largest public housing projects

---

* In Shakespeare's *Cymbeline*, Posthumus Leonatus queries his rival Iachimo whether "you have tasted her in bed."

in the western United States. A multitude of gangs have operated in the area and Boyle has buried numerous young men
during his time there. He has tried a number of tactics to relieve
some of the social problems of the area: peace treaties between
warring gangs, pleading with local companies to employ more
young people, opening spaces for gang members to hang out,
all to varying degrees of success. He uses mottoes like "Jobs not
jails," and "Nothing stops a bullet like a job."

In 1992 violent uprisings erupted across Los Angeles following the acquittal of Los Angeles policemen who had been videotaped beating motorist Rodney King. At that time, with some
startup funding from a movie producer, Boyle created Homeboy
Industries. Their first industry was a bakery. For two decades
now, former gang members, oftentimes from rival gangs, have
mixed and kneaded and baked bread together. This has given
many young men and women a new chance in life, and a number
of them go on to finish school or find other permanent work.
Homeboy Industries has added a number of other businesses,
employing more than four hundred people a year. It is now the
largest gang intervention program in the country. Homeboy Industries is about many things; a better life through bread is only
a part of it, yet the effects of bread making can be seen in the
re-creation of key social facets.[28]

The Navajo also know something of the bread of affliction
and wandering in the wilderness. What has emerged over the
past century and a half is a reverence for frybread. For many Navajo this has become sacred bread that honors and remembers
their displacement from their ancestral homeland (*dinetah*) in
northeastern Arizona to a less hospitable land in New Mexico.
In the late nineteenth century, the US Cavalry forced the Navajo
to make what came be called the Long Walk, more than three
hundred miles across desert landscapes. Many died of starvation, because the rations given to them were often rancid. What
seems to have sustained the Navajo was the combination of

white flour, sugar, salt, and lard. Out of these meager supplies frybread was born, preserving the people through their dislocation. Many now understand the bread to be one of the more vital symbols for contemporary Native Americans, especially as it has become a key part of powwows and it signifies resistance against oppression. Novelist Sherman Alexie says, "Frybread is the story of our survival."[29]

Yet this story too unfolds into more battle. As one might imagine from the ingredients, frybread is a deeply unhealthy food: the USDA estimates an average plate-sized piece has seven hundred calories and twenty-five grams of fat. With high rates of obesity and diabetes among many Native American tribes, a number of activists have campaigned against it. American Indian writer Suzan Shown Harjo wrote in 2005 that frybread is to blame for diabetes, hypertension, and obesity and is the cause of many deaths in general among Native Americans. Her reasoned plea was met with adversity as many came to its defense, feeling she had violated a sacred tradition. The battle continues.[30]

The eloquent writer on food M. F. K. Fisher also sees the bisection of baking and battles and the physical struggles of love. In the midst of food shortages during World War II, Fisher published a practical book called *How to Cook a Wolf*. She somewhat bemoans the contemporary lack of know-how for bread making, but espouses and encourages a return to its form, for the sake of economy if nothing else. If taken seriously, bread making has great side effects through its ritualistic, hypnotic motions, "like a dance from some ancient ceremony. It leaves you filled with one of the world's sweetest smells. But it takes a lot of time. . . . Make it, for probably there is no chiropractic treatment, no Yoga exercise, no hour of meditation in a music-throbbing chapel, that will leave you emptier of bad thoughts than this homely ceremony of making bread."[31] Writer James Baldwin in *The Fire Next Time* had this to say: "To be sensual, I think, is to respect and rejoice in the force of life, of life itself, and to be present in all that one does, from the effort of loving to the making of bread."[32]

Bread making, like ritual making, is born of the body. Bread making is a ritual at once secular and sacred, full of love and battle, testing and tasting. The Hebrew word used for bread in the Bible, *lechem*, looks like it should share a root with the word for fighting or doing battle, *lacham*. It does not; but though the words have different origins, the connection is inherent. Love-making can look like wrestling, and bread making could be confused with either.

While researching for this chapter, I came across a book published in 1944 called *Six Thousand Years of Bread: Its Holy and Unholy History* by H. E. Jacob, mentioned earlier. The book was favorably reviewed at the time in prominent places like the *New York Times* and the *Wall Street Journal* and is often referred to now in studies on bread, though usually with a grain of salt. While Jacob's research on bread initially was of interest to me, what became more interesting was Jacob's own life.

Heinrich Eduard Jacob was born in Berlin in 1889, during a time of increasing freedom for Jews within the dominantly Christian continent of Europe. Following the Enlightenment, nation-states in the eighteenth and nineteenth centuries began the processes of emancipation, as Jews struggled for and gained relative freedom and rights as citizens. The Fourth Lateran Council of 1215, the very same one that enacted the doctrine of the transubstantiation of bread and wine at the Eucharist, had required Jews and Muslims in Europe to wear particular clothing to distinguish them from Christians. This had been but one part of centuries full of discriminatory laws and attitudes that forced non-Christians to live in particular sections of towns (the term *ghetto* comes from this practice), without any significant civil rights, often with imposing tax structures, and occasionally forced conversion and baptism. Beginning with the French

Revolution in 1789, national laws were changed in Europe, and Jews began to play prominent roles in the socioeconomic life of cities and countries. Berlin became one of the great centers of Jewish life in Europe. With these new freedoms, Jacob was able to gain an education in literature, philosophy, and music; work as a journalist for a notable newspaper; and publish books on the histories of coffee, Mozart, film, and Johann Strauss.

The rise of National Socialism changed all that, reversing laws back to a previous age, and in much more severe terms. With the Nazi annexation of Austria in 1938, Jacob was arrested while working in Vienna and sent to concentration camps in Dachau and then Buchenwald. His writings, including the 1930 best seller *Blood and Celluloid*, were blacklisted. His ongoing research notes through the 1930s were kept hidden by his wife, Dora. Due to some key connections, and especially through the work of his wife, he was released a year later and immigrated to the United States, where he lived out his life as a writer and journalist. When he returned to his writing, settling into some space at the New York Public Library and Columbia University, the work to which he turned was *Six Thousand Years of Bread*. He wrote in German, and the book was translated into English and published not long before Dachau and Buchenwald were liberated.

When I learned about Jacob's life, something unsettled me. That he, a prisoner of some of the most notorious concentration camps of Nazi Germany, whose own life was almost wholly destroyed at the time, should turn to writing a history of bread during the years of the Holocaust seemed either escapism or something more profound. The answer, I think, comes in the final section of his book. After 350 pages of accounting for the history of bread in the Western world, Jacob turns to the rise of the Nazis and World War II. Here, Jacob does not make much mention of the anti-Semitic rules and regulations brought on by Hitler's powers; but he does attend to legal and political actions like the Reich Hereditary Farm Act of 1933 and to

Hitler's general duping of the peasants, what Jacob calls the "bread-producing class." The Nazis systematically starved the vast majority of the lands they had conquered, especially taking wheat from the lands and funneling it back to feed those within the party system. At the same time the Nazis mixed bread flour with potato flour and who knows what else, and gave this unwholesome mixture back to those they conquered.[33]

In the final twenty-five pages Jacob argues that the roots of both World Wars must be understood in agrarian terms. These wars were at heart about hunger, about feeding great masses of people, and bread is the staple through which this can be achieved. Jacob quotes Herbert Hoover from 1943: "World peace means a peace of bread. . . . The first word in a war is spoken by the guns—but the last word has always been spoken by bread."[34] For Jacob, Hoover here sums up the evidence of his argument. Jacob's book moves from the personal to the political and back again. The final two paragraphs of *Six Thousand Years of Bread* are worth quoting here:

In the Buchenwald concentration camp we had no real bread at all; what was called bread was a mixture of potato flour, peas, and sawdust. The inside was the color of lead; the crust looked and tasted like iron. The thing sweated water like the brow of a tormented man. . . . Nevertheless, we called it bread, in memoriam of the real bread we had formerly eaten. We loved it and could scarcely wait for it to be distributed among us.

Many died there without ever tasting real bread again. I still live. It seems remarkable to me that I can eat real bread. Bread is holy. And bread is profane. It is most wonderful when *all* can have it. In the six thousand years that men and bread have lived side by side there have often been moments when each of God's creatures had all they wanted. "And they were filled," the Bible says. No simpler words can be written to describe happiness, satisfaction, gratitude.

Jacob's account reminded me of another prisoner of Buchenwald, Elie Wiesel. In his book *Night*, Wiesel tells of the horrors of being taken to the concentration camps, and how people clamored over each other for chunks of bread thrown into boxcars headed for the camps. One man kills his own father for a piece, only to be killed by another.

But I'm also reminded of the Holocaust stories in which fragments of the precious commodity of daily bread rations were saved up through the week for the Sabbath. Yaffa Eliach in *Hasidic Tales of the Holocaust* tells of a Czech teenager named Ignac, prisoner at Mauthausen, who hid one crumb of bread each day in his uniform. "On Sabbath, at dusk after a long day of backbreaking slave labor, Ignac would manage to wash his hands, seek a corner where he would not attract too much attention, and celebrate his third Sabbath 'meal.'" He chewed the morsels, and remembered the Sabbaths of his childhood. "The peace and tranquility of the Sabbath would be upon him and the hell of Mauthausen would be overpowered by the Sabbath bliss."[35] Transcendence occurs through a crumb of bad bread. The memories of real, physical spaces and ancestors are enacted in the ritualized eating.

If bread is so engrained in world history, as Jacob argues, and if it is so deeply seated in religious consciousness, what happens when a community of the faithful comes from a culture that does not have bread at its base? What use is a metaphor when there is no physical reality on which to ground it? What happens to beliefs and behaviors when cultural specifics meet pancultural religious traditions? Is it the stuff itself that is central? Or the ritual surrounding it? Or can such matters be separated? As we come to the end of this chapter, tensions between the local and the global meet the already noted tensions between nature and culture and the sacred and the profane.

The worldwide Anglican Church has been asking some of these questions with regard to communion. In 2007 the church's liturgical department issued a report responding to increased needs to provide substitutes for wheat bread and alcoholic wine, since Christians in many parts of the world do not have access to these substances. Sometimes Christians live in dominantly Islamic nations in which the sale of alcohol is prohibited and thus wine is hard to come by. Or Anglican communities work with alcoholics, and the presence of alcohol hinders ministry. Or wheat is simply not the staple crop it is in the Western world, and rice is the common grain; not only might wheat bread be difficult to come by in this case but the whole metaphor of the staff of life also becomes meaningless in such settings. The Anglican report basically reconfirmed that wheat bread and alcoholic wine are best, but that the final practice should be dealt with in specific regions, on a local level.[36]

What gets used instead? In Uganda, during the years of Idi Amin's ruthless reign, it was difficult to obtain wine and bread, so Anglicans used banana juice, passion juice, or Coca-Cola in place of wine and biscuits for bread. During the height of the US economic embargo against Cuba, churches on the island began to brew their own "wine" from honey, fruit, and grain. In war-torn Sudan, bread has often been unavailable, and so cassava is eaten. There are Polynesian accounts of using coconut and Hawaiians who use poi instead of bread. East Asian Protestant churches in Los Angeles have used rice for communion—not because they can't find bread but because that's what was used in their homeland, in places where bread does not have comparable symbolic powers. The Church of Jesus Christ of Latter-day Saints (Mormons) uses water instead of wine, along with bread.

Similar circumstances affect the worldwide Jewish community. There is a Tunisian saying, "Shabbat is not Shabbat without couscous." Across North African Jewish communities, couscous is a staple food, though its use for Passover is debated. There are many Sephardic couscous recipes readily available for the seder, but Ashkenazi traditions generally don't include it, and many have argued that it is a pasta and thus *chametz*. But again, doctrine and culture do not readily align.

Throughout southern and eastern Asia, where bread grains are not regularly grown, there are various festivals that celebrate the planting and harvesting of rice, and it is this grass and not bread grain that is the staple. In India, rice is associated with the goddess Lakshmi, who is celebrated every autumn during Diwali, with rice playing a key role as part of her devotional offerings (*Lakshmi puja*). In China, rice was one of the Five Sacred Grains in ancient mythologies. And in Japan, the popular rice deity Inari Okami is associated with fertility, and offerings are made in the form of rice and the fermented rice drink, sake. The deities need to eat, as do the communicants and companions, and where bread is not a mainstay, rice generally is.

Naan. Chapati. Rye. Shami. Communion wafers. Matzoh. Tortilla. Roti. Wonder. Sourdough. Injera. Pita. All these can be called bread in an intelligible way. Bread can be flat or fluffy, black or white, soft or hard, moist or dry, airy or dense, formed into small or large units, eaten alone or as a utensil for other foods. The basic ingredients are a little water and some kind of flour. Typical additions include yeast, salt, and sugar, sometimes egg, sometimes fruits or nuts. The dough can be kneaded in order to rise or pounded flat, and then fried or baked.

Not only is bread a useful substance to use as a tool for comparison and contrast, as its making and eating is evident across a number of religious traditions, but it also works well metaphorically for religion itself. Among other things, "bread is a concept," says William Rubel in his global history of bread, "an invention of culture."[37] Bread works the tongue and the mind, makes us think and gives us the fuel for thinking: "The perfect vehicle," Apollonia Poilâne says, "to talk about really essential things."[38] The simple stuff of ground and baked grain mixed with water and one or two other ingredients becomes a powerful tool to carry us across the great reaches of continents and cultures, inventions and ideologies. All of which is not unlike the objects and activities of religious tradition.

But there is a caveat: bread is not universal. Bread connects us politically, cosmically, erotically, and gastronomically, but its religious applications make it distinct from the other widespread objects we have seen in the previous chapters. So, while stones, incense, drums, and crosses are prominently found in religious traditions around the globe, bread's religious use remains significantly Judeo-Christian. Muslims, Buddhists, Hindus, Taoists, and various animists may eat bread, but rarely does it find its way into so prominent a place as it does in the traditions of Judaism and Christianity. Even when we find it in multiple places, there are specific and special rules and customs accompanying its making, baking, and partaking. Widespread and everyday that it is, bread does not appear everywhere, in spite of its all-too-common epithet.

And so religion is like bread. It is an invention, a concept that changes from place to place, time to time. As I will explain further in the conclusion to this book, it has some basic ingredients (myths, rituals, and symbols, to name but three of the most prominent) and serves certain purposes (social cohesion, connection with supernatural forces, a sense of order and purpose), but when we get down to the nitty-gritty of it, the similarities between traditions can be difficult to sniff out. Which means that, against popular wisdom, I find it important to emphatically state that not all religions are the same. They do not want the same thing in the same way and are not structured for those purposes in the same way. Ideally, they might seek to offer a better life for their adherents, but how they go about this is different in each circumstance. We can say they are the same only if we remain in abstraction. If we look at a basket of pumpernickel and pita, chapatti and challah, we can say that's a breadbasket. If we look at Islam, Christianity, and Shinto, we can say those are religions. But the specificities are crucial to attend to.

Religion, like *bread*, is a useful term; just as *art*, *literature*, *history*, and *culture* are useful terms. We use these terms as concepts and conventions, even if what they point to is an invention. They help us live and offer us shorthand accounts for our experiences. Yet we must remain aware of the limits of our comparisons, be careful of the crunch when we are ready to chew.

SOUL

There was a child went forth every day;
And the first object he look'd upon,
    that object he became;
[. . .]
The strata of color'd clouds, the long bar of
    maroon-tint, away solitary by itself—
    the spread of purity it lies motionless in,
The horizon's edge, the flying sea-crow,
    the fragrance of salt marsh and shore mud;
These became part of that child who went forth
    every day, and who now goes, and will always
    go forth every day
        —Walt Whitman, "There was a Child went Forth"[1]

I often remind my students that there are no one-liner definitions of religion, or of anything of lasting significance in this world. And then against all that, I turn to a one-line, working definition that is a useful jumping off point for thinking about religion. It comes from Mark C. Taylor, current chair of the religion department at Columbia University. "Religion," Taylor says, "is a complex adaptive network of myths, symbols, rituals, and concepts that simultaneously figure patterns of feeling, thinking, and acting and disrupt stable structures of meaning and purpose."² This is not a perfect definition, nor could one really be achieved, but several things stand out here that I especially like.

First is that, like any good definition or any good recipe, Taylor gives the "is" and "does." Religion *is* made up of ingredients: myths, symbols, rituals, and concepts. This is the stuff of religion, the elements that we find multitudinously manifested in traditions across the globe. But these things are not the totality of the definition—just as a list of ingredients for sourdough bread will not on their own produce a steaming, leavened loaf. Religion also *does* things to people, for people, by people; it operates in the land of the living, moving, seeking, breathing, scared, and secure. So, religion creates (or "figures") patterns of order, meaning, and purpose. And it achieves this not by having beliefs but through "feeling, thinking, and acting." Religion is a noun that is nothing without its verb, a concept that is nothing without its embodiment. What this also entails is that simplistic definitions about religion being a "set of beliefs" are deeply deficient. In fact, beliefs (like god) are absent here.

Many of us will readily agree that some key functions of religious traditions are to establish order, meaning, and purpose. (Whether they do this effectively is not the question here.) What makes Taylor's definition advantageous is that disruptions to the stable orders of existence are also included among the functions of religions. Disruption, doubt, dis-ease, and disbelief are themselves part of the open-ended network. Religion, he suggests, is adaptive. Religion evolves. Every significant religious person of faith through history has gone through intensely important times of doubt, of feeling estranged from his or her own body, from past events, from significant others and must confront the chaos and cacophony of the cosmic realm. Most continue to ask questions and to go on quests, seeking new cognitive formulations and sensual connections as they live out their lives. Religious histories—of individuals and entire traditions alike—

oscillate between periods of stability and instability, constancy and volatility, ease and dis-ease, comfort and affliction, faith and doubt. Bodies at rest, bodies in motion. Religious traditions, then, include both sides of these opposing forces.

Guiding us through these alterations of faith, and undergirding the myths, rituals, symbols, and concepts, are objects. Religion, as I hope was convincingly conveyed in the preceding chapters, is impossible without these things. We sensually engage objects at a deep, bodily level and out of such encounters are born the languages of myths and doctrines, the structured performances of rituals and ceremonies, the meanings of symbols, and the very ability to think conceptually in the first place. Sensual objects give rise to primary metaphors, and these allow for the more abstract thinking, acting, and feeling that are part and parcel of religious life.

And so as I conclude this book I want to return to the suggestion made in the introduction that religion is technological, that religious people are not believers so much as *technologists*. We have to act. Belief is never enough. And we act with things, engaging them, using them as tools, creating art and organizations and cities out of them, just as the objects evoke actions and behaviors in us, call us to them, or scare us away. In this way, religious traditions instill *savoir-faire* and not merely *savoir*, know-how and not just knowing, as well as the know-how of working with technological objects. The French term *savoir* stems from the Latin *sapere*, which is also where we get the *sapiens* nomination of our species; *Homo sapiens* are the "knowing" or "wise" hominids. But just as bread is proofed, as we saw in the last chapter, the Latin roots of *sapere* also have to do with tasting. To be human is to taste and thus to test, ultimately to know and know how. The process is sensual through and through. Being wise depends on something outside us, the evocative objects to which we respond, and which we use to build our patterns and structures of existence. And yet the nice, neat, ordered worlds we build sometimes fall into disarray, scatter, and we are left to pick up the pieces in hopes of putting them together again, most likely in a new, improvised form.

The word *religion* stems from Latin roots and can be most directly rendered as "rebinding" or "reconnecting."* I explain this to my students and they dutifully write the fact down in their notes. When I push them a bit, two questions come to the fore. First, *what* exactly is bound? Maybe it's God and humans bound together. Maybe it's the binding force of the law. Maybe it's just humans bound together to form a community, strength in numbers and all that. And so go the better of the responses. Sometimes a second, more intriguing question emerges from these definitions: What happened to the first binding? *Rebinding* implies that something has come loose, the ties untied. Some disruption of stable structures has ensued.

My playfully serious suggestion here is that religion in its deepest forms aims to rebind the half body to the world, sensually connecting the interior realms of existence to the exterior realms, and thus crafting *soul*. And maybe, just maybe, soul is *produced* when humans consciously engage the things and bodies of the world. Soul craft. Soul, on this account, is not some interior, invisible substance, and it cannot have a definite article.† Rather, it is thoroughly material, stemming from physical connections (though not, à la Descartes, found in a specific part of the anatomy). It is not an immortal, immutable essence but a human technological production that comes and goes, ebbs and flows.

In 1930 the blues singer Blind Willie Johnson sought an an-

---

* From the Latin: *re* (again) + *ligare* (to bind; related to the terms *ligament* and *legal*).

† In other words, "the" soul. Thus also, this conclusion is not describing a *sixth* object in a history of religion.

swer to the question, What is the soul of a man? His song of that name tells of his travels and talks with people and his reading the Bible in search of an answer. Through it all, as far as he can tell, it's "nothing but a burning light." Soul is like the spark alighting from two stones rubbed together: fleeting, temporary, but potent nonetheless. An occasional flame erupts, yet even that burning light is codependent on oxygen and fuel to burn. An eternal flame is everlasting only in a relative way. The flame is new and different in each twinkling of an eye.

What I mean is that to understand soul, and thus the rebinding of religion, we would do well to listen to soul music, eat soul food. Soul emerges technologically, when the music is played, heard, felt; when the food is baked, tasted, shared. There is no real separation between body and soul, and so without some bodily sensing activity, soul doesn't exist or at least it goes dormant. It lies in a nascent state below the surface of things: within stones and drumbeats, broken bread and broken bodies, awaiting sensual contact. Soul comes forth, is birthed, awakens when head and heart meet the world. The spark alights through sensual connection.[3]

Even so, soul is ultimately untamed and untamable, though practice might improve the possibility for its presence. Poet Gary Snyder gets at this dichotomy in his Buddhist-rooted "practice of the wild": "a deliberate sustained and conscious effort to be more finely attuned to ourselves and to the way the actual existing world is. 'The world,' with the exception of a tiny bit of human intervention, is ultimately a wild place. It is that side of our being which guides our breath and digestion, and when observed and appreciated is a source of deep intelligence."[4] This practice does not make perfect, but puts us in our proper place of connecting with the deeper, wild reality of things. Adapting Snyder's comments, I suggest that soul materializes when the half body makes conscious contact with the wild and wooly elements of the world. Despite all the flaws and failures of religious and artistic traditions, they still retain something of this conscious contact among their core aims.*

One artist, the author D. H. Lawrence, offers something along these lines with his own credo, saying he believes:

That my soul is a dark forest.

That my known self will never be more than a little clearing in the forest.

That gods, strange gods, come forth from the forest into the clearing of my known self, and then go back.

That I must have the courage to let them come and go.[5]

Soul is wild and, as the educator Parker J. Palmer has noted, a bit shy. Palmer suggests that it doesn't like to be talked about and if you go into the woods shouting for it, it will hide in its hole. It doesn't want to be captured or civilized, and tenaciously survives.[6] Soul is not something we have; it is out of our possession. We don't own it, and often times we can barely find it.

The ancient Greeks used the word *psyche*—from which we get the words psychology and psychiatry—to denote the soul. The term also meant "breath" or even "wind." The Romans followed with the Latin word *anima*—from which we get *animation* and *animal*—which similarly was used for "soul," "breath," and "air." (*Unanimous* also stems from this root, meaning "of one mind or soul.") In the chapter on incense, we saw some translations of the Hebrew terms for wind and spirit and their connection to smell through the words *re'ach* and *ru'ach*. And we find correspondences in the Sanskrit, where the term most directly related to the Western concept of soul is *atman*, which is where we also get the word *atmosphere*. All this suggests that while it may be invisible, soul is still physical and acts in the

---

* Parallel to re-ligion, *art* comes from the Latin *ars*, meaning "connect" or "join."

world, guiding and moving us, breathed into us. Soul is blowing in the breeze.

As an undergraduate philosophy major, I struggled through my own intellectual and sensual connections with the world, believing in some kind of afterlife and thus a soul that might migrate to that great beyond. But my conceptions of it were disillusioning and often disturbing. None of the visions of heaven that I had heard and read about resonated in me (singing for a thousand years? Streets of gold? Floating on clouds?), and so, like Blind Willie before me, I went in search of the soul. I traveled, and I talked to people, and I read. And I set up some time with my philosophy professor to explore the ancient Western visions of the soul, reading Plato, Aristotle, and Augustine on the topic. The dualism that Plato, and later Augustine, proposed was a bit distasteful to me.* As a lover of the wilderness and music, of hot coffee and face-to-face conversations in far-off lands that last deep into the night, I had trouble viewing the body as a physical thing that would be transcended by the soul at the death of the body. Too much delight was given to the ethereal soul and too much disdain toward the sensual delights of the body. For me, my soul came alive *in and through* the material realities of life, as difficult as those might be. I don't know if a soul has an afterlife beyond the body, but I came to believe that is the wrong question.

And so it was to Aristotle that I kept coming back. I'm still not sure I fully get the old Greek: his relentless systematizing of such things as form and matter and body and soul and perception and intellect grow a bit wearying. But it is in his great treatise on the soul, *De anima*, that he states, "Soul is that by which

---

* Which isn't to say the senses aren't present in Plato and Augustine. Consider Augustine's deep entanglement with the senses through his famous conversion experience recounted in the tenth book of his *Confessions*: God calls and breathes and touches, while Augustine loses his deafness and blindness, beginning to hunger, thirst, and "burn" for peace (bk. 10, chap. 27).

primarily we live and perceive and think."[7] While his full account goes into significantly more complexities, it is this simple statement that haunts me and sustains me. There is a dualism involved, but Aristotle does seem to indicate that souls cannot be active without a body; a body may be animated by soul, but a soul cannot exist or act separate from the body. At heart: soul is implicated in our perceptions and thoughts, woven into the way we live now and not necessarily about the way we live *after* this life. Soul is animation, and we are animated through smelling and tasting, reading and believing, chewing over some idea or on a piece of fruit.

Such primary perceptions and conceptions are taken farther, not by philosophers in this case but by the children's book author Margery Williams in her 1922 *The Velveteen Rabbit*, subtitled *How Toys Become Real*. In the story, the wet-behind-the-ears, stuffed Rabbit seeks guidance from the wise Skin Horse on the ways of the world, asking, "What is real?" The Skin Horse gives some indication of the process needed to *become* real: "Generally, by the time you are Real, most of your hair has been loved off, and your eyes drop out and you get loose in the joints and very shabby." What animates the toys, what makes them alive is not something inside them—bells and buzzers and wind-up mechanisms—but a connection with something beyond the skin beneath their loved-off hair. The Real, the life force, is not a thing, but a relationship.

You don't have to believe this account of soul to get something from this book. I won't push anymore to convince you of it. But I will push for a rethinking and reexperiencing of religion as a deeply, thoroughly, unfailingly physical activity. The body cannot be disregarded, as some have considered, as a bag of bones to be left behind as the soul migrates onward and upward. Instead, the crux of religion itself is the sensual engagement with the physical objects of the world. I believe that starting a history of religion from this point also offers the potentials for a renewed take on dialogues between religions, an increasingly necessary task. Instead of asking whether all gods are the same thing (they aren't), we might have renewed respect for each other if we begin in wonder of why so many of us carry stones, burn incense, beat drums, regard crosses, and eat bread as part of our religious devotion.

My interest in writing this book has been in bringing us to our religious senses, to become aware of the objects we have come to love across ages and continents and to realize how central they are to our spiritual lives. And while we use objects on daily, even hourly bases, we often forget their power and stop listening for their evocations. More than likely, we are *taught* not to listen, *taught* not to believe these objects have any worth, no matter how much we use them. The spiritual life, we are often told, is not found "out there" in the land of things but is interior, invisible, silent. By investing in such stingy interpretations of the wisdom found across religious traditions, we forsake the rich depths of *this* world, *this* body, *these* things. As long as the spiritual realm is set in opposition to the material realm, we can only remain deeply and intractably *unaware*.

It is springtime here in Central New York. My daughters are playing outside, searching for branches that had fallen into the snow and are revealed in the thaw, and discovering the slow awakening of grubs and worms and salamanders that had gone dormant through the cold winter. In spite of feeble protests from the animal, they bring them back to life, not merely by waking them up but also by telling stories about them, by naming the salamanders and putting them in an old plastic take-away tub or by turning a stick into a magical weapon, a conjuring device. The objects are resurrected, made vibrant, liberated from their slumbers in a deep, dark kingdom. In so doing, the girls put their own half bodies into action, connecting with the backyard wild. In so doing, they participate in transformative rituals and imaginative stories akin to the basic activities of this much larger, much more global, sometimes violent, sometimes peaceful body-mind enterprise we have come to call religion.[8]

Maybe the original binding of inner and outer worlds and of body and soul, of *re-ligion* itself, was loosed when we became adults. We stopped believing in our senses and trusted only our intellect. We believed thinking and sensing were separate and separable functions. We were forbidden to put things in our mouths to figure out what they were: tasting and testing were once linked, but we severed those ties and were told testing is a thinking activity, not a bodily one. (Sit still! Don't touch!) We learned to ignore the pictures in our books and only read the words, since that's where we heard truth resided. Sigmund Freud once famously quipped, "Religion is comparable to a childhood neurosis, and he is optimistic enough to suppose that mankind will surmount this neurotic phase."[9] A hundred years after Freud, however, it's time for a renewed take on it all. If imagination and a greater connection to the stuff of nature are childish things, then so be it. This world is weary of grown-up ideas.

There is no way back to an imagined childhood life, but one hope I have with this book is that we will begin to feel again, to acknowledge the basic stuff around us, to see and hear and taste and touch and smell with renewed senses and sensibilities, and thus come to a deeper spiritual life. Perhaps you too have your objects, kept in your pocket, on your bed stand, above the fireplace, on your desk. This book celebrates some of these objects; it celebrates the materiality of religious life and offers an explanation of why religions continue to invest in the objects of the world.

It may sound strange to say, but if up to this point you've understood my fledging attempt to justify the role of objects in our spiritual lives, you'll understand when I say, we need stuff, even junk, and old broken branches in our lives.

Acknowledgments

Travel to several research locations was aided by an Individual Research Grant from the American Academy of Religion and a Franklin Research Grant from the American Philosophical Association. Hamilton College's Dean of Faculty office was especially helpful with travel funds for research and provided me the means to work in Istanbul and Kyoto for some time.

I would also like to thank many of the people who have offered support, suggestions, and advice along the way: Diane Apostolos-Cappadona, Annette Baehne, Timothy Beal, Betsy Flowers, Chaz Gay, Norman Girardot, Rosalind Hackett, Simon Halliday, David Howes, Tod Linafelt, Peter Manseau, Jeff McArn, Birgit Meyer, Darren "Dazza" Middleton, David Morgan, David Nienhuis, Crispin Paine, Wanda Rodríguez, Janet Stanley, Isaac Weiner, Tom Wilson, and the members of Tel Mac. I would especially like to thank David Patterson, my agent; Amy Caldwell at Beacon for continual encouragement and sharp ideas; Andrea Lee, Susan Lumenello, Beth Collins, and Will Myers, who each worked to get the final product in great shape; Nina Ergin for a tour of Ottoman mosques in Istanbul; Hannah Grace O'Connell, who provided significant research assistance; and the Guyot-Bender family, especially Paul and Larry, for some much needed hospitality at a crucial time in this book's development.

Notes

1/2

1. Colin Cheney, "Half-Ourselves, Half-Not," *Poetry* 194, no. 5 (September 2009): 430–31.
2. Federico Fellini, *8 ½* (Cineriz, 1963).
3. Julian Barnes, *A History of the World in 10 ½ Chapters* (New York: Vintage Books, 1989).
4. Plato, *Symposium*, trans. Benjamin Jowett (Oxford, UK: Oxford University Press, 1953), sections 189a–193e.
5. Quoted in Maurice Merleau-Ponty, "Cézanne's Doubt," *The Merleau-Ponty Aesthetics Reader*, ed. Galen Johnson (Evanston, IL: Northwestern University Press, 1993), 67.
6. Diane Ackerman, *A Natural History of the Senses* (New York: Random House, 1990), xv.
7. Mircea Eliade, *Myths, Dreams and Mysteries*, trans. Philip Mairet (New York: Harper & Row, 1960), 74.
8. Ibid., 81.
9. Paul Stoller, *The Taste of Ethnographic Things* (Philadelphia: University of Pennsylvania Press, 1989), 3.
10. Paul Stoller, *Sensuous Scholarship* (Philadelphia: University of Pennsylvania Press, 1997), xi–xii.
11. Evelyn Fox Keller, *A Feeling for the Organism: The Life and Work of Barbara McClintock* (New York: W. F. Freeman, 1983), 197–98.
12. Sherry Turkle, *Evocative Objects: Things We Think With* (Cambridge, MA: MIT Press, 2007), 10.
13. Ibid., 4, 10.
14. T. S. Eliot, from "The Dry Salvages," in *The Four Quartets* (London: Faber and Faber, 1944), 31.
15. Ibid.
16. See Mark Johnson, *The Meaning of the Body* (Chicago: University of Chicago Press, 2008), and George Lakoff and Mark Johnson, *Philosophy in the Flesh* (New York: Basic Books, 1999).

17. James Geary, *I Is an Other: The Secret Life of Metaphor and How It Shapes the Way We See the World* (New York: Harper, 2011), 3.

18. Cynthia Ozick, *Metaphor and Memory* (New York: Alfred Knopf, 1989), 270, 283.

STONES

1. Andy Goldsworthy, *Stone* (New York: Harry Abrams, 1994), 6.

2. Matthew 7:24–27. All biblical quotations are from the Revised Standard Edition.

3. Qur'an 17, "al-Isra."

4. Emile Durkheim, *Elementary Forms of Religious Life* (New York: Simon & Schuster, 1995), 13, 15.

5. Nelson Goodman, *Ways of Worldmaking* (Indianapolis: Hackett, 1978), 67.

6. Information on the "sorry rocks" from Jasmine Foxlee, "Stories in the Landscape: The Sorry Rock Phenomenon and the Cultural Landscape of Uluru-Kata Tjuta National Park," PhD diss., University of Western Sydney, 2008. Some of the study is summarized in Foxlee's "Meaningful Rocks," *Material Religion* 5, no. 1 (2009): 123–24.

7. Francesco Petrarch, *Letters on Familiar Matters*, vol. 2, trans. Aldo S. Bernardo (Baltimore: Johns Hopkins University Press, 1982), 260.

8. John Janovy Jr., *Vermilion Sea: A Naturalist's Journey in Baja California* (Boston: Houghton Mifflin, 1992), 5.

9. Norman O. Brown, *Hermes the Thief* (Madison: University of Wisconsin Press, 1947).

10. Sechin Jagchid and Paul Hyer, *Mongolia's Culture and Society* (Boulder, CO: Westview Press, 1979).

11. See Isamu Noguchi, *The Isamu Noguchi Garden Museum* (New York: Harry Abrams, 1987); and Diane Apostolos-Cappadona, "Stone as Centering: The Spiritual Sculptures of Isamu Noguchi," *Art International* 24, nos. 7-8 (1981): 79–89.

12. Andy Goldsworthy, *Hand to Earth* (New York: Harry Abrams, 2004), 151–53. See also Goldsworthy, *Stone.*

13. For more on the Japanese tea ceremony, see Jennifer Lea Anderson, *An Introduction to Japanese Tea Ritual* (Albany: State University of New York Press, 1991).

14. Martin Fackler, "Tsunami Warnings, Written in Stone," *New York Times*, April 20, 2011.

15. Annie Dillard, *Teaching a Stone to Talk: Expeditions and Encounters* (New York: Harper & Row, 1982), 68, 76.

16. 2 Samuel 23:3; Psalm 31:3; Isaiah 17:10; Isaiah 26:4; Isaiah 44:8.

17. See Matthew 3:9 and Luke 3:8; Matthew 7:9; Luke 19:40; Matthew 4:3 and Luke 4:3.

18. Numbers 15:36.

19. John 8:1–11.

20. A German company called Crowd Dynamics Ltd. rebuilt the *jamarat* after a stampede led to the deaths of four hundred hajjis in 2006.

21. See Qur'an, 37:100–109, "As-Saaffat."

22. From Psalm 118:22; quoted in Matthew 21:42; Mark 12:10; Luke 20:17.

23. Herbert Thurston, "Corner Stone," in *The Catholic Encyclopedia*, vol. 14 (New York: Robert Appleton, 1912). Accessed online: http://www.newadvent.org/cathen/14303a.htm.

24. Heine and Grimm both quoted in George Smith, "On Kirk-Grims," *Cornhill Magazine* 8, no. 55 (1887).

25. Matthew 16:18.

26. Several books are the sources of my references here and throughout to Japanese gardens: David Slawson, *Secret Teachings in the Art of Japanese Gardens* (Tokyo: Kodansha International, 1991); Francois Berthier, *Reading Zen in the Rocks*, trans. Graham Parkes (Chicago: University of Chicago Press, 2000); Jiro Takei and Marc Peter Keane, *Sakuteiki: Visions of the Japanese Garden* (Tokyo: Tuttle, 2001); and Marc Peter Keane and Haruzo Ohashi, *Japanese Garden Design* (Tokyo: Tuttle, 1996). Background information on the gardens is also rooted in the many lectures I attended and my experiences with the Japanese Garden Intensive Seminar, 2010, at the Research Center for Japanese Garden Art and Historical Heritage, Kyoto University of Art and Design. Wybe Kuitert's lectures, conversations, and writings are of particular importance here.

27. Gert J. Van Tonder and Michael J. Lyons, "Visual Perceptions in Japanese Rock Garden Design," *Axiomathes* 15 (2005): 353–71.

28. Many of these references to the Oneida come from Anthony Wonderley, former official historian of the Oneida Nation, and his book *Oneida Iroquois Folklore, Myth, and History* (Syracuse, NY: Syracuse University Press, 2004), and from the Oneida Nation's Shako:wi Cultural Center located in Oneida, New York.

29. Henry Rowe Schoolcraft, *Historical and Statistical Information Respecting the History, Conditions, and Prospects of the Indian Tribes*

of the United States, Parts 1–6 (Philadelphia: Lippincott, Crambo, 1851–57), 134, quoted in Wonderley, *Oneida Iroquois Folklore, Myth, and History,* 2.

30. Quoted in Silas Conrad Kimm, *The Iroquois: A History of the Six Nations of New York* (Middleburgh, NY: P. W. Danforth, 1900), 36.
31. Joshua 4:3–7.
32. Francis Ponge, "The Pebble," in *Things,* trans. Cid Corman (New York: Grossman, 1971), 38–44.

INCENSE

1. See Rachel Herz, *The Scent of Desire: Discovering Our Enigmatic Sense of Smell* (New York: HarperCollins, 2007).
2. Helen Keller, quoted in Dorothy Herrmann, *Helen Keller: A Life* (Chicago: University of Chicago Press, 1998), 159.
3. Jean-Jacques Rousseau, *Emile: Or, On Education,* trans. Alan Bloom (New York: Basic, 1979), 120.
4. General information on smell and culture comes from Constance Classen, David Howes, and Anthony Synnott, *Aroma: The Cultural History of Smell* (London: Routledge, 1994).
5. Historical resources on incense come from several studies, most notably Nigel Groom, *Frankincense and Myrrh: A Study of the Arabian Incense Trade* (London: Longman, 1981); the dated but still interesting E. G. C. F. Atchley, *A History of the Use of Incense in Divine Worship* (London: Longmans, Green & Co., 1909); and Susan Ashbrook Harvey, *Scenting Salvation: Ancient Christianity and the Olfactory Imagination* (Berkeley: University of California Press, 2006).
6. Exodus 30:34–38.
7. Leviticus 10:1–2.
8. Maimonides, *Guide for the Perplexed,* pt. III, chap. 45.
9. Psalm 141:2.
10. Isaiah 1:13.
11. John Chrysostom, "Eight Homilies Against the Jews," Homily 1, VII.3.
12. Origen "Against Celsus," VIII.LX.
13. Tertullian, "To His Wife," II.VI.
14. Mar Jacob, "Homily on Habib the Martyr," trans. B. P. Pratten. From *Ante-Nicene Fathers,* vol. 8 (Buffalo, NY: Christian Literature Publishing Co., 1886).

15. *The Russian Primary Chronicle*, trans. Samuel Hazard Cross and Olgerd P. Sherbowitz-Wetzor (Cambridge, MA: Medieval Academy of America, 1953).

16. Ibid.

17. Isaiah 11:2.

18. Isaiah 11:3–4.

19. Hildegard of Bingen, *Book of Divine Works with Letters and Songs*, ed. M. Fox (Santa Fe, NM: Bear and Company, 1987), 130. Quoted in Constance Classen, *The Color of Angels* (London: Routledge, 1998), 59.

20. 2 Corinthians 2:14–15.

21. The tenth-century Persian historian and Qur'anic exegete Muhammad ibn Jarar al-Tabari makes this argument. See Brannon Wheeler, *Mecca and Eden* (Chicago: University of Chicago Press, 2006), 81–85.

22. David Howes, "Olfaction and Transition," in *The Varieties of Sensory Experience*, ed. David Howes (Toronto: University of Toronto Press, 1991), 128–47.

23. Susan Rasmussen, "Making Better 'Scents' in Anthropology: Aroma in Tuareg Sociocultural Systems and the Shaping of Ethnography," *Anthropological Quarterly* 72, no. 2 (1999): 65.

24. Diana Eck, *Darshan: Seeing the Divine Image in India* (New York: Columbia University Press, 1998), 11.

25. J. Douglas Porteous, "Smellscape," *Progress in Human Geography* 9, no. 3 (1985): 362.

26. Tiranga website, http://www.tirangaagarbatti.com/.

27. Timothy Beal, *The Rise and Fall of the Bible* (New York: Houghton Mifflin, 2011), 77–79.

28. For more on the spatial setting, in distinction to the Western time-based connection, see James McHugh, *Sandalwood and Carrion: Smell in Indian Religion and Culture* (New York: Oxford University Press, 2012).

29. "The Incense Seal of Avalokiteshvara Bodhisattva," quoted in Silvio Bedini, *The Trail of Time: Time Measurement with Incense in East Asia* (Cambridge, UK: Cambridge University Press, 1994), 75. Much of the section here on East Asian incense clocks is drawn from Bedini's study.

30. See Aileen Gatten, "A Wisp of Smoke: Scent and Character in *The Tale of Genji*," in *The Smell Culture Reader*, ed. Jim Drobnick (Oxford, UK: Berg, 2006), 331–41.

31. Robert Klara, "Something in the Air," *Adweek*, March 5, 2012. Accessed at http://www.adweek.com/news/advertising-branding/something-air-138683.

32. ScentAir website, http://scentair.com/the-big-idea/.

33. Sturgess quoted in Klara, "Something in the Air."

34. Walter Savage Landor, "Praise and Censure," from *Selections from the Writings of Walter Savage Landor* (London: Macmillan, 1889), 284.

35. C. S. Lewis, "Afterword to the Third Edition," *The Pilgrim's Regress: An Allegorical Apology for Christianity, Reason and Romanticism* (Grand Rapids, MI: Wm. B. Eerdmans, 1992).

36. Diane Ackerman, *A Natural History of the Senses* (New York: Random House, 1990), 8–9.

DRUMS

1. Chinua Achebe, *Things Fall Apart* (Oxford, UK: Heinemann, 1996), 31.

2. Charles Darwin, *The Descent of Man* (New York: Penguin Classics, 2004), 639.

3. Igor Stravinsky, *Poetics of Music*, trans. Alfred Knodel and Ingolf Dahl (Cambridge, MA: Harvard University Press, 1970), 18.

4. Janna Levin has been working on these ideas and discusses them in various interviews and lectures, including the TED talk, "The Sound the Universe Makes," March 2011.

5. Joseph Campbell, *The Flight of the Wild Gander: Explorations in the Mythological Dimension* (Novato, CA: New World Library, 2002), 34.

6. Yehudi Menuhin, *Theme and Variations* (New York: Stein and Day, 1972), 9, quoted in Anthony Storr, *Music and the Mind* (New York: Free Press, 1992), 33.

7. Luther G. Jerstad, *Mani-rimdu: Sherpa Dance Drama* (Seattle: University of Washington Press, 1969).

8. Stravinsky, *Poetics of Music*, 23.

9. Plato, *The Republic*, trans. Benjamin Jowett, bk. 3.

10. Chun-Fang Wang, Ying-Li Sun, and Hong-Xin Zang, "Music Therapy Improves Sleep Quality in Acute and Chronic Sleep Disorders: A Meta-analysis of 10 Randomized Studies," *International Journal of Nursing Studies* (April 11, 2013): 10.1016/j.ijnurstu.2013.03.008.

11. David H. Rosenthal with Art Blakey, "The Big Beat!," *The Black Perspective in Music* 14, no. 3 (Autumn 1986): 275–76.

12. Ingrid Monson, "Art Blakey's African Diaspora," in *The African Diaspora: A Musical Perspective*, ed. Ingrid Monson (New York: Garland, 2000), 339.

13. On some of the jazz-Africa links, see Samuel A. Floyd Jr., *The Power of Black Music* (Oxford, UK: Oxford University Press, 1995).

14. Bonnie Greer's quote, and most of this section, derives from the chapter "Akan Drum" in Neil MacGregor, *A History of the World in 100 Objects* (New York: Viking, 2012).

15. David Tame, *The Secret Power of Music* (Rochester, VT: Destiny Books, 1984), 189.

16. Gabriel Okara, "The Mystic Drum," online at the Poetry Foundation Ghana: http://www.poetryfoundationghana.org/index.php/ traditional-poems/item/656-the-mystic-drum.

17. From Joseph A. Gilfillan, "The Ojibways in Minnesota," *Collections of the Minnesota Historical Society* 9 (1901): 114. Quoted in Thomas Vennum Jr., *Ojibwe Dance Drum* (Washington, DC: Smithsonian Folklife Studies, 1982), 33.

18. Tore Ahlbäck and Jan Bergman, *The Saami Shaman Drum* (Åbo, Finland: Donner Institute for Research in Religious and Cultural History, 1991), 28.

19. Ibid.

20. Bryant quote in Mike Rimmer, "Terl Bryant: Christendom's Master Percussionist Writes *A Heart to Drum*," in CrossRhythms, July 13, 2007, http://www.crossrhythms.co.uk/articles/music/Terl _Bryant__Christendoms_master_percussionist_writes_A_Heart_ To_Drum/28005/p2/. See also Terl Bryant, *A Heart to Drum* (Eastbourne, UK: Kingsway Publications, 2006).

21. Information on the *kabaro* in the Ethiopian Church comes from Michael Powne, *Ethiopian Music* (London: Oxford University Press, 1968), and the works of Kay Kaufman Shelemay, especially the article "The Musician and Transmission of Religious Tradition: The Multiple Roles of the Ethiopian *DABTARA*," *Journal of Religion in Africa* 22, no. 3 (1992): 242–59.

22. Most information on the Drum Dance is based on Thomas Vennum Jr., *Ojibwe Dance Drum*.

23. Louise Erdrich, *The Painted Drum* (New York: HarperCollins, 2005), Kindle location 2452.

24. Achebe, *Things Fall Apart*, 31.

25. Franz Kafka, *Parables and Paradoxes* (New York: Schocken Books, 1961), 93.

26. Stuart Brown, *Play: How It Shapes the Brain, Opens the Imagination, and Invigorates the Soul* (New York: Penguin, 2009), 3–4.

27. For an overview of several studies on drumming as therapy, see Michael Winkelman, "Complementary Therapy for Addiction: Drumming Out Drugs," *American Journal of Public Health* 93, no. 4 (April 2003): 647–51.

28. Mickey Hart, with Jay Stevens, *Drumming at the Edge of Magic: A Journey into the Spirit of Percussion* (New York: HarperCollins, 1990), 18. See also Mickey Hart and Fredric Lieberman, with D. A. Sonneborn, *Planet Drum* (Petaluma, CA: Acid Test Productions, 1991).

29. Stephen Cramer, "What We Do," in *Shiva's Drum* (Urbana: University of Illinois Press, 2004), 7.

CROSSES

1. Schoenmaekers, *Het nieuwe Wereldbeeld* (The New World Image), quoted in Mark C. Taylor, *Disfiguring: Art, Architecture, Religion* (Chicago: University of Chicago Press, 1992), 76.

2. Agnes Martin, quoted in Ann Wilson, "Linear Webs," *Art and Artists* 1, no. 7 (October 1966): 49.

3. Piet Mondrian, *The New Art—The New Life: The Collected Writings of Piet Mondrian*, ed. Harry Holtzman and Martin S. James (Cambridge, MA: Da Capo Press, 1993), 339.

4. Schoenmaekers quoted in Mark C. Taylor, *Disfiguring* (Chicago: University of Chicago Press, 1992), 76.

5. Adolf Loos, "Ornament and Crime," in *The Industrial Design Reader*, ed. Carma Gorman (New York: Allworth Press, 2003), 75.

6. Information on Chinese cosmologies comes primarily from Sarah Allan, *The Shape of the Turtle: Myth, Art, and Cosmos in Early China* (Albany: State University of New York Press, 1991); Norman Girardot, *Myth and Meaning in Early Taoism* (Berkeley: University of California Press, 1998); and Michael Nylan's introduction to Xiong Yang, *The Elemental Changes: The Ancient Chinese Companion to the I Ching*, trans. Michael Nylan (Albany: State University of New York Press, 1994).

7. Gary Urton, *At the Crossroads of the Earth and the Sky: An Andean Cosmology* (Austin: University of Texas Press, 1981).

8. Sherry B. Ortner, "On Key Symbols," in *A Reader in the Anthro-pology of Religion*, ed. Michael Lambek (Oxford, UK: Blackwell, 2002), 158–67.

9. Ibid., 161.

10. Stanislaw Chojnacki, *Ethiopian Crosses: A Cultural History and Chronology* (Milan, Italy: Skira, 2006).

11. See the exhibition catalog by Jeffrey Spier et al., *Picturing the Bible: The Earliest Christian Art* (New Haven, CT: Yale University Press, 2007), 228–29.

12. See Timothy Beal, *Religion and Its Monsters* (New York: Routledge, 2002).

13. See Peter Manseau, *Rag and Bone: A Journey among the World's Holy Dead* (New York: St. Martin's Press, 2010).

14. Adolf Hitler, *Mein Kampf* (Boston: Houghton Mifflin, 1939), 737.

15. Information on the swastika comes primarily from Thomas Wilson, *The Swastika: The Earliest Known Symbol, and Its Migrations* (Washington, DC: Government Printing Office, 1896); and Malcolm Quinn, *The Swastika: Constructing the Symbol* (London: Routledge, 1994).

16. Edward Butts, *Statement No. 1: The Swastika* (Kansas City, MO: Franklin Hudson, 1908), 9.

17. Quinn, *The Swastika*, 119.

18. Steven Heller, *The Swastika: Symbol beyond Redemption?* (New York: Allworth Press, 2008), 3.

19. Heiner Bastian, "Signs Are Senses," in *Joseph Beuys—Zeichnungen, Tekeningen, Drawings*, ed. Heiner Bastian and Jeannot Simmen (Berlin: Nationalgalerie, 1979), 83. Exhibition catalog.

20. Eusebius, *The Life of Constantine*, I.XXVII.

21. Sabine Baring-Gould, "Onward, Christian Soldiers," 1865.

22. Miguel Angel Astor-Aguilera, *The Maya World of Communicating Objects: Quadripartite Crosses, Trees, and Stones* (Albuquerque: University of New Mexico Press, 2010).

23. Alison Lurie, *The Language of Clothes* (New York: Holt Paperbacks, 2000), 3.

24. Ezekiel 9:4.

25. Job 31:35.

26. See Kate Shellnutt, "Tattoos Spread Montrose Church's Lenten Message," *Houston Chronicle*, February 22, 2012, http://www.chron.com/news/article/Montrose-church-spreading-its-message-through-3354183.php.

27. Susanna Elm, " 'Pierced by Bronze Needles,' " *Journal of Early Christian Studies* 4, no. 4 (1996): 409–39.

28. René J. A. Weis, *The Yellow Cross: The Story of the Last Cathars, 1290–1329* (London: Penguin, 2001).

29. Virginia Ann Guess, *The Spirit of Chiapas: The Expressive Art of the Roof Cross Tradition* (Santa Fe: Museum of New Mexico Press, 2004), 29.

30. Jon Stewart, *The Daily Show*, Comedy Central, broadcast August 4, 2012.

31. David Freedberg, *The Power of Images: Studies in the History and Theory of Response* (Chicago: University of Chicago Press, 1989), 1.

BREAD

1. Berrigan quote is found in Sister Corita Kent's 1965 artwork *Breadbreaking*.

2. Julie Ault, *Come Alive! The Spirited Art of Sister Corita* (London: Four Corners, 2006).

3. Harvey Cox, *Commonweal*, October 24, 1986, quoted in Ault, *Come Alive!*, 20.

4. See Lauren Collins, "Bread Winner," *New Yorker*, December 3, 2012, 78–85.

5. See Richard Wrangham, *Catching Fire: How Cooking Made Us Human* (New York: Basic Books, 2010).

6. Genesis 3:19.

7. Muhammad al-Bukhari, *Sahih al-Bukhari*, Book 81, Hadith 109.

8. John Muir, "The American Forests," *Atlantic*, August 1897, http://www.theatlantic.com/magazine/archive/.

9. For more on the North American setting, see Daniel Sack, *Whitebread Protestants: Food and Religion in American Culture* (New York: Palgrave Macmillan, 2000).

10. Stephen Benko, *The Virgin Goddess* (Leiden, Netherlands: Brill, 1993), 190.

11. Felipe Fernandez-Armesto, *Near a Thousand Tables: A History of Food* (New York: Free Press, 2002), 97.

12. Michael Pollan, *Cooked* (New York: Penguin, 2013), 207.

13. H. E. Jacob, *Six Thousand Years of Bread* (Garden City, NY: Doubleday, Doran, and Co., 1944), 27.

14. Pollan, *Cooked*, 234.

15. Deuteronomy 16:3.

16. Yosef Hayim Yerushalmi, *Zakhor: Jewish History and Jewish Memory* (Seattle: University of Washington Press, 1996), 44.
17. Quoted in Yerushalmi, *Zakhor*, 45.
18. Many of the historical elements of challah described here come from Maggie Glezer, *A Blessing of Bread: The Many Rich Traditions of Jewish Bread Baking around the World* (New York: Artisan, 2004).
19. John 6:51.
20. See Benko, *The Virgin Goddess*, 181–83.
21. *The Canons of the Fourth Lateran Council, 1215*, Canon 1. See the *Internet Medieval Sourcebook*: http://www.fordham.edu/halsall/basis/lateran4.asp.
22. Mechthild's quote and much of the information in this section are taken from Caroline Walker Bynum, *Holy Feast and Holy Fast* (Berkeley: University of California Press, 1987).
23. Ibid., 4.
24. Quoted in Bynum, 184.
25. Cardinal Joseph Ratzinger, "Letter to All Presidents of the Episcopal Conferences Concerning the Use of Low-Gluten Altar Breads and Mustum as Matter for the Celebration of the Eucharist," July 24, 2003, http://www.vatican.va/.
26. "Communion Wafers Box of 1000," Amazon.com page, http://www.amazon.com/.
27. Proverbs 4:17; Proverbs 20:17; Isaiah 30:20.
28. See Gregory Boyle, *Tattoos on the Heart* (New York: Free Press, 2010).
29. Sherman Alexie quoted in Jen Miller, "Frybread," *Smithsonian*, July 2008.
30. Ibid.
31. M.F.K. Fisher, *How to Cook a Wolf*, republished in *The Art of Eating: 50th Anniversary Edition* (New York: Houghton Mifflin, 2004), 247.
32. James Baldwin, *The Fire Next Time* (New York: Vintage, 1993), 43.
33. See the chapter, "Hitler's 'Pacte de famine,'" in Jacob, *Six Thousand Years of Bread*.
34. Quoted in Jacob, *Six Thousand Years of Bread*, 380.
35. Yaffa Eliach, "The Third Sabbath Meal at Mauthausen," in *Hasidic Tales of the Holocaust* (New York: Oxford University Press, 1982), 172–76.
36. Cynthia Botha, Ron Dowling, and Ian Paton, "Eucharistic Food and Drink: A Report of the Inter-Anglican Liturgical Commission to

the Anglican Consultative Council," Anglican Communion, 2007, http://www.anglicancommunion.org/.

37. William Rubel, *Bread: A Global History* (London: Reaktion, 2011), 8.

38. Collins, "Bread Winner," 85.

SOUL

1. Whitman, "There was a Child went Forth," from *Leaves of Grass* (Philadelphia: David McKay, 1900).

2. Mark C. Taylor, "Defining Religion," *Chronicle of Higher Education*, November 5, 2004. A similar but slightly differently worded definition is found in Taylor's *After God* (Chicago: University of Chicago Press, 2007), 12.

3. I am intrigued by and indebted to the writings of French philosopher of science Michel Serres and his work *The Five Senses* (New York: Continuum, 2008; original French, 1998), a meandering, metaphorically rich excursion into the cultural, historical, philosophical, and scientific understanding of the senses. Serres begins by telling of an experience he had in which his soul was "saved." The experience was a shipwreck, an autobiographical tale that made him realize the deep relations of the senses not only with the struggle between life and death but of life itself. He did not find his soul through some inner calm, some prayer, but rather as his senses struggled, worked together and against each other in the dark, watery chaos.

4. Gary Snyder, *The Practice of the Wild* (Berkeley, CA: Counterpoint, 2010), viii–ix. Snyder is not using the term *soul* in the way I am suggesting, but I mean to insert into soul making something like the "practice of the wild" that Snyder discusses.

5. D.H. Lawrence, "Benjamin Franklin," *Studies in Classic American Literature* (Cambridge, UK: Cambridge University Press, 2003 [orig., 1923]), 26.

6. See Parker J. Palmer, *A Hidden Wholeness: The Journey Toward an Undivided Life* (San Francisco: Jossey-Bass, 2004).

7. Aristotle, *De Anima*, bk. II, chap. 2.

8. Some of my speculative conceptions here are indebted to Lynda Sexson's marvelous work *Ordinarily Sacred* (Charlottesville: University of Virginia Press, 1992).

9. Sigmund Freud, *The Future of an Illusion* (Toronto: Broadview Press, 2012), 103.

Index

½ (meaning of), 1–22; and crosses, 143, 173; and drum playing, 133; in *8½* (movie), 1–2; and half bodies, 5–6, 223–24; and half lives, 16; in *A History of the World in 10½ Chapters* (Barnes novel), 2; in *Symposium* (Plato), 2–3

Achebe, Chinua, 99, 131
Ackerman, Diane, 5–6, 97
agriculture: deity of, 184–85; as sign of culture, 180, 185
aloeswood, 83, 86, 88
Aristophanes, 2–3
Aristotle, 221–22
Augustine (saint), 196, 221, 221n
Avatar (movie), 5
Ayers Rock (Uluru), 31–32, 33

Baldwin, James, 205–6
Barnes, Julian, 2–3
Battle Creek (MI) Sanitarium, 183
Beal, Timothy, 84, 133
Béatrice of Planisoles, 166–67
Bedini, Silvio, 230n29
Bellah, Robert, 134
Benedictine Sisters of Perpetual Adoration, 200
Berrigan, Daniel, 175
Beuys, Joseph, 160–61
Bible: as authority, 120; bread in, 195, 203, 206, 208; music in, 119; role of remembrance in Hebrew, 191; stones in, 42–43, 45; stoning in, 44–45
Blake, William, 33, 59

Blakey, Art, 114–15, 118, 133, 135
bodies: in devotion, 155; in ritual, 117; and symbols, 173. *See also* ½
Boyle, Greg, 203–4
bread, 17, 175–213; in Adam and Eve story, 180; and Anglican Church, 209–10; baking, 177, 179, 189, 205–6; baking of, as mystical encounter, 177, 189; in the Bible, 195, 203, 206, 208; as blessing, 194; "bread eaters," 179; "breaking bread," 194; challah, 193; in Christianity, 186, 194–98, 202, 209–10; complexity of, 176–77, 180; as deity, 197n, 198; and development of agriculture, 179, 185; and divine encounters, 198; and doctrine of transubstantiation, 197, 201, 206; as Eucharist, 186, 195–200, 210; and fasting, 198–99; frybread, 204–5; in *Gilgamesh*, 179; in Holocaust literature, 207–9; and Holy Communion, 176, 190, 196, 199–202, 209–10; in *The Iliad*, 179; importance as food source, 180; in Jewish culture, 189–94, 209, 210–11; and Kollyridians, 186–87; at Last Supper, 190, 195; leavened, 187–88, 202; as "magical" food, 188–89, 196; matzoh, 190, 191; as metaphor for religion, 211–12; as metaphor